DATE DUE

DEC. 1 6 1982		
JAN. 1 3 1989		
MAR. 1 2 1983		
FEB. 1 1 1984		
DE 0 4 85		
APR 2 8 97		

Tragedy on the High Seas

Tragedy on the High Seas

A History of Shipwrecks

Kenneth Hudson and Ann Nicholls

First published in the United States of America in 1979 by
A & W Publishers, Inc.
95 Madison Avenue
New York, New York 10016
By arrangement with Macmillan London Ltd

Library of Congress Catalog Card Number: 78–55108

ISBN 0–89479–024–2

Printed in Great Britain

Contents

The publishers and authors would like to thank the following sources for supplying illustration material:

British Museum 15, 16; Central Press Photos 85; F. E. Gibson 61, 63, 77; Keystone Press 96; The Kyrenia Ship Project/courtesy Michael Katzev 100 (John Veltri), 101; *Illustrated London News* 3 (William Morris, Bath), 73, 79 (William Morris, Bath), 82, 87, 92, 93; The Mansell Collection 8, 9, 10, 58; Mary Evans Picture Library 1, 2, 5, 14, 17, 22, 23, 34, 44, 45, 46, 50, 51, 54, 55, 56, 57, 60, 66, 67, 69, 71, 74, 75, 76, 90; Musée Borely, Marseilles 12; Museum of London 13; National Library of Australia 41; National Maritime Museum, London 6 (J. R. Freeman), 7, 32, 36, 39, 40 (J. R. Freeman), 43, 47 (J. R. Freeman), 53, 59, 68 (J. R. Freeman), 70, 81, 91, 97, 98; Nova Scotia Museum 4; Peabody Museum of Salem, Massachussetts 37, 42, 48, 49, 52; Popperfoto 25, 26, 35, 62, 65, 78, 80, 83, 84, 88, 89, 94, 95; Statens Sjöhistoriska Museum, Stockholm 28 (drawing by Gunnar Olofsson), 29, 30, 31, 64, 99; The Sutcliffe Gallery, Whitby 72; Ulster Museum, Belfast 27; Universitets Oldsaksamling, Oslo 18, 19; U.S. Environmental Protection Agency, Las Vegas 86; Viking Ship Museum, Roskilde 20, 21.

Line maps and illustrations by R & B Art.

Jacket photograph by Syndication International.

The Perils of the Sea

A wreck is not an isolated event. Its full interest and importance become apparent only when we study it within the context of the period when it happened. This involves knowing something about the technology of shipbuilding at the time, the skill and experience of seamen, the conditions of life on board, the risks that were deliberately run, the navigational and life-saving equipment available, the cargoes carried and the routes followed.

The enormous improvements in ship design, navigational aids and life-saving equipment during the past hundred and fifty years should theoretically have made life at sea a good deal safer and on the whole this is what has in fact happened. A young man going to sea for the first time today has a very good, if not certain chance of living to the age of fifty-five or sixty and of drawing a pension, but the proportion of seventeenth-century sailors who had spent all their life at sea and were still alive and well at sixty was very small. Until well into the present century, working on ships was an exceedingly hazardous occupation. It can now be classified as merely hazardous.

The list of dangers has not changed in any significant way during the three thousand years with which this book is concerned. Ships still run into hurricanes, hit rocks, collide with one another and break down because they are old or poorly maintained. Officers and their crews still fail to take, on occasion, all the precautions they should take. The weather and the sea continue to do freakish and unpredictable things. Mutinies and wars are still with us.

The sea is not a gentle or a controllable animal, although a modern supertanker is better able to cope with its moods than a Viking ship was. Waves rarely exceed twenty-five feet from trough to crest, although a sea as rough as this represents a very real threat to a small ship. In 1956, the captain of a ship sailing near Cape Hatteras saw a wave 100 feet high and another, even higher, was seen by the USS *Ramapo* in 1933.

Waves are most destructive when they meet an obstacle, particularly a rocky coast. It has been reckoned, for instance, that the force of breakers on the coast of Scotland can be as much as six thousand tons a square foot. Nothing, even the strongest of fixed structures, can stand up to poundings of this order.

In 1854 the steamship *Royal Charter* was returning from Melbourne to Liverpool with 388 passengers, a large quantity of wool and three quarters of a million pounds in gold. She was caught in a hurricane between Queenstown and Liverpool. Her engines could do nothing to save her from being driven on to the beach at Anglesey and she broke up very quickly. All but a very few of the passengers and crew were battered to death by the sea, the force of which was so great that a piece of ironwork picked up later had a gold ingot and several

1

sovereigns embedded in it, as if the iron had been in a molten state when the gold was thrown against it.

At one time, fire ran wind and waves close as a major cause of disaster at sea. In the days of wooden ships, sailors feared it even more than the weather. Sailing ships, with spars, tarred rigging and canvas above deck, and ammunition, spirits and often an inflammable cargo such as cotton or spices below, were very vulnerable. Spontaneous combustion of the cargo is one of the most frequent causes of fire. Ships carrying coal, cotton or oil are particularly likely to be endangered for this reason. Gas accumulates in the holds and if the hatches are not periodically removed or ventilation ensured in some other way so that the gas can escape, the slightest spark can cause a disaster.

Fires have also occurred during rough weather by chemicals which form part of the cargo spilling over on to inflammable material. Nitrate can burst into flames through the bags first becoming wet and then drying, a process which causes the nitrate to heat up to a dangerous extent. Some commodities – copra is a good example – can catch fire as a result of friction caused by careless stowing. The cargo moves about, causing first heat and then fire.

Fires continued to devastate ships, despite modern methods and equipment. In 1963, the *Lakonia*, an old ship which like many others had been converted to cruising purposes, was on her maiden voyage. Fire broke out in the hairdressing salon, probably because of faulty electrical equipment, and the ship was destroyed, with considerable loss of life.

Nowadays, every precaution is taken to make sure that fires do not occur or, if they do, that they can be put out quickly. Automatic sprinklers are fitted, as a matter of ordinary routine, an ample supply of regularly-inspected chemical fire extinguishers are scattered about the ship and a fire in the hold can now be brought under control by stifling it with a mixture of steam and a non-inflammable gas. Electric wiring has to be exposed and easily examined, switches and plugs must be of an approved type and all electrical equipment of good quality.

But, very regrettably, to say that certain precautions should be taken does not necessarily mean that they will be taken. Now, as in Greek and Roman times, owners are sometimes prepared to gamble with adequate equipment and poor maintenance, and every year accidents and wrecks occur for this reason alone. All one can say is that the methods of fireproofing ships and of dealing with any fire which should happen to break out (one cannot prevent a drunken cruise passenger from smoking in bed and setting his cabin on fire) should make it unlikely that a modern ship will be destroyed by fire. Disaster need not happen today, but it still does, often in quite unpredictable circumstances.

Collisions are still perhaps surprisingly much the most common cause of accidents, either at sea or in confined waters. Despite radar, ship-to-shore communication and other technical aids which were denied to nineteenth-century captains and navigators, approximately 150 collisions still occur each month in one part of the world or another. The worst region of the world for collisions is the Straits of Dover, which are used by 750 ships each day. During 1967 there were twenty-five serious collisions here, five times as many as ten years previously when navigational equipment was of a less advanced standard.

The coming of the steamship greatly increased the dangers of collisions. Steamships travel faster than the old sailing ships and they hit one another with a greater impact. Once their engine-room is hit or becomes flooded they are completely incapacitated.

Radar, primitive versions of which existed as early as 1935, should allow ships to avoid collisions, but it is only a piece of equipment, not a magician's wand, and like any other tool it can be mishandled. This is well illustrated by the fate of the *Andrea Doria* in 1956. This Italian liner collided with the *Stockholm* off Nantucket in thick fog. Both ships had radar. The navigating officer of the *Andrea Doria* believed the *Stockholm* was on an opposite course, but the two ships were actually converging. It is not possible to see this from radar alone, unless one plots courses from a series of radar signals. In this particular instance, the ships hit one another at a combined speed of forty knots.

Many accidents at sea have been and are still being caused by what can only be described as commercial greed, the urge to make more profit by shortening the duration of a voyage. This was not unknown in the days of sailing ships – the masters of the clippers going to and from Australia and the Far East took great risks in order to beat their rivals – but the situation became much worse with the introduction of steamships. From the beginning, the captains of passenger liners were under great pressure from their employers to drive their expensive ships at the maximum possible speed under all conditions in order to please those passengers who were willing to pay for punctuality and a fast ship. This not infrequently led to disaster.

The liner operators of the 1940s and 50s, unlike their predecessors, could at least excuse themselves by claiming that they had equipment which allowed them to know their position and speed with great accuracy and to pass this information on to other ships. Before the twentieth century captains often did not know where they were and many wrecks must have occurred because of this.

The first step towards more precise navigation was taken early in the Middle Ages. The magnetic compass was used by the Arabs at least three centuries before Columbus made his voyage to America in 1492. In its earliest form, it consisted of a circular card marked out with thirty-two points around its circumference. Fixed to it was a magnet formed by stroking an iron rod with a piece of natural lodestone. The card pivoted on a needle point and, for a long time, it was believed always to point to the true north. This was nearly always the case when ships were built of wood and had very little metal in their construction, but the increasing use of iron and, especially on warships, the numerous guns, produced serious compass deviations and many ships were lost as a result.

Ignorance of a ship's longitudinal position was equally, if not more, serious. The British Admiralty was so worried about the problem that it established a special Board of Longitude in 1714. The Board offered twenty thousand pounds, an enormous sum for the time, to the first person who would prove that he had invented a practicable and reliable way of finding longitude at sea. In 1735, John Harrison claimed the reward for an extremely accurate watch, which he called a chronometer. Harrison's principle was simple. If one took a fixed point on land – Greenwich Observatory was the one selected – and travelled either east or west away from it, sunrise and sunset would occur either earlier or later each day, according to the direction in which one was sailing. The same would be true of the sun's midday zenith. There is actually a difference of one hour for every 1020 miles or fifteen degrees of longitude.

If, then, one kept a watch permanently set on Greenwich time, and compared it with the midday sighting, the difference in hours or minutes between the two could be converted into miles sailed. The latitude was found by observing the angle of the sun at midday and once one had both the latitude and the longitude the position of the ship could be established precisely. Until Harrison's chronometer, however, there was no watch accurate enough to be used for navigational purposes. An error of only three seconds each day would cause an error of thirty miles in position in three weeks. This could be disastrous for eighteenth-century ships, which could easily be at sea for several weeks between ports.

Until that time, navigators used various rough and ready methods to establish longitude. The British called their method 'dead-reckoning', which stood for 'deduced reckoning'. They calculated the speed of the ship and then worked out the distance since leaving the last port or land feature. The Dutch estimated their speed by throwing chips of wood over the side and finding how long they took to pass between two marks on the gunwales. The British used a triangular piece of wood known as a chiplog. This scooped up water and remained stationary while the ship moved forward. It was fixed to a line marked with knots tied at intervals of forty-two feet. As the line slipped away the ship's speed in 'knots' could be calculated. An offical 'knot' was equal to one nautical mile (one and an eighth land miles) or one-sixth of a degree of latitude or longitude. It was a crude system and mistakes were very easily made. While travelling across the Atlantic or the Indian Ocean, it was quite possible to be faced with an error of several hundred miles in the calculation of longitude. When the *Batavia* was wrecked in 1629, she was six hundred miles further east than her captain reckoned. This kind of mistake is no longer possible.

Human error is as inevitable in navigating and running a ship as in any other kind of activity and many wrecks have undoubtedly been caused by just this. But the number of wrecks which were, by any definition, accidents with no blame attachable to anyone are equally numerous. One thinks, for example of what happened in 1902, at St Pierre in the West Indies. The volcano of Mont Pelée suddenly erupted, devastating an area of forty square miles, killing forty thousand people, destroying the town of St Pierre and wrecking and burning all but one of the ships in harbour. Nothing that any captain could have done, no matter how good his equipment and how great his skill and experience, could possibly have saved his ship on such an occasion.

The shipping situation and the wreck situation have been completely transformed during the past twenty years by the introduction of monster and, as some would say, monstrous oil tankers of 250,000 tons and more. The world tanker fleet now represents about half the total tonnage afloat. A high proportion of these ships are of the very large type, which presents problems of navigation and safety of a kind which previous generations of sailors never had to face. That supertankers are regarded as extremely dangerous by their insurers is shown by the fact that insurance premiums have now risen to seventy per cent of the total operating cost. Supertankers are deliberately not built to last. Their life, with few exceptions is reckoned to be about ten years, and the owners reckon to have got their money back long before that. What they order is consequently a cut-price job and many accidents are due to this, and to this alone.

Technically most modern tankers have nothing in reserve. They have only a single screw and rudder, and their so-called auxiliary engine is usually laughably small and quite insufficient to provide the ship with electricity or any other essential services. Because of this, when the main engine stops, for whatever reason, the ship loses all power. It cannot be steered and it has no lights and no radar. It simply drifts as a vast hulk, a danger to itself and to any other vessel in the vicinity. For cheap construction and maintenance, nearly all large tankers are steamships. They are not powered by the more conventional marine diesel engine. Unlike traditional steamships, however, they normally have only one high-pressure boiler – the *Queen Mary* had twenty-four – and, once this fails as it not infrequently does, everything necessarily comes to a halt.

For some extraordinary reason, the early supertankers, which came into service during the 1960s, were designed as if they were only half or a quarter their actual size. This led to gross mis-calculation of the stresses involved and ship after ship cracked and broke up in heavy seas. A permanent and increasing source of weakness lies in the fact that the average tanker, of whatever size, loses two per cent of her steel each year from the corrosion which takes place in the holds as the result of the action of the oil on the metal. If the thickness of the metal has been reduced to a minimum anyway in order to save money, one can easily see that after five years, let alone ten, the ship has been considerably weakened and may be potentially dangerous for this reason alone.

To run a 200,000-ton tanker without every item of equipment in perfect order is to court disaster from the moment it leaves port. A ship of this size, with the bridge, engines and control mechanisms all in the stern, must rely on automation and electronics if it is to be navigated with any safety at all. It is controlled from a point a quarter-of-a-mile away from its bows. It cannot respond to split-second timing in the way a small ship can, it cannot manoeuvre at all at low speeds and it takes three miles and something like twenty minutes to stop. It drives itself through the waves, instead of riding them and the navigating officer has so little feel of the ship that it is perfectly possible for him to run a small ship down without being aware of it.

Because of the great size of the ship and the weight of its cargo, the depth of water below the keel is often frighteningly small. It may be as little as two feet. Conventional charts and methods of taking soundings were never intended to meet such a demand. Shifting sands and wreckage on the sea-bed can easily turn a two-feet clearance into nothing at all.

The supertankers have transformed the function and the skills of a ship's officer. He is no longer required to use his instincts and his judgement or to acquire a feel for his ship; the computer and comprehensive set of electrical equipment does much of the job for him. When these aids break down, however, both he and the ship are in a very unenviable situation. With a ship like this, it is all or nothing. One cannot extemporise.

It is fair to assume, however, that few shipowners at any period have actually wanted their ships to sink, although since the days of insurance some have certainly seen the commercial advantages of such an event. We can therefore reckon that such technical innovations as lighthouses, foghorns, radar and, when the worst has happened, lifeboats, will have met with widespread support both from the people who owned ships and from those who sailed them. Lighthouses must be placed high on the list of such innovations.

The earliest recorded lighthouse was the celebrated Pharos of Alexandria, erected in 300 BC, but it is extremely unlikely that this magnificent structure can have been the pioneer. However, between 300 BC and the end of the fourth century AD the sites of thirty lighthouses have been identified. Most of them were on the northern side of the Mediterranean, but there were at least four to assist mariners bound for the Atlantic coast of Spain and France and for the English Channel ports, including one at Boulogne and one at Dover to guide them across the Straits. The light was provided by wood fires and torches kept burning in the open. With the collapse of Rome's power in Europe, all reference to sea lights comes to an end, although it is possible that some continued to exist. They were certainly in use again by the beginning of the twelfth century at the entrance to some of the Italian ports and between then and the sixteenth century they spread gradually northward. In the Mediterranean and in western Spain and France, the usual method of illumination was by oil lamps or by candles fitted into lanterns, but in northern Europe coal beacons were more common. By the end of the sixteenth century, in addition to lighthouses, the navigable channels of Dutch and German rivers were indicated by means of buoys and beacons.

Important improvements in building lighthouses and in providing them with illumination were made between the end of the seventeenth century and the end of the eighteenth. These included the first towers directly exposed to wave action on the Eddystone Rocks; lightships on sandbanks; lights with parabolic reflectors; oscillating lights; and eventually, in 1781, the first revolving light. Oil lamps gradually took the place of coal fires, not because they provided better illumination – the opposite was the case – but because it was possible to shelter them against winds and rain. The pioneering revolving light in the Carlsten lighthouse near Marlsten in Sweden used a number of oil lamps, each with its own reflector. They were fixed to a vertical axis and rotated by clockwork to give flashes at regular intervals.

With the early lighthouses or beacons, there was always the problem of distinguishing one light from another. In the days of coal fires, the only method available was to have more than one light on the same site or as was done in some instances to put two lights on one tower.

The first North American lighthouse was built in 1716 at Boston and by 1800 there were thirty regularly-maintained navigation lights along the east coast, from Cape Breton in the north to Charleston in the south. They all used oil lamps without reflectors and their chief purpose was to guide ships into harbours, not to prevent wrecks.

The first lightship was placed in position in 1731, close to the Nore buoy in the Thames Estuary. It was paid for by means of subscriptions from the owners of ships engaged in the coastal trade. The lighting consisted of two ship's lanterns suspended twelve feet apart from cross-arms on the mast. Trinity House put its own lightship on the Goodwins in 1795. The men on it were armed, to deal with privateers. The main danger to the lightships, however, was the real possibility of being run down in fog, which increased as ships became larger, noisier and faster. To warn vessels of the presence of the lightship, the crew had various forms of fog-signal, ranging from muzzle-loading guns to giant horns driven by compressed air. Radar has considerably reduced the risks, but work on lightships is understandably not popular under modern conditions and the modern trend is to replace them by automatic illuminated buoys.

Fog is as great a problem on the north-east coast of America as it is along the

English Channel. The principal navigation risks for ships using American ports may be summed up as fog in the north, hurricanes in the south. The Lighthouse Board in the United States came into existence in 1852. At that time, it was generally recognised that the United States had a system of lighthouses and other aids to navigation which has inadequate, out-of-date and badly administered. Wrecks were consequently much more numerous than they need have been. The need for good facilities can be seen from the extent to which fog warning systems are used nowadays. On the New England, Pacific and Alaskan coasts it is not at all uncommon for some lighthouse stations to have their fog signal working for twenty-five per cent of the time, i.e. for anything between 1500 and 2000 hours in the year.

The Royal National Institution for the Preservation of life from Shipwreck was founded in 1824. By 1850, there were about a hundred lifeboats in existence around the coasts of Britain. Thirty belonged to the Institution, which was and still is a wholly voluntary body, and the remainder to various other societies. Many, however, were in a far from seaworthy condition. In 1851, the Institution took over all the existing stations and undertook to keep the boats manned and in good repair. In the hundred and fifty years between 1824 and 1974 the Royal National Life-Boat Institution (it was renamed in 1854) saved fifty-seven thousand lives.

The Americans, like most other countries, have a state-run life-saving service. This was set up in 1850 when the Federal Government decided to build its own lifeboat stations. Previously, the Revenue Service, set up in 1790 to enforce the country's laws on the high seas, had done what it could to help people in distress at sea and to save the cargoes of wrecked vessels. Life-saving operations on the coast began in 1786 when the Massachusetts Humane Society was formed. This kind of rescue organisation was given official shape in 1871 when Congress established the Lifesaving Service. The Coastguard Service as it is known today did not come into being until 1915 when a Revenue Cutter Service and the Life Saving Service were merged into the US Coast Guard.

Under international regulations, all sea-going vessels have been obliged since the loss of the *Titanic* in 1915 to carry suffcent life-boats and life-rafts to accommodate every passenger and member of the crew, to maintain these in good working order and to organise regular and thorough life-boat drills. Over and over again, however, it has been discovered during the enquiries which take place after a ship has been wrecked with loss of life that the life-saving regulations had not been properly observed. Since Samuel Plimsoll's Merchant Shipping Act of 1876 – and there has been corresponding legislation in most other countries – it should be impossible to send out a British ship which is overladen.

Wrecks of the Prehistoric and Classical Periods

The Principal Routes and Cargoes

It is known from archaeological evidence that ships, or perhaps more accurately, boats, were being sailed or rowed over quite long distances of the eastern Mediterranean nine thousand years ago. By 300 BC seafarers had crossed the Aegean, the Adriatic and the open sea between Egypt and Crete and they had ventured into the Red Sea and the Persian Gulf. The third millenium BC, the Early Bronze Age in the Aegean, produced three exceptionally energetic cultures, known to archaeologists as the Early Minoan on Crete; Early Helladic on the Greek mainland; and Early Cycladic on the islands of the Cyclades. Longboats from these three areas, almost certainly rowed, not sailed, made regular trading journeys as far as Sicily and the Dalmatian coast in one direction and to Asia Minor on the other. Sails were being used on ships coming from all three areas during the second millenium, probably under the influence of the Egyptians. Minoan pottery of this period has been found in Italy, Greece, Egypt and along the coast of Palestine and Syria, indicating that trade was carried on with these countries, in some of which the Minoans had colonies.

Knossos was destroyed in 1400 BC and after this Mycenean (Late Helladic) naval and trading power took the first place in the Mediterranean, with ships crewed by as many as thirty men. At the same time, the Canaanites, who came from the Syrian coast and were later known as Phoenicians, were playing an increasingly important maritime role. They traded particularly in grain and metals, and they had ships big enough to transport about 450 metric tons of grain.

The founding of the Hellenistic kingdoms at the beginning of the first millenium changed the situation fundamentally. The new urban civilisations of these regions greatly increased the need for trade because a much higher proportion of the population than ever before were consumers not producers of food. Commerce began spreading on a large scale into the central and western Mediterranean, with the Greeks, Phoenicians and Etruscans taking the leading part. The Phoenicians were the most adventurous and probably the best sailors.

During the fourth and fifth centuries BC, it has been estimated that the total population of Greece was about three million of which perhaps two-thirds lived in towns and cities. If one-third could be fed from home resources and the other third had to live off grain brought from the Black Sea area and from Egypt, three hundred ships, each making four voyages a year, were required to transport grain alone with perhaps another three hundred for other kinds of food and drink. Goods from Greece had to be taken in exchange and consequently the pattern of trade routes in and around the Mediterranean was laid down in the first place by the need to keep the Greek population fed, a pattern which repeated itself soon afterwards as a result of even greater demands of the same kind from Rome. Since foodstuffs and liquids were normally shipped in amphorae, there had to be a major industry concerned with making these containers and it was widely distributed around the coastal areas of the Mediterranean, wherever there was suitable clay. The amphora was the barrel of antiquity.

The Romans had no tradition of seafaring when the Republic began to expand down through Italy during the fourth and third centuries BC. Two hundred years later, with Carthage defeated, they were controlling and administering the whole of the Mediterranean. The rise of Roman colonial power and the acquisition of colonies stimulated more complex and more sophisticated demands on the part of the Roman ruling class. Imports of luxuries came from as far afield as India and even the finer qualities of building stone were brought great distances by sea. To maintain this flow of trade and to reduce transport costs, ships became much bigger. The carrying capacity of the ships used for bringing marble from the Eastern Mediterranean was as much as two hundred tons, a figure not greatly exceeded until the seventeenth century.

The wrecks which are to be discussed in this section are nearly all in the Mediterranean. This is where shipping was mostly to be found during the Classical period and where the level reached by several civilisations had produced a need for trade. In Roman times, however, there was a second major concentration of ships between Gaul and Britain and along the Channel coasts. The ships serving these routes were built in the area and never left it. Until the time of the Vikings, seafaring was restricted wherever possible to routes holding close to land, as the map shows.

The cargoes carried were of three types: heavy, bulky goods, such as wine, grain, stone, timber, tiles and metals; luxury and semi-luxury products, like works of art, the finer types of pottery, fabrics and spices; and, to an increasing extent, as the imperial power of Rome grew, people.

The Ships

The appearance of Egyptian ships is well-known from paintings, inscriptions and models. They rose sharply at both ends, often with a high stem and sternpost. Those used by the Syrians, Canaanites and Mycenaeans were similarly designed. No remains of ships belonging to this culture have survived, however. By the first millenium BC, however, evidence from wrecked ships can be combined with what is known from paintings, drawings and coins to produce fairly reliable information about the size and design of ships, the materials used and the methods of construction. It is clear that there was by this time a fundamental distinction between warships, which were light, slender and fast, and merchant ships, which were heavy, broad and slow. The merchant ships were usually built of pine and the warships of fir. For a warship, the essential features were that it should be fast and manoeuvrable since the aim was to drive it as fast as possible at an enemy ship in an attempt to cripple it or sink it. To achieve this degree of speed

9

it was rowed in some cases by as many as 170 men sitting in three banks.

The square-sail was most common, but there is evidence that a fore-and-aft rig was sometimes employed by merchantmen. Steering was always by means of an oar at the stern. The hook type of anchor was introduced at some time during the first millenium BC. It was sometimes of iron, but more frequently of wood tipped with iron. The hull was often, although by no means invariably, sheathed in lead fixed with copper tacks to defeat attacks by the teredo worm.

All the Greek ships so far found were constructed by laying the keel, setting up the stern and stemposts and then building the hull by laying each plank overlapping the one below. The frames and floors were fitted in afterwards to provide extra strength. This was the Egyptian system, too. The Romans used this method, but also built ships by first fixing ribs to the keel and then fixing the hull-boards to them. The wrecks of ships belonging to the classical period have two kinds of planking. One uses long boards, of which there was a reasonably good supply around the Mediterranean, and the other shorter pieces of wood, mortised and tenoned together at the ends. Even when long timbers were available, the Roman shipbuilders always used mortise and tenon joints where one plank joined another. The standard of craftsmanship revealed by the Roman wrecks is very high. The planking was up to four inches thick, carefully worked so that it fitted together closely, giving, once the wood had swelled, a water-tight joint without the need for any caulking. The frames, placed very close together, were made of roughly-hewn hardwood logs. Above the waterline extra longitudinal strength was provided by two or more wales, heavy external timbers running continuously from stem to stern. The hulls were usually made of pine, cypress or cedar, and occasionally elm. Oak was employed for the frames. Merchant ships were often lead-sheathed. A merchant ship of the Roman period was consequently very solid, heavy and slow. Its thick timbers had a better chance of surviving the attacks of decay and boring insects than the much more lightly-built warships.

A single square mainsail on a centrally placed mast was normal, with the occasional use of a triangular topsail. There was a heavy spar called an *artemon* raked sharply forward over the bow and with a small headsail fixed to it. This sail helped the steering and allowed the ship to be held on a steady course. After the collapse of the Roman Empire, the *artemon* and its sail fell completely out of use and were only revived in the late fifteenth century in a modified form known as bowsprit and topsail. Fore and aft sails were known in Roman times, but they were not common. The square sail needed at least ten men to handle it; ships rigged in this way had to have a much larger crew than was required for vessels of the same size with a fore-and-aft rig. On all Roman wrecks there is evidence, in the form of tiles, of an attempt to guard against fire spreading from the galley where food was cooked on an open fire or brazier. No charred timbers have so far been found which would suggest a ship had been destroyed by fire.

Anchors of stone or of wood sheathed in lead were in use until the second century BC when iron anchors became more normal. Navigation was entirely by the stars and the captains had to know where and when the winds would blow at different seasons of the year and at different times of day. Sailing instructions based on this kind of information have survived from Roman times, mostly drawn up for the benefit of Greek seamen. No charts are extant, but it is probable that they were used.

10

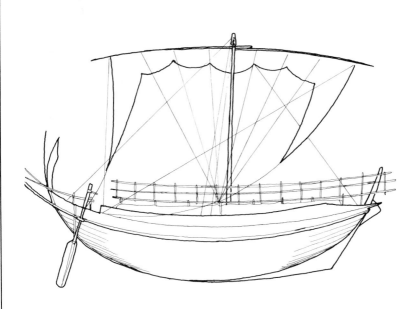

Greek trading vessel, eighth century
(from *The Ship* by Bjorn Landström)

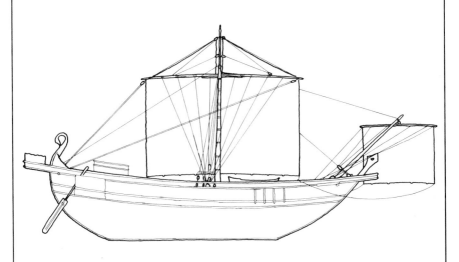

Roman grain ship, first century AD
(from *The Ship* by Bjorn Landström)

The Wrecks in Approximate Date Order

It has been estimated that between 3000 BC and AD 500 the number of ships sailing within the Mediterranean and between Mediterranean ports and north-west Europe totalled about half a million. Some of these were undoubtedly very small and in some cases little more than sailing barges engaged in coastal and river trade. But they were all potential wrecks and a high proportion of them undoubtedly ended their days on the bottom of the sea. Many, perhaps most, have rotted away entirely. The waters of the Mediterranean are not kind to sunken wooden ships or indeed to wooden ships while they are still afloat. The high salinity and warmth of the water provide perfect conditions for wood-boring worms and most wrecks would undoubtedly have had their timbers destroyed within fifty years. The lower parts of the ships usually had some protection against worms from the sand which covered them. How much more than this has survived has depended almost entirely on the depth of sand and mud which accumulated over the ship very shortly after she sank.

c. 2500 BC. Near island of Hydra, Greece

During the summer of 1975 a team of archaeologists, led by the American expert on ancient ships, Peter Throckmorton, discovered the remains of an Early Bronze Age ship lying at a depth of about sixty-five feet off the island of Hydra, in an area where more than twenty other shipwrecks dating from Classical times have already been located. The ship probably went down in about 2500 BC. She was loaded with pottery typical of that period – cooking pots, jugs, cups and the vessels shaped like sauce-boats which are a special feature of Cycladic ware. Something like a twentieth of the timbers have survived – a very rare occurrence – and this makes it possible, once the wood has been brought to the surface and given preservative treatment, to reconstruct the size and shape of the ship. Until now, the appearance of ships of this period has been known only from representations on pottery. From their peculiar shape, they are known to archaeologists as 'frying-pan' ships, but it would be equally correct to describe them as centipedes, because they had between twenty and thirty oars sticking out from each side. It is not too difficult to imagine how the ship was wrecked. She was probably trying to get out of harbour, but the wind suddenly changed and drove her back towards the shore. She hit a submerged rock and broke in two. The ballast fell out and was found by the divers about twenty-five feet down, probably near the point where the ship struck the rock.

c. 1500 BC. North Ferriby, Yorkshire

Three Bronze Age boats were discovered on the bed of the River Humber in 1946 and 1963. They were primitive vessels without a keel, consisting of broad planks sewn together edgeways. They are the earliest known plank-built boats to have been found in Britain.

c. 1400 BC. Near Bodrum, Turkey

The remains of this ship and her cargo were found in 1957. The date of the wreck has been placed at about 1400 BC. Many ships came to grief on this treacherous reef around Yassi Island, where the rock rises to within six feet of the surface. Among the cargo recovered from the wreck are bronze tools, broken amphorae, and a large number of copper ingots, twenty-four inches across, shaped exactly like an ox-hide. Originally, these probably weighed about fifty-six lbs each and their value in metal was probably that of a cow or ox. The archaeological material also includes a number of scarabs from Syria inscribed with hieroglyphs suggesting that the ship may have traded with that country. The site of the wreck is directly on the course from Cyprus to Greece, the Aegean Islands or the western coast of Anatolia. The 'ox-hides' came from Cyprus, the great source of copper in Classical times. The tools included hammers, chisels, axes, adzes, knives and ploughshares. Some of these had inscriptions in Cypro-Minoan script used in Cyprus during the Bronze Age. There were also blanks for making tools, suggesting to the excavators that the ship may have been engaged in the business of selling new tools and taking old ones in part exchange.

c. 1200 BC. Bodrum, Turkey

A Canaanite (Phoenician) ship about thirty feet long found in a hundred feet of water off the Turkish coast near Cape Gelidonya, on a rocky bottom, with little sand coverage, and nearly all trace of her hull gone. The cargo was copper, bronze, and tin ingots from Cyprus with remnants of baskets containing scrap bronze (broken tools) hammer-heads and other metal-working tools.

c. 800–700 BC. Béziers, France

Nothing of the hull has survived. The cargo includes copper and bronze ingots, tools, weapons and ornaments.

c. 700–600 BC. Estuary of the river Huelva, north-west of Gibraltar

Cargo of bronze objects, including swords, spear-heads, arrowheads, helmets and brooches was discovered in 1923 during dredging operations. The material, which was apparently being transported as scrap, came from the Eastern Mediterranean, Sardinia and the Atlantic coast.

c. 600 BC. Off Rochelongues, France

During excavations carried out from 1964 onwards, a varied cargo was discovered on a wreck site here. It included bronze objects, probably metal scrap, and a large quantity of copper and tin ingots. Metal-working tools found on the site suggest that the ship had a craftsman on board who made objects to order at the various ports where the ship called, using both new and scrap metal for the purpose. The trade items carried included buckles, chains, razors and arrowheads.

c. 570 BC. Cap d'Antibes, France

This ship, the remains of which were excavated in 1950, was probably Etruscan. It contained two types of cargo, fine quality Etruscan pottery being transported for trade purposes, and about 150 amphorae, which contained wine. An anchor stock, made of lead, was also discovered on the site.

c. 400 BC. Straits of Messina, Sicily

The cargo of this ship appears to have been pillaged at some time. What remained showed that the ship was carrying amphorae of wine and olive oil, bronze statues, lead ingots and silver. The surviving fragments of the hull show that the ship had been built hull first with the frames inserted later and was lead-sheathed.

c. 306 BC. Kyrenia, Cyprus

Greek merchant ship, about fifty feet long. More than half the hull was preserved and lifted. Carbon dating of almonds in the cargo and of the ship's planks show that the ship was at least sixty years old when she sank. Three types of cargo: millstones, wine and almonds. Spoons, bowls, salt-dishes and oil-jugs suggest a crew of four. The 400 amphorae were of ten types, each representing a different port of call. Cooking utensils were on board, but there was no trace of a hearth, making it probable that cooking was done on shore. This, coupled with the discovery of fragments of only one small lamp, suggests the ship did not run at night. The absence of coins and remains of personal belongings may mean that the crew abandoned the ship during a storm and made for the coast.

c. 300 BC. Kyrenia, Cyprus

This ship, built for coastal trading, was forty-seven feet long and had a beam of about fourteen feet. Her weight when new was something like 14 tons and she probably carried seven tons of cargo. When she was fully loaded, the top of her rail was only two feet above the level of the water. We can estimate her speed at between four and five knots. She was fitted with two steering oars and her hull was sheathed in lead, to protect it against attacks by worms. There was a crew of four. They started their last voyage at Samos, where a small number of amphorae of wine were loaded. Millstones were put aboard at Kos and the ship then went on to Rhodes to pick up the bulk of the cargo, a further three hundred amphorae of wine. Cloths of woven matting protected the wine from the sun and from seawater. All this can be deduced from the archaeological evidence. Off Kyrenia the joint between two timbers opened. The crew abandoned the ship and she sank in ninety feet of water. She was discovered in 1967 and all the cargo was raised the following summer. When the mud was being flushed out of the hull, preparatory to lifting it, piles of almonds were discovered with their shells still perfectly preserved. The sacks in which they were being transported had, of course, long since rotted away. Almonds were not at that time a luxury commodity. They formed a regular part of the ancient Greek diet. The hull was dismantled before being brought to the surface as it was in a very fragile condition. Each timber was carefully mapped, photographed and labelled before it was lifted and taken ashore for conservation treatment. The ship was reconstructed in the medieval castle at Kyrenia, where she still remains.

c. 300–200 BC. Motya, Isola Lunga, off western coast of Sicily

Excavations carried out in 1971–72 showed this vessel, possibly a warship, to have been about 100 feet long. The maple, oak and fine timber used in her construction was well preserved. Some of the timbers had incised guidelines and painted signs in the Punic alphabet, probably shipwrights' marks. The dunnage used to protect the hull from the ballast was in excellent condition. It included beech, oak, maple, cedar, myrtle and olive, all of which grow in the Lebanon (Phoenicia) today. Pottery found near the wreck shows, in conjunction with carbon dating of the timbers, that the ship was built towards the middle of the third century BC at the time of the Punic wars. It was carrying no cargo.

c. 200 BC. Grand Congloué, Marseilles

Noteworthy as having been the first to be excavated by divers equipped with aqualungs (1953). The site was complicated, since it almost certainly contained the remains of two ships, one of which had settled on top of the other. The finds included a cargo of about 8000 amphorae, mostly Italian and Greco-Italian, and about 12,000 pieces of Campanian pottery. The amphorae, which were signed, were of two dates. Those from the upper layer were larger and presumably came from the second ship; they contained wine from the estate of Lucius Titius near Naples. The lower layers were seventy years older and had come from the vineyards of Marcus Sextius, who lived on the Greek island of Delos in the middle of the third century BC. The site of the villa there is known and has been excavated. It was never completed and it is possible that the loss of the ship bankrupted him. The excavation was the first occasion on which underwater television was used to direct divers and a suction system used to shift mud.

c. 120–100 BC. Island of Spargi between Corsica and Sardinia

The excavation of this site, which lies in shallow water, showed the wrecked ship to have been about a hundred feet long. The bottom of the ship had been ripped out on a reef. Three thousand amphorae were found together with plates, bowls and a large quantity of Campanian dishes and cups.

c. 100 BC. Albenga, Italian Riviera

The remains of a large Roman amphorae carrier were discovered here in 1949, but are still unexcavated. The ship appeared to have been about a hundred feet long and twenty-six feet wide. It was lead-sheathed.

c. 100 BC. Cap Dramont, France

This ship appears, from its remains, to have been about eighty feet long and flat-bottomed. She carried about 1000 amphorae.

c. 100 BC. Mahdia, Tunisia

At the beginning of the present century, sponge-divers found a wreck just off Mahdia, on the Tunisian coast between Susa and Sfax, in 150 feet of water. A large part of the cargo was raised between 1907 and 1913 and is now in the Bardo Museum, Tunis. Most of it consisted of marble columns and statues, but there were some bronzes, which suffered less than the marble from their long immersion in the sea. The shipwreck seems to have taken place early in the first century BC. The ship was loaded at Athens, which had been captured and plundered by Sulla in 86 BC. The consignment was a curious mixture of original works and copies, ornamental pieces and furniture, produced in Greece and intended for the Italian market, which it never reached. The sixty marble columns in the cargo formed part of a complete pre-fabricated temple.

c. 100 BC. Titan, Ile du Levant, France

Excavations show this ship to have been between eighty and ninety feet long. The keel and the lower part of the hull were well preserved. The cargo consisted of more than 1,000 amphorae.

c. 100 BC. La Chrétienne, Anthéor, France

The wreck of an amphorae carrier was found here in 1949, deeply buried in sand. Some of the amphorae had inscriptions in Oscan, a language still in use in the area around Naples in the first half of the first century BC. They also bore the name of the importer of the wine.

c. 80 BC. Island of Antikythera, between Crete and Kythera

The first Roman sea-going vessel to be examined by divers (1901). Cargo of marble and bronze statuary, now in National Museum, Athens. Many of them have been identified as copies of original Greek works. The statues may have formed part of Sulla's booty en route to Rome. A complex astronomical computer was also discovered, the only truly scientific instrument to survive from classical times.

First half of first century AD. Lake Nemi, near Rome

When the lake was drained in the 1930s, two luxury barges, two hundred feet long and sixty feet wide, dating from Imperial Roman times were uncovered. They are reputed to have been pleasure boats built for the Emperor Caligula (37–41 AD). Although not intended for use on the open sea, the barges were lead-sheathed, a quite unnecessary precaution, since Nemi was a fresh-water lake. One of the barges and the museum containing them were set alight and destroyed by German soldiers in 1944.

c. 100–200 AD. Marzamemi, Sicily
This ship, of about 170 tons, was carrying a cargo of sections of stone columns.

c. 100–200 AD. Blackfriars, London
During excavation work in connection with a new embankment in 1962, the remains were found of a Romano-British ship dating from the second century AD. She was flat-bottomed, about fifty-five feet long, with a beam of twenty-two feet, oak-built and almost certainly of native construction. She probably sank as the result of a collision. Her cargo consisted of building stone, quarried near Maidstone in Kent. Parts of a number of Roman-type shoes were found.

c. 100–200 AD. San Pietro, Gulf of Taranto, Italy
The remains of a ship of about 150 tons were discovered here. She had been carrying a cargo of marble sarcophagi.

c. 100–200 AD. St Tropez, France
The remains of a second-century ship, of an estimated two hundred tons, were located here. She had been carrying blocks of marble and worked sections of marble columns.

c. 100–200 AD. Torre Cianca, southern Italy
This ship carried four marble columns, each 9 × 1 metres.

c. 180 AD. Torre Sgarrata, near Taranto
The wreck of this Roman freighter, about 2000 years old, was found in 1967 in the Gulf of Taranto, in southern Italy. The cargo was marble from Afrodisias, in Asia Minor, mostly in the form of unfinished sarcophagi. Many of the pine timbers were remarkably well-preserved, still looking yellow and fresh. They show how the Greek and Roman shipwrights used mortise and tenon joints to fasten the planks of the hull edge to edge, relying on the water to swell the wood and keep the ship water-tight. Patches of inferior wood fixed to the hull with iron nails suggest that the ship had been repaired when she was already old for an owner who hoped to be able to sail her a few years more.

c. 100–200 AD. Isole delle Correnti, Sicily
The remains of a ship of about 350 tons were found near here. Her cargo had consisted of marble blocks.

c. 100–300 AD. Cape Spitta, Pelaponnese
The absence of any hull remains makes it difficult to date this wreck, the evidence of which is its cargo of four granite sarcophagi, with ballast stones and roof-titles. The sarcophagi were only partly finished, suggesting that the rest of the work was to be completed on arrival.

c. 100–200 AD. New Guy's House, London
A small, flat-bottomed barge made of oak was discovered during building of the surgical wing of Guy's Hospital in 1958, near the Thames. It was covered with pitch outside and caulked with hazel twigs. The vessel could not be completely excavated because it lay under drains and service roads in the hospital grounds.

c. 300 AD. Near Westminster Bridge, London
This was the first ship built during the Roman period to have been properly excavated and recorded (1910). A merchant ship, sixty to seventy feet long, she had been built of oak, either in Britain or northern France, for the coastal trade. She apparently sank at her moorings, for no ascertainable reason.

Medieval Wrecks

The Meaning of 'Medieval'

One can argue for hours as to when the Middle Ages began and ended, and each kind of specialist sets limits to suit his own particular field. For shipbuilding and navigation the problem is particularly difficult because very few technical advances of any note were made between the fifth century when Rome's empire finally disintegrated and the fifteenth when the long-distance ocean voyages and exploration of the Portuguese, the Genoese and the Venetians both necessitated and were made possible by new types of ship, new navigational techniques and new commercial possibilities. But within this period the Scandinavians – the Vikings – were performing extraordinary feats of seamanship in boats which marked little advance on what was available in Roman times, making regular voyages across the North Sea and the Baltic and even to North America.

This section of the book, for the reasons just given, uses 'medieval' in a special sense. The Middle Ages of voyaging and ship-design are taken here as the years between about AD 500 and 1400, the period during which north-west Europe was becoming increasingly important as a trading centre and when Africa, Asia and America were beginning to lose something of their vague, mythological quality. This expansion of interest should be observed, from a European point of view, with proper modesty, because, when the Roman Empire was falling to pieces under the attacks of the barbarians, the Polynesians, in their outrigger pirogues, were navigating and colonising the Pacific.

The Routes

During the first five centuries AD the Vikings successfully explored the Scandinavian coasts from Denmark to beyond the North Cape. They used long boats made of skins stretched over wooden frames. Between the seventh and twelfth centuries the great Swedish conquerors, the Varangians, undertook plundering and trading voyages down the Russian rivers to Kiev, the Caspian and the Black Sea. In this way, Chinese silk found its way up to the Baltic. In the ninth, tenth and early eleventh centuries the Vikings, now using wooden ships, sailed down the coasts of the North Sea and the Atlantic and into the Mediterranean. These voyages of invasion and looting eventually led, in the eleventh century, to the annexation of the British Isles. To the north-West, they went from Norway and the Shetlands to Iceland, from Iceland to Greenland, from Greenland to Labrador and Newfoundland and then down the American coast to Cape Cod. By the eleventh century, the Vikings were settling down to

17

become farmers and traders in the countries they had invaded and occupied. They established regular sea-links with the rivers of Europe, which allowed them to trade with the Bosphorus and the Eastern Mediterranean. They set up the pattern of European commerce on a scale far beyond what was achieved by the Romans.

Within this long period of Viking power, six new trade routes were established from centres in and around the Mediterranean.

From Constantinople (Byzantium) to Venice
This lasted from the fifth century until the capture of Constantinople by the Turks in 1453.

From Tana on the Black Sea to Constantinople
This was the silk route, the goods being brought overland from China, through Central Asia. It existed from the thirteenth to the fifteenth century.

From Modone and Crete to Alexandria
Between the eighth and the fourteenth centuries, this was the main route by which Europeans got the spices which were essential as medicaments and for preparing and preserving foodstuffs.

From Gibraitar to Alexandria
Thirteenth–fifteenth centuries. This brought gold from the Sahara to Venice and north-west Europe.

From Venice and Genoa to north-west Europe
The wool route, operating during the fourteenth and fifteenth centuries. Its main depots were in London and Bruges.

From Venice to Aigues-Mortes, Barcelona and Valencia
Important during the fourteenth and fifteenth centuries, this route served the exchange of oriental products with those from France and northern Europe, reaching the Mediterranean via the Rhône valley.

Interlocking with parts of the Viking trading network was a secondary system, involving the Hanseatic ports of Hamburg and the Baltic. This was developed during the twelfth, thirteenth and fourteenth centuries. It was concerned with the transport of ores and metals from Central Europe and Sweden; wool, furs, cloth, tin, corn and hides between Flanders, Novgorod, London, Rostock, Bergen and Lisbon; salt and wine from France; Baltic grain to Italy; oriental goods from Venice; salt fish from the Baltic to ports throughout Europe.

By the beginning of the fourteenth century, there was a European system of trade routes which had three origins: the network of ports and routes surviving from classical times; the routes established by the Vikings; and the routes developed by the new commercial powers in the Mediterranean, especially Venice. The importance of Venice dates from the eighth century. It was one of the few ports in the western Mediterranean to resist the Saracens. By the beginning of the thirteenth century, Venice controlled the commercial traffic of the whole of the Mediterranean. Her ships travelled in highly-organised convoys, which depended for their success and survival on good ships, good crews and improved methods of organisation, all of which the Venetian government provided. The fall of Constantinople in the mid-fifteenth century destroyed the system. Ships from the West were forbidden to enter the Black Sea and one by one the Aegean ports used by the Venetians were taken over. The trading links with Asia were cut and the economic basis of Venice's prosperity had gone. But the habits and methods of trade developed by Venetian merchants over a period of more than eight centuries remained as an inheritance for the new trading nations, especially the English, the Spanish, the Portuguese and the Dutch.

From the professional archaeologist's point of view, the Mediterranean is an unusually convenient laboratory. The smaller Greek and Roman ships hugged the coasts wherever possible and, when they were wrecked, this usually happened in conveniently shallow water. The medieval ships were less obliging. They were better built and probably better sailed and, within the Mediterranean, they came to grief less frequently than their predecessors. As cargoes became valuable, the danger from pirates increased, and it seems very likely that by the twelfth century piracy was a more serious menace than storms or shipwreck. Pirates, however, are more likely to seize a ship and sail it to a port of their own choosing or, having taken what they want of its cargo, to set the ship on fire.

During the medieval period the North Sea, the English Channel, the Bay of Biscay and the Baltic must have sent thousands of ships to their graves but these areas for the most part are very unpromising for underwater exploration. A high proportion of wrecked ships went down in deep water where location and exploration is so difficult as to be almost impossible. Where evidence of ships and their cargoes of this period has survived, it is nearly always in the old Greco-Roman places, in harbours or in estuaries.

The Ships

There are two separate traditions in the building of wooden ships. The first, characteristic of Mediterranean ships until the end of the Roman period and of ships in Gaul and Britain, used carvel or edge-to-edge planking. The second, clinker building, had each plank of the hull overlapping the one below. It was already known before the beginning of the Christian era and it became the usual system in northern Europe early in the medieval period.

What is known as the Sutton Hoo ship was discovered in 1939 in a burial mound near Woodbridge in Suffolk. The clinker-built boat, eighty-nine feet long and fourteen feet broad, is reckoned to date from about AD 600, and it was probably constructed in Britain. There is no trace of decking or of a mast, although the boat was almost certainly capable of being sailed. It had a permanent rudder, an oar fixed to the right-hand side of the hull. The Nydam ship, found and excavated in Schleswig in 1864, was probably built between AD 350 and 400. Carvel-built, it represents the older tradition and is probably typical of ships used in southern Scandinavia and for journeys across the North Sea during the fourth and fifth centuries. Both the Sutton Hoo and the Nydam ships could be equally well described as warships and merchant ships, since the Vikings made no distinction between these two functions. Their ships were multi-purpose. Boats of the seventh, eighth and ninth centuries found preserved in bogs in Denmark, Sweden and Norway confirm this general picture of the size and technical features of Viking boats. They make it clear that ocean voyaging at that time was not a comfortable experience for crew or passengers – the sea ran in when the boat keeled over even slightly – and was not calculated to maintain any freight carried in a good condition.

The first Scandinavian vessel to be discovered with definite evidence of a mast and a sail is the Oseberg ship, of about AD 800. With two other Norwegian ships, the Gokstad and the Tune, of approximately the same period, the example from Oseberg shows the high standard of craftsmanship which had been reached in Scandinavia at this time.

Shipbuilding design in Northern Europe changed during the medieval period because the demand changed. Larger quantities of cargo had to be transported over longer distances. This meant bigger, stronger ships, which had to be lived in for weeks on end. The traditional system of sleeping and cooking on shore was no longer possible once long voyages became inevitable. This in turn meant that clinker-building had to be replaced by carvel-building and that the use of several masts and sails was necessary in order to drive the bigger, heavier ships. The chunky, straight-stemmed ships, the cog or hulk, was found to be the answer to the problem. It was probably developed in the Frisian islands and it ousted the traditional and much more elegant Scandinavian type because it made it possible to transport grain, timber and salted herrings in large quantities. (In medieval times fish could be transported only after it had been salted. From the fourteenth century onwards, the pattern of trade established by the Hansa towns was to take Baltic grain and Scandinavian timber to the Atlantic coast of France and to bring back salt in exchange.)

In the Mediterranean, as in the north, however, merchant ships were tubby, round and slow, warships long, sleek and fast until well into the fifteenth century. The galleys built in Byzantium and Italy from the eight century onwards were up to 165 feet in length and were propelled by a hundred and more oars. A variant of the galley was used for trading purposes where the urgency and value of the traffic demanded it.

Navigation was transformed during the thirteenth century by the invention of the maritime compass. This is usually supposed to have taken place in Amalfi. This early compass did not have North, South, East and West points. The circular card to which it was attached showed the directions of eight winds. These eight directions were subdivided to make sixty-four points. Detailed sailing directions for the whole of the Mediterranean were collected into a book, *Lo Compasso da Navigare*, published in 1296. This gave bearings, distances and local conditions. When this information was converted into a picture, one had a chart. The earliest known chart, the *Carta Pisana*, dates from about 1275. It shows compass bearings and scale distances. With it, the captain of a ship could, for the first time, plot a course with reasonable accuracy.

Fourth century. Yassi Ada, Turkey

Yassi Ada is a small island between the Turkish mainland and the island of Pserimos. Two ships, which hit a reef off the coast of Yassi Ada, were located and investigated in 1958, and one of these wrecks was fully surveyed in 1967–69. The ship, sixty-two feet long and nearly twenty-two feet wide, was built of cypress, with an oak keel. The galley equipment found included pottery, glass vessels, a copper jug, lead weights for a fishing net, lamps and a steelyard. The cargo was carried in 1100 amphorae. The fact that only a hundred stoppers were found, and that the ship was apparently bound for a major wine-producing area, suggests that most, if not all, of the amphorae were new and empty. The presence among the finds of pottery from the Black Sea area, mussel shells from the Bosphorus and coins from Constantinople makes it probable that the voyage began

20

somewhere in the area of the Straits of Bosphorus.

Also among the discoveries were three sets of scales. Two used the balance-pan method, with bronze weights inlaid with silver, and the third was a steelyard, with the counterweight in the form of a bust of Athena.

c. 550. Marzamemi, Sicily

The famous 'churchwreck', a consignment of prefabricated marble interior fittings of a church, made in Byzantium and probably being shipped to North Africa. The ship struck submerged rocks and sank in only thirty feet of water. Investigations carried out in the 1960s showed that nothing of the timbers remained, but there were signs of a galley and of iron nails used in the ship's construction.

Sixth century. Pantano Longarini, Sicily

Remains of a ship broken up on a reef outside the ancient port of Edissa, on the south-eastern coast of Sicily. A number of timbers were destroyed in 1963 before their significance was realised. They included a very rare item, the ship's name in Greek letters on a hardwood plaque. The overall length was about 130 feet and the capacity 200–300 tons.

Seventh century. Yassi Ada, Turkey

The second ship found on the site, excavated 1961–64. The hull was sixty-two feet long and seventeen feet wide. The galley was exceptionally well furnished and equipped, and there is no doubt that the crew took their meals on board. The hull was built in the modern manner, with the frames put in first and the hull planking added afterwards. The vessel had been sunk in AD 625 or 626, with a cargo of about nine hundred amphorae, probably filled with wine.

Late eighth century. Utrecht, Netherlands

The remains of 'hulk', fifty-six feet long and twelve feet broad, were found (1930) embedded in mud in the former bed of the Rhine. The ship was built, without keel or stem, of planks converging at both ends with a thick curved oak bottom plank instead of a keel and a mast-step fitted well forward. It had probably been used for river transport.

Eleventh century. Roskilde, Denmark

At some time between 1000 and 1050 the navigation channel of Roskilde fjord was blocked against invaders by sinking five ships at Skuldelev. The ships were then covered with boulders. The site was excavated and the ships salvaged within a coffer dam in 1957–59. They have since been conserved and restored and are now on exhibition in a specially-built museum at Roskilde. The five ships, fortunately for the historian, are of different types.

1. *The ocean-going merchant ship.* About thirty-six feet long and fifteen feet broad, with high sides, this is the only example yet found of a cargo and passenger ship known as a *knarr.* Ships of this type sailed from Scandinavia to England, Iceland and Greenland. This particular one was probably built in south Norway. It had a half-deck fore and aft, but there was nowhere for the people travelling in it to take shelter. It was propelled by a single square sail.

2. *The small merchant ship.* About forty-four feet long and eleven feet broad, this type of ship was used for carrying cargo across the Baltic, up large rivers and, on occasion, across the North Sea. The freight was stowed amidships under a hide tarpaulin and the crew, probably of six to eight men, remained on the half deck fore and aft. The ship could be rowed, but usually relied on its square sail.

3. *The warship.* About fifty feet long and ten feet broad. Usually propelled by a

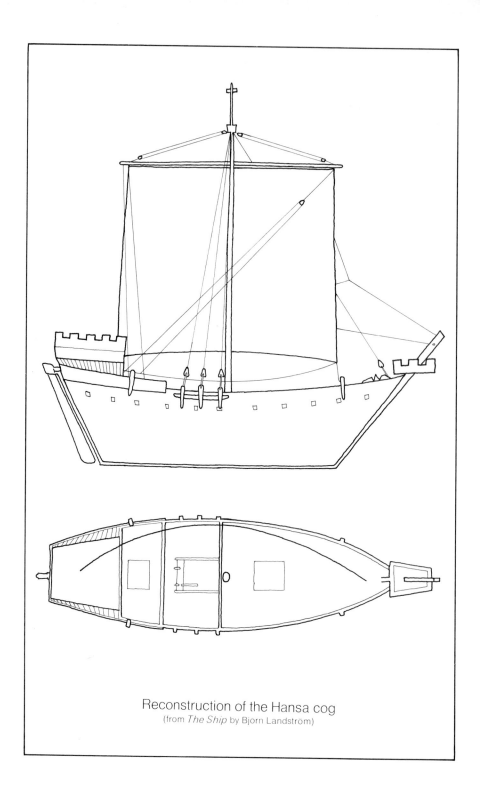

Reconstruction of the Hansa cog
(from *The Ship* by Bjørn Landström)

sail, it could be rowed. The three upper strakes had come from another ship.

4.   *The longship.* About a hundred feet long, this is the only example of the Viking long-distance raider so far discovered. It carried a crew of forty to fifty men and had a single sail. In battle it was rowed, not sailed.

5.   *The ferry or fishing boat.* About thirty-nine feet long and eight feet wide. There are broad cross-beams, but no deck. It had a mast and sail, but there are no traces of oar-holes.

Twelfth century. Zuider Zee, Netherlands
During the draining of the north-east polder during the 1950s, the remains of 156 ships were found, mostly from the sixteenth to the nineteenth centuries. Wreck Q75, however, was sunk in the twelfth century. The lower part has survived and shows the ship to have been clinker-built, with a flat bottom board.

Early thirteenth century. Asker, Norway
The remains of a fifty-foot merchant ship were found as a result of excavations within a coffer dam.

Early thirteenth century. Bergen, Norway
At some time in the middle of the thirteenth century twenty-five parts of a large ship were used to build a wharf. These sections, of pine, had come from a ship eighty-five feet long and about thirty feet wide, showing that the Scandinavian ship-builders were fully as competent as those of Holland and the Hansa towns in constructing large ships and that they had adopted the cog design.

Thirteenth century. Kalmar, Sweden
During the clearance of accumulated mud from this medieval harbour in 1933–34, a number of wrecks were discovered. One was that of a small thirteenth century merchant ship.

Thirteenth century. Kolding Fjord, Denmark
The wreck of a cog, flat-bottomed, with a straight stem. It was sixty feet long, twenty feet broad and a Stern-rudder. There is evidence of primitive-type galley.

Late fourteenth century. Bremen, Germany
During the deepening of the harbour in 1962, parts of a wooden ship were discovered. Archaeologists succeeded in salvaging nearly all the timbers and planks and the ship, a cog with a length of seventy-seven feet, has been reconstructed in the Maritime Museum at Bremerhaven. The ship did not appear to have been completed and, since a winch and capstan showed no signs of wear and a tar barrel and shipwright's tools were found on board, it was concluded that the nearly-finished ship had been swept from its slipway during a flood.

Fifteenth century. Lake Garda, Italy
Venetian galley, *c*.1439, part of a fleet brought overland from Venice during the war between the Republic of Venice and the Duchy of Milan. Two thousand oxen were used to tow the ships. The remnants of the fleet to which this galley belonged were scuttled in 1509. The ship was located in 1962 and parts of it were raised. The hull was about two hundred feet long.

The Age of Exploration: Wrecks of the Tudor and Renaissance Periods

It is difficult to find a satisfactory label for the period of a little over 150 years between the end of the fifteenth century and the middle of the seventeenth, during which the world was opened up to international shipping and trade to an extent which would have seemed both impossible and pointless during the Middle Ages. By one of history's conveniences, however, the first Tudor king in England, Henry VII, began his reign just before Christopher Columbus made his first voyage of exploration to Central America and when the Portuguese were finding the way to the East round the Cape of Good Hope. 'Tudor' therefore indicates this phase of Europe's expansion reasonably well. It is roughly the last quarter of the fifteenth century and the first half of the sixteenth. Once the gold and silver of the New World was flowing back to Europe regularly and in huge quantities, as it was by 1550, the style of life began to change rapidly, at least among the middle and upper classes. What had previously been considered great luxuries became much more easily available, the scale of trade vastly increased and, as a consequence of both these developments, the major European nations became much more greedy and combative, anxious to establish empires of their own and, wherever possible, to destroy or weaken those of others. This raising of the level of technical knowledge, living standards, awareness of the world, curiosity and national arrogance can be defined as the Renaissance. It was noticeable in some countries of western Europe rather earlier than others, and it had made an unmistakeable impact everywhere by the first quarter of the seventeenth century.

The Routes and Cargoes

Between 1271 and 1295 the Venetian, Marco Polo, travelled overland to Central Asia and returned by sea, via Indonesia, Baluchistan and the Persian Gulf. His account of what he had seen made the East seem real to Europeans in a way which it had not been before. This, coupled with the fact that Turkish control of the sea-routes in the eastern Mediterranean made spices, on which the Turks levied exorbitant customs duties, impossibly dear, produced a determination on the part of the Portuguese to find a route to the East which was not subject to Turkish interference. Prince Henry, known because of his seafaring interests as

Henry the Navigator, had a new type of ship, the caravel, constructed and began to encourage and finance the exploration of a route going south from Portugal, down the African coast, mainly in the first instance to look for sources of spices, which the otherwise dull diet of Europeans had made almost a necessity. Bartolomeo Dias reached the Cape of Good Hope in 1487 and in 1498 Vasco da Gama sailed as far as Mozambique, where he found plenty of spices, and then went on to India. Twenty years of fighting, colonisation and conquest established the Portuguese firmly on both sides of the Indian Ocean and by 1516 they were in Canton, having set up ports and trading posts all along their route to the East.

At the same time as the Portuguese were exploring eastwards, the Spaniards were interesting themselves in the possibilities westwards across the Atlantic, not, in the first place, to reach America, of the existence of which they were unaware, but as a means of getting to Asia by sailing round the world in the opposite direction from the Portuguese. A Spanish expedition led by Christopher Columbus left Europe in 1492 and discovered Cuba, in the belief that it was China. Once it had returned with the news that the new continent was flowing, not precisely with milk and honey, but certainly with gold and silver, whole fleets were fitted out to colonise and explore the New World. Within fifty years the Spaniards had explored both coasts of South America, built a network of towns, ports and harbours, conquered the native populations with utter ruthlessness and established regular routes to bring the treasure back to Spain. Eventually two fleets went out each year, one to Cartagena and the other to Vera Cruz, collecting the gold, silver, tobacco and Oriental goods which had been accumulated throughout the year at the depots. Towards the end of the sixteenth century the Spanish ships and colonial towns were regularly attacked by French and English pirates, a process which continued with increasing vigour into the following century.

Between approximately the end of the fifteenth century and the beginning of the nineteenth, the Spaniards shipped an average of seventeen million pesos of gold and silver back to Spain each year, together with an unknown but certainly large quantity of unregistered metal which was, from the point of view of the Spanish government, contraband. Economically, this trade was of immense importance both to Spain and to Europe. The unprecedented amount of precious metal put into circulation as coinage was a powerful stimulus to international commerce and for Spain herself, with no significant industrial development, it was of vital importance. Her political and social order was founded on the products of the American mines. Once her dominating position as an owner and supplier of gold and silver had gone, as it had by the beginning of the nineteenth century, she withered away as a world power.

Conversely, so long as her gold and silver Empire existed, Spain pursued a single-minded policy in order to safeguard what she understood to be her interests. The ships, traders and colonists of other countries were kept out of the area by all possible means, slave labour was employed at the mines and every attempt was made to salvage rapidly the cargo of any ship which had been wrecked. No humanitarian considerations were allowed to interfere with this. If Negro women were able to withstand cold longer, Negro women, not Negro men were used as divers. If the best way of extracting silver from the ore was to spread it out mixed with mercury and then to drive horses and mules round and round over it, that was done, even if the animals' feet were rotted away by the mercury within a short time. Mercury has been unreasonably neglected in the accounts of the Spanish hunger for silver. It was a vital commodity, so much so that its possession and supply was made a crown monopoly. The loss of a ship carrying mercury was almost as great a disaster as a wrecked treasureship, especially since the mercury could rarely be salvaged.

The English, Dutch and French established themselves as colonists in the Caribbean between 1620 and 1670 after many years of piracy and privateering in the area. The capture of Jamaica in 1655 by the British was particularly significant, since it provided a base for trading both with England itself and with the North American colonies. By the end of the century very large convoys of English ships were involved in a varied trade, with a special concentration on cotton, tobacco, indigo, spices, timber and rum. The Dutch began to come to the New World after about 1580, the main reason being their desperate need of salt for pickling herring. Until that time they had bought most of it in Portugal but when the Spaniards put an end to the trade it was necessary to find other sources of supply. The deposits in Central America provided the answer, and by 1600 the Dutch were bringing back two hundred shiploads a year, mostly from Punta de Araya. They were also beginning, very willingly, to take over the Portuguese role of supplying the Spaniards with African slaves.

The Dutch, with Amsterdam as their trading base, began following the Portuguese routes to the East in the last quarter of the sixteenth century. By 1600 they had discovered Mauritius and established trading posts in Indonesia and the Moluccas and in 1602 they set up the Dutch East India Company. This had good relations with the Japanese, broke through into the Mediterranean, where they became the main agents for Europe's trade and sailed right round Australia. By the middle of the seventeenth century they were the most powerful naval power in the world, with much the best-trained navigators and the most efficiently organised commercial and banking systems.

Interlocking with this expansion of trade was the new pattern of shipping routes brought about by emigration and colonisation in North America. The Atlantic was a difficult ocean for sailing ships making for the eastern seaboard of North America. Given the prevailing westerly winds, they had to go either to the north via Greenland and Iceland – the Viking route – or to the south along the line followed by the Spaniards. Jacques Cartier reached the St. Lawrence by the northern route in 1534, John Smith went south to Virginia 1604, the Pilgrim Fathers took a more direct route to Cape Cod in 1620. From then onwards, new settlements sprang up all along the Atlantic coast of North America and the business of transporting and supplying them and of bringing back timber, cotton and tobacco created a new system of shipping routes.

The Ships

Until somewhere about 1550, the usual ocean-going ship was small, for the most part less than a hundred tons. The *Niña*, in which Columbus crossed the Atlantic and explored the New World was only thirty to forty tons, that is, thirty-five feet long and twelve in the beam, the size of a Thames sailing barge or a rather broad yacht. The carracks, the work-horses of northern Europe, were bigger, but

1 *A seventeenth-century artist's impression of the Pharos of Alexandria. Built on the orders of Ptolemy, it was dedicated to him by the architect, Sostrates Gnidius.*

2 *Smeaton's Eddystone lighthouse. The smooth masonry of the tower offered the minimum resistance to waves and so increased the chances of the lighthouse's survival.*

3 *Brown's steam-driven siren, ready for action on the cliff. Its size can be judged by the height of the man leaning on it.*

4 *The Sambro Light, Nova Scotia. The first American lighthouse was built near Boston in 1716. By 1800 there were thirty oil-fuelled navigation lights along the east coast.*

5 *Captain Manby's travelling hammock for rescuing victims of shipwrecks, 1808.*

6 *The Ramsgate lifeboat attempting to rescue a ship wrecked on the Goodwin Sands, c. 1850.*

7 Clearing a Wreck, *a painting by Templeton, c. 1830. The picture makes clear how important a source of supply a wreck could be for local people. In conditions such as this, nothing of value was likely to be left once the 'clearing' operation had been concluded.*

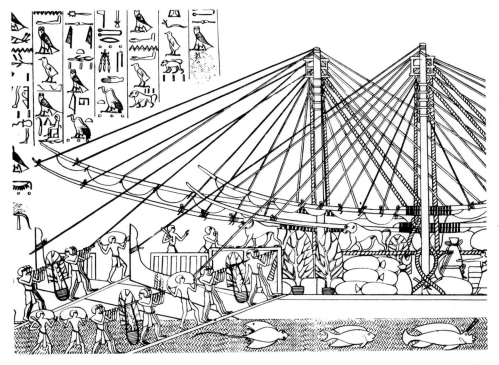

8 *Sea-going Egyptian merchant ships of c. 1500 BC from a fresco, showing the expedition by Queen Hatshepsut to Somalia to buy incense trees and other exotic goods.*

9 *A Greek bireme of about 500 BC, which has two tiers of oars. Early Greek ships were very similar to those of the Phoenicians.*

10 *A mosaic from the Church of S. Apollinaire Nuovo, Ravenna, showing Roman merchant ships of the first century BC in harbour.*

11 *In 1968 excavation was carried out at Kyrenia, Cyprus, on a trading vessel and its cargo which*

11 *In 1968 excavation was carried out at Kyrenia, Cyprus, on a trading vessel and its cargo which sank c. 300 BC. The cargo contained amphorae of wine and piles of almost perfectly preserved almonds.*

12 *Timbers from a Roman ship wrecked off Grand Congloue, Marseilles, c. 200 BC. It was the first wreck to be excavated by divers equipped with aqualungs in 1953.*

13 *Moving the remains of a Roman merchant ship* c. *AD 300, excavated in 1910 near Westminster Bridge, London.*

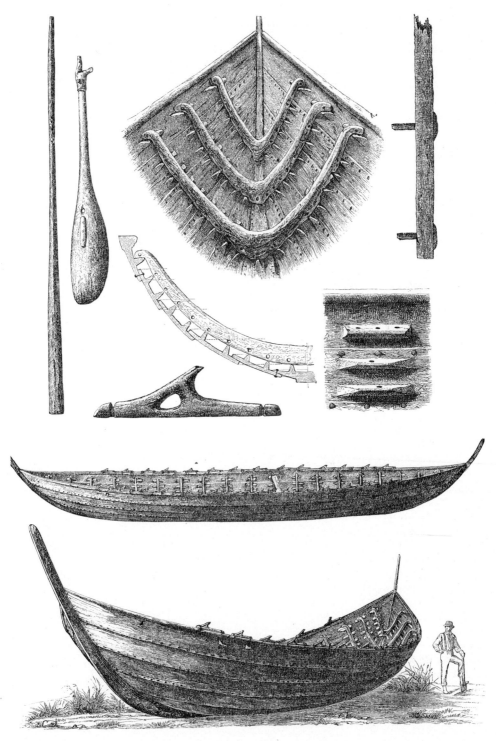

14 *Details of construction of the carvel-built Viking ship found in a peat bog at Nydam, Schleswig, in 1863. The ship probably dates from* c. *A D 350-400.*

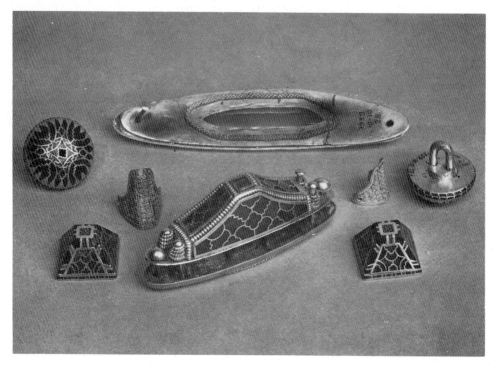

15 *Treasure from the Sutton Hoo ship: (above) gold and garnet sword fittings, a saddle pommel in the form of a cocked-hat, scabbard bosses, pyramids, filigree hilt-mounts and quillons; (below) gold and silver strap-mounts, a buckle, dummy buckle and strap distributor from sword harness.*

16 *The Sutton Hoo ship was discovered in 1939 in a burial mound in Suffolk. The clinker-built boat is thought to date from about A D 600.*

17 *A contemporary engraving of the Gokstad ship, discovered in a burial mound in Norway in the nineteenth century, and dating from A D 800.*

18 *The Oseberg Viking ship of about AD 800, during its excavation in Norway. It was the first Scandinavian vessel to be discovered with definite evidence of a mast and sail.*

19 *The reconstructed Oseberg ship shows the high level of craftsmanship which had been reached in Scandinavia by this time.*

20 *Excavation and salvage of the Roskilde ships being carried out within a coffer dam in 1959. At some time between AD 1000 and AD 1050 the navigation channel of Roskilde fjord was blocked against invaders by the deliberate sinking of five ships.*

21 *One of the salvaged ships, a knorr or sea-going cargo ship.*

22 *Fifteenth-century warships, still following the Viking pattern but broader and stronger. These boats were very small, of no more than twenty or thirty tons.*

23 *A German woodcut of a shipwreck, with the two survivors clinging to part of the wreckage.*

24 *(Facing page) A fifteenth-century astrolabe, supposedly used by Columbus during his first voyage to the New World in 1492.*

25 *The voyages of the Age of Discovery led to the development of a new type of ocean-going vessel, the Spanish caravel. The ships were still small, less than 100 tons and about 35 feet long.*

26 *In the English Channel in 1588 the Spanish Armada was forced to retreat in the face of English galleons. The galleon was a hybrid developed by combining the advantages of the huge Spanish carrack and the fast oar-driven galley.*

27 *Two silver coins from among the treasures salvaged from the* Girona, *one of the Armada ships wrecked off the Irish coast in 1588.*

very slow and difficult to manoeuvre. The galley, which had to be rowed as well as sailed, was fast, but vulnerable to storms. As a way of combining the special advantages of the carrack and the galley, the Spaniards developed the galleon. It was a successful mongrel, with the carrying capacity of the carrack, the lines and speed of the galley and the sails and rigging of the caravel. The galleons were usually three to six hundred tons, but towards the end of the sixteenth century they were occasionally being built much larger, up to 1000 or 1200 tons.

The galleons were smaller than warships for four reasons. Many of the ports at which they had to call would not take larger vessels; it was felt to be uneconomic to have large crews, which would, in any case, have been difficult to recruit; the smaller the ship, the easier it was to find suitable timber; and, by having two small ships instead of one large ship, the risk was spread.

The naval ambitions of the major European powers produced a few much larger ships – Henry V's *Grace Dieu*, launched in 1418, was of 1400 tons and Henry VIII's *Harry Grace à Dieu* or *Great Harry* 1000 tons – but they were floating fortresses, built entirely for fighting in the Channel and never more than twenty-four hours' sailing time from their base. The galleons, on the other hand were away for months at a time. But, although the development of the galleon produced an effective sailing design, it left the fundamental problems of long-distance voyaging unsolved. Every captain's main worries were about keeping the people on board healthy and adequately fed. Losses from sickness and disease were much greater than from enemy action or wrecks and the more people a ship carried and the longer the voyage, the smaller the passenger's chances were of arriving at his destination alive.

Voyages within Europe

1545, 18 June. Portsmouth

The *Mary Rose* was built at Portsmouth in 1529 and rebuilt and increased in size, also in the Royal Dockyard at Portsmouth, in 1536. She was then a four-masted sixty-gun carrack of six hundred tons and one of the first warships to have gun-ports. In 1545 she was lying at anchor in calm water together with the rest of the British fleet, waiting for a French attack. She heeled over in a sudden breeze and sank immediately, probably as a result of water entering the open gun-ports. Of the seven hundred men on board, fewer than fifty-six survived. In 1965, when she was found by divers, she was under fifteen feet of mud. Archaeologists who worked at the site from 1973 onwards found the timbers of the *Mary Rose* in excellent condition and much of the ship has now been raised.

1588. Destruction, by enemy action and wreck, of *La Felicissima Armada*

The great fleet assembled by Philip II of Spain for the invasion of England, consisted of 130 ships. After the English victory in the Channel, some of the ships tried to escape by sailing round the north of Scotland, a route of which the navigators had no experience and no charts. At least twenty were wrecked in the attempt. Among them were:

La Trinidad Valencera. Sank in the Bay of Kinnagoe, near Glenagivney.
Santa Maria de la Rosa. Went down off Great Blasquet, on the Dingle Peninsula.
El Gran Grifón. Went down in the narrow inlet of Stroms Hellier, off Fair Isle.

San Pedro Mayor. After rounding Scotland and the west coast of Ireland, she was blown ashore near Hope Cove, Devon.

Girona. Wrecked on the Rock of Bunboyes, at Port La Spaniagh near Port Ballantrae, on the north Antrim coast.

1627, 26 November. Coast of Devon

The Duke of Buckingham's fleet were at anchor off the coast of Devon, having recently returned from the Île de Rhe, when a severe gale blew up and drove fifteen vessels on to the Hamoaze and five more into the Cattewater.

1628, 10 August. Beckholmen, Stockholm

King Gustavus II's first warship, the *Wasa*, was designed by a Dutchman, the Swedes at that time having little experience of large warships. She was 180 feet long, with a displacement of fourteen thousand tons and was square-rigged. She sank soon after beginning her maiden voyage, having heeled over in a gust of wind. She was topheavy – a floating castle and a monument to royal vanity – and with water rushing in through open gun-ports she sank immediately. After being raised in 1959 and floated into dry dock the following year, the timbers of the *Wasa* were found to be in excellent condition – the ship-worm does little damage in the Baltic and she has been conserved with great skill. The ironwork was less fortunate; the water in this area is not kind to iron. But a wide range of other objects, including clothing, has been wonderfully well preserved, as visitors to the *Wasa* can see for themselves. The instability of the *Wasa* had two causes: the elaborately sculptured superstructure and the two continuous gun-decks, carrying guns with a total weight of more than seventy-one tons. Together, these made the ship's centre of gravity dangerously high.

1675, 26 March. Ilfracombe, Devon

The 350-ton *Arms of Bristol*, on her way from Bristol to Barbados, was wrecked in a gale near Ilfracombe. Forty survivors reached the shore in boats and on pieces of wreckage, but sixteen drowned and little of the cargo was saved.

1686. Silver Carn, Isles of Scilly

The *Princesse Maria*, eleven hundred tons, left Texel for the East Indies, with four hundred people on board and a valuable cargo, much of it in pieces of eight. She was wrecked by Scilly and her cargo plundered. James II sent the royal yacht, *Isabella* secretly to the island to collect his share of the loot. Archaeological work, carried out from 1970 onwards, located the wreck and produced a number of objects from it, including a very rare discovery, a Bellarmine flagon containing forty pounds of mercury.

1689, 25 December. Mount Batten, Devon

In fierce storms two ships were driven ashore and wrecked here, HMS *Centurion*, thirty-four guns, and the *Henrietta*, sixty-two guns.

1691, 3 September. Plymouth, Devon

HMS *Coronation*, 1346 tons, and HMS *Harwich*, 993 tons, sailed into Plymouth Sound with the remainder of Admiral Russell's fleet to shelter from bad weather. They were sailing so fast and so close together that a number collided and others ran ashore, among them the *Harwich*, which went down with four hundred and twenty men, and the *Coronation*, with more than five hundred. After the loss of the *Harwich*, the Admiralty buoyed the channel leading into the Hamoaze. These buoys and others in Plymouth Sound are named after famous naval vessels.

Europe to India and the Far East

1561. Sumatra
The Portuguese carrack, *São Paolo*, six hundred tons, sailed with five other ships from Lisbon in April 1560. She carried five hundred passengers and was seriously overloaded. Because of the contrary winds her captain decided to make first for Brazil, instead of rounding the Cape of Good Hope. After repairs and re-provisioning, the *São Paolo* crossed the Atlantic again but, having passed the Cape, she was wrecked off the coast of Sumatra. Three hundred and thirty of the passengers and crew were saved. Some tried to make their way overland to the nearest Portuguese settlement, others built boats from the wreckage and reached safety that way.

1594. Punta Negra, Faial, Azores
The Portuguese *Las Cinque Chagas*, 2000 tons and probably the largest ship afloat at the time, was sunk off the Azores by British privateers on her return voyage from India and the East Indies. There were only thirteen survivors out of a total of one thousand people on board. Nothing of the cargo has ever been salvaged.

1622. Monte Bello Islands Reef, Barrow Island, Western Australia
The East India Company's ship, *Tryal*, left Plymouth for Java in 1621, with 143 people on board. Inadequate sailing directions caused the captain to set a wrong course on the last stage of the journey. The ship hit the rocks and broke up quickly. Between forty and fifty of the passengers and crew reached Batavia in two boats. The remains of the ship were discovered in 1970.

1629, 3 June. Wallabi group of islands, Western Australia
The 600-ton Dutch East Indiaman, *Batavia* left Holland on her maiden voyage on 27 October 1628, bound for Batavia (the modern Djakarta) with three hundred passengers and crew and a cargo which included cloth, wine, cheese and a considerable quantity of jewels and silver coin. She was in a convoy of eight ships, several of which hit a coral reef in the Wallabis and were wrecked. A group from the *Batavia* got away in a small boat with as much of the valuable cargo as they could carry. When they returned from Java with help they found that a small group of the castaways had murdered most of the rest of the survivors, with the intention of taking possession of the relief ship and making off with the remainder of the treasure. Seven of them were hanged and two left to their fate on the island. Others were brought back for execution in Batavia. The 250 men originally left behind were the first white people to live in Australia.

Voyages around the coasts of North and South America

1492. Hispaniola
Christopher Columbus's flagship, the *Santa Maria*, was wrecked in Caracol Bay, near Cape Haitian. The ship was completely dismantled to build a fort, which the survivors could use as a base until they were rescued on Columbus's second voyage.

1504. Jamaica
During his fourth voyage of discovery in Panama and Central America, Columbus was using two ships which were leaking and waterlogged because of

worm-attack on the timbers. Both ships were run aground in St Anne's Bay to prevent them from sinking and the crews lived in the castles of the ships – the only parts above water – for more than a year until they were finally rescued.

1524, 20 January. Los Triángulos, Mexico
The Governor of Santiago de Cuba was wrecked on a voyage to meet Cortez in Mexico. The survivors built a boat from the wreckage and reached Veracruz.

1526. Hispaniola
The small Spanish merchant ship, *Santa Maria*, 110 tons, sank in the harbour of Puerto de Plata after taking on a cargo of sugar there.

1526. Isla Cancun, Mexico
La Nicolasa, bound from Cuba to Veracruz with supplies for the conquistadors went down here. Cannon from the wreck were recovered in 1959.

1540. Near San Diego, California
The small caravel, *Trinidad* was on a voyage of exploration up the Californian coast. There was sickness on board and the crew had to be put ashore. The anchor cable broke in a storm and the ship drifted away and was wrecked.

1545, 20 August. Santo Domingo, Hispaniola
A hurricane destroyed many of the ships in port. A later and worse hurricane wrecked most of the remaining twenty ships.

1550, c. 27 August. Near San Juan, Puerto Rico
The *Santa Maria de Jesus*, on a voyage from Spain to Mexico with an exceptionally valuable cargo, went down in a storm close to the port of San Juan. Very little of the cargo was salvaged.

1551. Fort Pierce, Florida
The merchant ship *San Nicolas*, 200 tons, was wrecked here on her return voyage from Cartagena and Nombre de Dios to Spain. Much of the cargo was salvaged by Indians.

1553. Colombia
The merchant ship *Santa Maria de Villacelan*, 120 tons, bound from Nombre de Dios to Cartagena, was wrecked south of Cartagena. The cargo of treasure was saved by Indian pearl divers brought from Margarita Island.

1553. Padre Island, Texas
The twenty ships of the treasure fleet bound from Veracruz to Cuba and Spain were hit by a hurricane in the Gulf of Mexico. Only three reached port.

1563, 18 July. Cuba
Six ships of the New Spain Fleet, the *San Juan Bautista*, *San Juan*, *San Salvador*, *Nuestra Señora de la Consolación*, *Nuestra Señora de la Concepción* and *Santa Margarita*, were wrecked on the Los Jardines Reefs off the southern coast of the island. All the ships were carrying mercury, and the *San Juan Bautista* had, in addition, an archbishop and a large consignment of church plate and ornaments.

1567. Dominica
Six small (120–150 tons) treasure ships of the New Spain Fleet were lost off here in a storm, while following an unusual route back to Spain in order to avoid two English fleets waiting to intercept them, one at Havana, the other near the Bahama Channel. Those who reached shore were massacred by Indians.

1568, 21 September. San Juan de Ulúa, Mexico
The Fleet of New Spain, en route from Sanlúcar to Spain, found an English fleet, under the command of John Hawkins, anchored in the harbour of San Juan. In the battle which followed, a number of ships on both sides were sunk including

the *Santa Clara*, which included in its cargo the extremely valuable item of a hundred pounds of mercury. The English flagship, the *Jesus*, was lost.

1571, October or November. Tabasco, Mexico

Four merchant ships of the Fleet of New Spain, on a voyage from Sanlúcan to Veracruz, were wrecked here. The ships, the *San Juan*, *La Maria*, *Santa Catalina*, and *La Magdalena*, were carrying, among other commodities, mercury and wine, most of which was salvaged.

1572. Isla Tesova, Colombia

The galleon, *San Felipe*, 550 tons, caught fire on a voyage from Nombre de Dios to Cartagena. She was beached but exploded before her treasure could be salvaged.

1584. Hispaniola

The galley *Santiago* was sent from Santo Domingo to look for pirates. It hit the reef outside the harbour and was wrecked with the loss of all the galley slaves.

1597, 30 August. San Juan de Ulúa, Mexico

The Fleet of New Spain, with sixty-eight ships, arrived here after a two-month journey from Cadiz. Two merchant vessels, the *San Buenaventura*, and *La Pandora*, collided and sank at the entrance to the harbour. The two ships were sailing much too close together, so that the anchor on the bow of one caught the rigging of the other.

1599. Near San Francisco, California

The large Manila-based galleon, *San Agustin*, was wrecked on a voyage from the Philippines to Acapulco, with the loss of nearly everyone on board. Her cargo consisted mainly of spices, silks and porcelain from the Far East.

1600. North of San Diego, California

A squadron was sent from Peru to look for Dutch warships reported near Panama. Off Panama, the leading ship, the *Capitana*, lost her rudder in a storm, drifted northwards for several weeks and was wrecked off the California coast.

1600, September. At various points along the Mexican coast

Two hurricanes struck the sixty ships of the Fleet of New Spain. Fourteen ships were lost, together with about a thousand men and a great quantity of cargo, ranging from wine to muskets and from olive oil to mercury. It was one of the worst disasters to have hit the convoys sailing between Spain and the New World.

1603. Guadeloupe, Antilles

The Fleet of New Spain anchored here to take on water. Three of the ships were wrecked at anchor. Two hundred and fifty men were left behind to salvage the cargo, but they were attacked by Indians and left the island with all speed. Shortly afterwards, Spanish ships captured a French privateer near Puerto Rico and found that she had on board a number of bronze cannons abandoned on one of the three wrecked ships.

1604, 5 September. Veracruz, Mexico

The *Santa Maria de Begonia*, part of the Fleet of New Spain, was sunk in the harbour here during a gale, with a cargo of mercury and general merchandise.

1605. Punta de Araya, Venezuela

The Dutch had established an important salt industry here. An armada of Spanish ships destroyed the twenty-two Dutch ships at anchor and wiped out the settlement.

1605. Serranilla Bank, Central America

Seven galleons of the Tierra Firme Fleet were struck by a hurricane and four, the

San Roque, Santo Domingo, Nuestra Señora de Begonia and *San Ambrosio* were wrecked on the reef here, with no survivors. Salvage teams attempted to locate the wrecks and rescue the treasure for more than sixty years, but failed.

1609, Bermuda

The English ship, *Sea Venture*, on a voyage from Plymouth, England, to Jamestown, with supplies for the colony, was wrecked here. The survivors established the first European settlement on the island.

1615, 4 September. Veracruz, Mexico

The small merchant ship, the *Espiritu Santo*, belonging to the Fleet of New Spain on its way home, ran aground. She was pulled off the shoals, but then sank in deeper water. While she was sinking, most of her cargo was saved by being thrown into small boats alongside.

1621. Bermuda

The armed Spanish merchant ship, *San Antonio*, bound for Spain with a cargo of hides, brazilwood, indigo, tobacco, sarsaparilla, tortoise-shell and a small amount of gold and silver, was wrecked here in a storm. Most of the cargo was recovered by Bermudans.

1622, 6 September. Dry Tortugas, Florida

The galleon *Nuestra Señora del Rosario*, was wrecked with a cargo of silver, all of which was recovered by divers.

1622, 6 September. Matacumbe Key, Florida

The Havana-built galleon, *Nuestra Señora de Atocha* 600 tons, went down in deep water during a hurricane with a cargo of silver and tobacco. This hurricane was an especially bad disaster for the Spanish treasure fleet, with the loss of at least fifteen ships. The galleon, *La Margarita*, 600 tons, also carrying silver and tobacco, sank close to the *Nuestra Señora de Atocha* during the same hurricane, but in shallower water, where it was possible for divers to recover most of the cargo soon afterwards.

1623. Isla Mujeres, Mexico

The *Nuestra Señora de la Piedad*, with a cargo of 282 negro slaves from Angola, was wrecked here. The crew and 170 of the slaves were rescued.

1623. Near Ais, Florida

The galleon, *Espiritu Santo el Mayor*, 480 tons, sank in a hurricane. All her treasure was lost, together with two hundred and fifty of the three hundred people on board.

1623. Near Ais, Florida

The galleon, *Santissima Trinidad*, 600 tons, was wrecked in a hurricane. She went down slowly, however, and all her cargo, passengers and crew were taken off in smaller ships.

1625. Salvador, Brazil

Salvador was captured by a Dutch fleet in 1624, a number of Portuguese merchant ships being sunk in the attack. In 1625, a large fleet of Spanish and Portuguese ships was sent to recapture the town. Three Dutch ships were sunk by gunfire and a Portuguese warship wrecked on the rocks outside the port.

1626, December. Nauset, Massachusetts

The *Sparrowhawk*, a small ship bound from England to Jamestown, Virginia, with about twenty people and supplies for the new colony, ran into bad weather off Cape Cod and had to be beached. The ship was repaired with the help of colonists at the Plymouth settlement and resumed its voyage. Further bad weather forced the *Sparrowhawk* to return to Plymouth where those on board spent the winter. Indians burned the upper part of the hull and the rest was sucked down into a marsh at Naunset. In 1863, after a storm had left the remains of the ship on the surface again, they were recovered and put on display.

1628, 8 September. Cuba
A Dutch West Indies fleet forced the Fleet of New Spain into Matanzas bay, where all twenty-four of the Spanish ships were wrecked on the sandbanks. Some of the treasure was thrown overboard, but the Dutch got most of it. The quantity was so great that, even after the twenty-eight Dutch ships had been fully loaded, four of the wrecked Spanish ships had to be repaired and refloated in order to help with transporting the treasure back to the Netherlands.

1631, October. On the coast of Mexico, between the Bajo de las Arcas and Tabasco
The Fleet of New Spain was struck by a hurricane on its way from Veracruz to Spain. All nineteen ships were lost. The cargo lists illustrate the nature of the trade at this time, the items including gold, silver, cochineal, indigo, Chinese raw silk, hides, brazilwood, chocolate and molasses.

1632, 27 February. Las Hormigas, near Callao, Peru
A merchant ship, Spanish owned, was sailing for Callao from Panama with a valuable mixed cargo and a hundred and twenty-five slaves. It hit the rocks at Las Hormigas and broke up. The pilot was subsequently hanged for having caused the loss of the ship.

1632, 2 April. Off Miami, Florida
Two ships of a Spanish convoy bound from Havana to Spain became separated from the convoy and were forced by the current too close to the shore. One of the ships was carrying a luxury cargo, cocoa.

1636. Martinique
The warship, *San Salvador*, bound from Spain to Venezuela with a cargo of munitions was wrecked off the island, which had been colonised by the French. The crew set fire to the ship before getting away in the boats. The *San Salvador* exploded before the French were able to get possession of any of the cargo.

1636, 20 January. Cap San Antonio, Cuba
A Spanish merchant ship, carrying a cargo of cocoa from Maracaibo to Havana, was forced aground here by Dutch privateers. The crew were put ashore and the Dutch then plundered the ship of everything of value.

1640. Colombia
Three ships of the Portuguese armada were deliberately wrecked near the entrance to the harbour at Cartagena to prevent them from falling into the hands of the Spanish. None of the cargo of gold, diamonds and other precious stones appears to have been recovered.

1641. Near Hispaniola, on a reef known as Silver Shoals or Silver Bank
The *Nuestra Señora de la Concepción* was one of a convoy destroyed by a hurricane. Most of the cargo of silver was recovered in 1687 by an English expedition, backed by Charles II and the Duke of Albemarle and led by William Phips of Boston. Phips used native divers and a device known as a Catalan bell, which allowed men to work underwater by refilling their lungs from time to time with the air trapped in the top of the bell. Thirty-four tons of treasure were brought back to England, Phips being rewarded with one sixteenth of its value and a knighthood. He was also made Governor of Massachusetts.

1650, 26 March. Punta Dotolauquen, Chile
The Spanish warship, *San José*, left Concepción with soldiers and supplies for garrisons in the south. After it was wrecked, most of those on board managed to get ashore, but were massacred by Indians.

1656. Little Bahama Bank, Bahamas
The galleon *Nuestra Señora de las Maravillas* sank after colliding with another galleon during the night, with a loss of 650 people. During the next three years Spanish salvage teams recovered one and a half million of the five million pesos of treasure carried on the wreck, before shifting sands covered it completely. In 1657, two small ships taking some of the salvaged treasure to Puerto Rico were wrecked on Gorda Key. The survivors buried as much of the cargo as they could get on shore and it was later found and taken to safety by the Spaniards.

1666. Bay of All Saints, Martinique
The Governor of Barbados received news of six French ships lying at anchor in the Bay and sent five British ships to capture them. The French set fire to their ships, but the British managed to save five. When the cargoes were being loaded into the British ships, a sudden storm sank them all.

1673. Guadanillas Islands, Puerto Rico
The warship *Ogeron* was built by order of the governor of the French island of Tortuga, near Haiti. It was sent to take part in the capture of Curaçao, crewed by five hundred pirates of several nationalities. The ship was wrecked on the rocks near the Guadanillas Islands. The crew reached Puerto Rico overland, but were massacred by the Spaniards there.

1683. Veracruz
The 70-ton Spanish ship, *El Santo Cristobal*, bound from Spain to Tabasco, stopped at Veracruz for repairs, since she was leaking badly. The ship was careened on the beach to allow the hull to be inspected and put to rights but, while the work was being carried out, she caught fire and was destroyed.

1666, 14 August. Guadeloupe, Antilles
In a battle here between a British and a French fleet, the French lost twelve ships and the British two. Two days later, however, a hurricane struck the island and all fifteen survivors of the British fleet were lost.

1673, 25 February. Isle de Vache, Hispaniola
The *Jamaica Merchant*, an English privateer based on Port Royal, Jamaica, was wrecked here as a result of faulty navigation. The crew were taken back to Jamaica by another privateer, and salvage vessels sent by the Governor of Jamaica recovered twenty cannon from the site of the wreck.

1683, 31 July. Charlotte Amalie, Virgin Islands
The British warship HMS *Francis*, attacked the pirate ship, *La Trompeuse*, as she lay at anchor in the harbour. *La Trompeuse* caught fire and exploded.

1694, 27 September. Carlisle Bay, Barbados
Twenty-six English merchant ships were sunk at their moorings during a hurricane, with the loss of more than a thousand men.

War and Commerce: the Eighteenth Century

From the point of view of seafaring and exploration, the eighteenth century began in 1662, when the British staked a firm claim in the East by establishing themselves in Bombay, hitherto a strongly Portuguese base. The eighteenth and nineteenth centuries were the great period of British overseas power, dependent on a dominant navy and on ambitious, successful and well-organised merchants. It was the period, too, in which London became the world centre of marine insurance. *Lloyd's List*, the first comprehensive record of disasters at sea, began publication in 1740. It provides modern historians with the kind of record which had never previously existed. By establishing itself as the major institution for insuring ships, Lloyd's was committed to becoming a registry of shipping and at the same time a body for ensuring that certain minimum rules of safety at sea were laid down and complied with.

During the seventeenth century, the British established themselves on both sides of India. Bombay and Madras looked after the trade of the Indian Ocean, from the Persian Gulf and Arabia to the spice islands further south. Calcutta was the base for commerce with the Far East. Between 1650 and 1800, the average size of a merchant ship sailing from England to the East doubled from 500 to 1000 tons. The speed of voyages increased at the same time. London to Canton and back took between two and three years in the seventeenth century; it was reduced to twenty months during the eighteenth.

The British bought their way into Indonesia and China with opium, in which the East India Company had a monopoly. They used it to buy spices and Philippine dollars, which in turn were exchanged for the Chinese products, especially tea and porcelain, which were becoming increasingly popular in Britain and in the wealthier towns of the American colonies and which formed a very important part of the British trade with the East. A ship carried about 1500 cases of tea and, since the quantity of tea imported into England rose from a hundred thousand pounds a year in 1700 to nearly thirty million in 1800, ship-owners were assured of prosperity, merely from this single commodity. The difficulty, however, was to pay for Chinese goods. The balance of trade somehow had to be maintained, and the East India Company found the answer in opium. Traditionally, the Chinese used it only as a medicament, but the English, helped by local merchants, deliberately and profitably turned it into a habit-forming drug, as tea had already become in England. The habit of smoking opium spread throughout Chinese society and millions of people were brutalised by it.

Tens of thousands if not millions were brutalised, too, by the slave trade, which

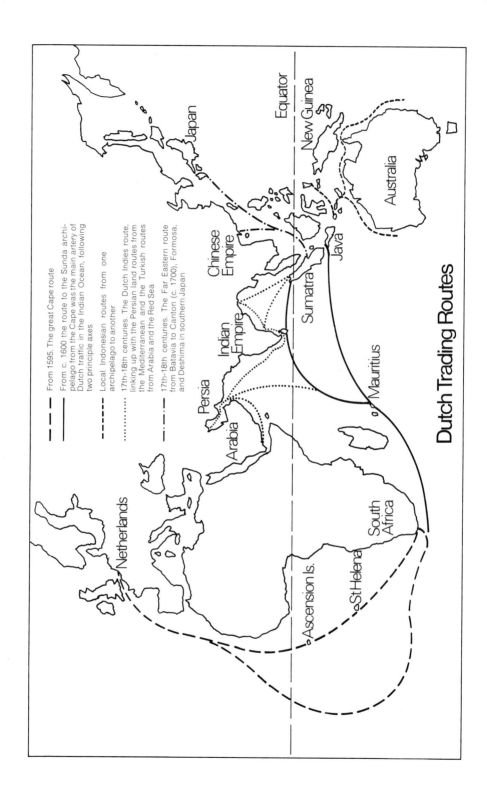

Dutch Trading Routes

- - - From 1595. The great Cape route

——— From c. 1600 the route to the Sunda archipelago from the Cape was the main artery of
Dutch traffic in the Indian Ocean, following
two principle axes

– – – Local Indonesian routes from one
archipelago to another

········· 17th-18th centuries. The Dutch Indies route,
linking up with the Persian land routes from
the Mediterranean and the Turkish routes
from Arabia and the Red Sea

–·–·– 17th-18th centuries. The Far Eastern route
from Batavia to Canton (c. 1700), Formosa,
and Deshima in southern Japan

Netherlands

Ascension Is.

St Helena

South
Africa

Arabia

Persia

Indian
Empire

Chinese
Empire

Japan

Mauritius

Sumatra

Java

New Guinea

Equator

Australia

from the seventeenth century onwards became so important commercially as a means of supplying cheap labour to the new colonial territories of America that it had its own routes. The slavers followed the African coast down to the Gulf of Guinea where they anchored at the estuaries of the big rivers linking the coast with the interior. Here they traded slaves for cheap goods brought from Europe, took their new cargo across the Atlantic to South and Central America, exchanged the Negroes for gold, silver, spices, sugar and coffee and returned to Europe. The routes and the system were established by the Portuguese, but by the seventeenth century the Dutch, French and British all had a hand in it. It was easy to build up a quick fortune and many of the leading European merchant families acquired their wealth in this way.

During the century and a half from the end of the Thirty Years War until 1800, merchant ships became bigger, stronger, faster and much more numerous and large navies with greater fire-power somehow had to be financed in order to protect merchant shipping and to prevent colonial territories from being invaded. Taken together, these two developments necessitated during the eighteenth century a doubling or trebling of the number of men required to build, navigate and man the ships. To find builders and navigators was not a great problem, but to get seamen every form of compulsion and bribery had to be resorted to. The work was dangerous and extremely unhealthy. Few men were willing to do it voluntarily and many wrecks must have been caused at least in part by the inexperience and incapacity of the crews.

The Ships

The average European-built merchant ship of the mid-seventeenth century was of about 180 tons, the size of the *Mayflower*. It was three-masted, with a very simple sail-plan: two square sails to the foremast and mainmast, a lateen sail on the mizzen mast and a spritsail under the bowsprit. By the end of the eighteenth century, the East Indiamen were of 1000–1200 tons and carried a great deal more sail – three or four square sails on the foremast and main-mast, a triangular sail and a square sail on the mizzen mast, and two jibsails on the bowsprit. To deal with this great quantity of sail, a large crew was required. A hundred to a hundred and fifty men was normal for an East Indiaman. They included, besides seamen, a number of specialists such as caulkers, gunners and coopers. The bigger ships became, the more need there was of expert knowledge and skills, and for this reason particularly deaths during a long voyage were an extremely serious matter since a boatswain or navigating officer were just as likely to die as the most inexperienced seaman and to replace them at the Cape of Good Hope or any other port en route was virtually impossible. To improve ship design to produce more living space and more ventilation, to avoid overcrowding, to provide a good diet and to take only healthy people on board were the constant preoccupation of those who had the management of large ships. One has to remember, however, that, given luck, there was a great deal of money to be made from operating a ship and that then as now many owners were prepared to gamble with old, ill-maintained ships, overloading and overcrowding, and incompetent crews, in the hope that fortune would be with them as indeed it often was.

Voyages to Australasia

1656, 28 November. Cape Leschenault, Western Australia
The Dutch East Indiaman, *De Vergulde Draeck* (The Gilt Dragon) left Texel,
Holland, in 1655 with 193 people on board and a valuable cargo which included a
large quantity of pieces of eight, mainly from the Mexican mint. She made an
unusually short stop at the Cape of Good Hope, probably because her passengers
and crew were in exceptionally good health. A few deaths occurred between the
Cape and Australia. Off the Australian coast, the captain evidently reckoned he
was much further from land than he actually was and struck a reef near Ledge
Point, Cape Leschenault, in good weather and under full sail. The ship split open
under the impact and sank immediately, many of those on board being drowned
in their sleeping quarters. The seventy-five survivors included the captain. They
reached land in two boats, which carried some provisions and fresh water. A
small party then left for Batavia to report the wreck and to bring help to the
survivors. The two rescue boats failed to find anyone at the site and returned to
Batavia, and other attempts made the following year were also without success,
although the original camp and items of wreckage from the ship were discovered.

1712, June. Near the mouth of the Murchison River, Western Australia
In 1711 the Dutch East Indiamen, *Zuytdorp* and *Belvliet*, both of about 400
tons, sailed from Flushing to the East. They made unusually slow progress
to the Cape. Scurvy had caused heavy casualties in both ships – the *Zuytdorp*
had lost 112 men out of 286 and the *Belvliet* sixty out of 164. In order to be
able to continue their voyage, both ships had to take on extra crew at the Cape.
Belvliet arrived safely in Batavia, but *Zuytdorp* was driven ashore in a gale on to
the Australian coast and totally wrecked. The remains of the ship and her cargo
were found in 1927 and identified in 1958 by means of coins, a special minting
made by the Middleburg Mint for the *Zuytdorp* and *Belvliet* to take to Batavia.
The fate of the survivors is uncertain. One piece of evidence suggests that some of
the Dutch settled. Aborigines in the areas have been discovered with unmis-
takably Dutch build, hair and faces.

1727, 9 June. Gun Island, southern Abrolhos group, Western Australia
The *Zeewyk*, a new ship belonging to the Dutch East India Company, hit the
Half Moon Reef near Gun Island. She did not sink immediately and twenty out
of thirty of the crew continued to live on her for four months. Others found safety
on an artificial island formed by the masts and rigging, which drifted away from
the wreck, and were afterwards ferried away, with provisions, to Gun Island. The
ship's longboat, sent to Batavia for help, failed to arrive, and having realised this
the eighty-eight survivors of the 208 who had originally sailed from Holland then
built themselves a small ship from the wreckage of the *Zeewyk*. Eighty-two of
them reached Batavia safely. Of the sixty members of the crew who died during
the time spent on Gun Island, two were boys who were marooned and left to die
on separate islands as a punishment for homosexuality. The captain of the
Zeewyk was charged with carelessness and with not following his sailing orders,
and also with having altered the ship's journals to cover up his offence. He was
convicted, all his belongings were confiscated and he was banished for life from
everywhere under the administration of the East India Company.

1788. Whanoo and Paiou Islands, between the New Hebrides and Santa Cruz group
The French exploring ships, *Astrolabe* and *Boussole* left Botany Bay with the

intention of surveying the Gulf of Carpentaria. Those in the ship wrecked on Whanoo were all killed by natives; the survivors who got ashore on Paiou bought the natives off with presents and managed to construct the boat which got them away, presumably to be wrecked in its turn.

1790, 19 March. Norfolk Island, New South Wales

The *Sirius* was built on the Thames for the east-coast trade. She caught fire while loading and was burnt out to the waterline. The British government bought her in this condition and rebuilt her. She became the flagship of Captain Phillips's expedition which founded Sydney as a penal establishment in 1788. While unloading stores at Norfolk Island in heavy weather, she dragged her anchors and was thrown on to a reef. Most of the cargo, including livestock, which were simply thrown overboard, was got on shore before the ship finally broke up.

1790. Pitcairn Island, Pacific Ocean

After a mutiny, the commander of HMS *Bounty*, Lt. William Bligh, was put off, together with eighteen other men, in a longboat. They all arrived safely at Timor, more than 3500 miles away. The leader of the mutineers, Fletcher Christian, sailed the *Bounty* to Tahiti where sixteen of the crew decided to stay. Christian himself went on with the remainder of the crew, eight men and twelve Polynesian women and eight Polynesian men to Pitcairn Island, 1300 miles from Tahiti, where they scuttled the ship. In 1808, the Boston ship *Topaz* called at Pitcairn and found the survivors, together with a number of children who had been born there. Only one mutineer was still alive. The others had either killed one another or been killed by the Tahitians.

1791, 28 August. Great Barrier Reef, Australia

HMS *Pandora*, was sent from England to look for the mutineers of the *Bounty*. When she reached Tahiti, fourteen either gave themselves up or were captured. On board the *Pandora* they were kept in irons and caged on deck in a box eleven feet long. On her return voyage, the *Pandora* struck the Great Barrier Reef sixty miles north-east of Cape Grenville. Although she filled with water fast, the Captain refused to release the prisoners. The master-of-arms did so, however, and eleven escaped as the ship was being abandoned. The survivors reached Timor in the boats. The convicts, who were extremely badly treated, were sent to the Cape and then to England, where three were eventually executed.

1797, 9 February. Preservation Island, Australia

The *Sydney Cove*, a Calcutta-owned ship, sailed from Bengal to Port Jackson, Australia in 1796, with a cargo which included seven thousand gallons of spirits. During heavy weather off the Tasmanian coast, she sprang serious leaks and had to be run ashore on Preservation Island. Seventeen of the crew made for Sydney in the longboat in very bad weather and two weeks later they were wrecked on Ninety Mile Beach, 220 miles from Sydney. The men attempted to walk to Sydney, but fourteen died or were killed by aborigines on the way. The terrible journey had a bonus; the survivors reported the first discovery of coal in Australia.

Voyages to North America

1710, 7 July. Long Island, New York

The *Herbert*, and the *Palatinate*, bringing German emigrants to America, were wrecked on the east end of Long Island. No lives were lost.

1738, 10 September. Sandy Point, Rhode Island

The *Prinzessin Augusta*, carrying 350 German emigrants from Amsterdam to New York, was wrecked on Sandy Point, Rhode Island. At the time, only one hundred of the passengers were still alive, two hundred and fifty of them having previously died through drinking contaminated water.

1750, 18 August. Cape Hatteras, North Carolina

The Fleet of New Spain was struck by a hurricane near here. Four ships were lost off Cape Hatteras and three off Cape Charles, Virginia. The *Nuestra Señora de Guadeloupe* and the *Zumaca* reached Norfolk, but both were lost during another hurricane a few weeks later.

1751. Wallops Island, Virginia

The British merchant ship, *King's Fisher*, on a voyage from New England to South Carolina with prisoners, was taken over by the prisoners, who murdered the crew and then wrecked the ship.

1752. Block Island, Rhode Island

On the last stage of her voyage the Dutch immigrant ship *Palatine* ran into tremendous storms which damaged the ship and resulted in the death of the captain. The crew then looted the ship and took to the lifeboats, leaving the passengers to fend for themselves. The ship drifted for some days before running aground on Block Island. There the inhabitants allowed the immigrants to land, then plundered the vessel and set fire to it. Blazing fiercely, it was set adrift with one demented passenger still on board, who had refused to leave the ship. The legend has grown up that on the anniversary of the looting a ghostly ship, blazing from stem to stern, can be seen gliding along the coast past Block Island.

1752, 15 September. Charleston, South Carolina

During a hurricane, twenty English merchant ships and three warships were sunk in harbour here. When a second hurricane struck on 30 September, twelve more ships were sunk.

1757, 22 April. Sable Island, Nova Scotia

The English merchant ship, *Buchanan*, en route from Gibraltar to Maryland, was captured by a French privateer. On her way to Louisburg she was wrecked on Sable Island.

1757, 24 September. Louisburg, Cape Breton Island

The English warships, HMS *Tilbury* and HMS *Ferret*, were sunk in harbour here during a hurricane.

1758, 18 June. Louisburg, Cape Breton Island

A British fleet was preparing to attack Louisburg and the French scuttled four of their ships in the harbour – the *Apollon*, *Fidèle*, *Chère* and *Biché* – because there were no crews to man them. Shortly afterwards, three of the large French warships, the *Entreprenant*, *Capricieux* and *Célèbre*, were accidentally destroyed by fire.

1777, 28 August. Sable Island, Nova Scotia

The English ship, *Aurora* was wrecked here. When the survivors reached shore, they found seven Negro women still alive from a French ship wrecked here sixteen years earlier.

1778, 2 November. Cape Cod

The British frigate, *Somerset*, was on duty in the North American colonies. She was present at the landing of British troops at Charlestown, Massachusetts, in preparation for the Battle of Bunker Hill. Her captain had the reputation of sending his chaplain ashore to preach in Provincetown in exchange for Ship's provisions. While chasing French merchant ships, she ran into a storm at Cape Cod, tried to get back to Provincetown Harbour and was wrecked on Peak Hill Bars. The survivors were imprisoned in Boston by the colonists and the cannon used for coastal fortifications. Wreckers cleared the ship of everything else of value and the upper parts of the ship were gradually cut away for souvenirs.

1779, 14 August. Portland, Maine
Four American warships, the *Warren*, *Diligent*, *Hazard* and *Tyrannicide* were set on fire and destroyed in harbour here, in order to prevent them from falling into the hands of the British.

1783, 23 November. Oswego, Lake Ontario
The English ship, *Ontario* sank here with the loss of 190 passengers and crew and a considerable quantity of gold and silver coins.

1794. Delaware Bay
The Spanish merchant ship, *San Joseph*, on her way from Philadelphia to Cuba sank as a result of ice crushing her hull.

Voyages from Europe to the Far East

1749. Hastings, Sussex
The Dutch East Indiaman, *Amsterdam*, began her maiden voyage to the East in January 1749, with 203 sailors, 127 soldiers and five passengers on board. A fortnight afterwards when she had got no further than the Sussex coast, she struck a sandbank and lost her rudder. The captain anchored her offshore, waiting for suitable wind and weather to reach Portsmouth for repairs. With eighty of those on board suffering from yellow fever, he decided the task was impossible and drove the ship up a narrow estuary at Bulverhithe, and beached her. By that time, the majority of the crew were drunk, having looted the *Amsterdam*'s wine store. A large number of wreckers got to work on the cargo, despite the efforts of the Dutch soldiers and of a small British detachment to prevent them. The salvage engineer blew himself up while trying to blast a way to the remaining cargo and although the main treasure chests were rescued it was impossible to get at the main part of the cargo, because the ship had sunk so deep into the mud. Two weeks after the wreck had occurred, the Dutch East India Company gave all attempts at further salvage. A rapid and far from scientific investigation carried out in 1969, when a new sewer outfall was being constructed nearby, allowed archaeologists to recover a good deal of further material, including cannon, bottles of wine and a lady's fan, and to observe that the hull was still at least three-quarters complete.

1782. Pondoland coast, Cape Province, South Africa
The East Indiaman, *Grosvenor*, sailed from Trincomalee in Ceylon with 150 passengers and crew and jewellery and bullion valued at more than two million pounds in money of the time. The ship struck a submerged reef off Pondoland, 750 miles from the Cape, and sank rapidly into the sand.

1790, *c.* 22 December. False Bay, South Africa
The frigate, HMS *Guardian*, left Spithead for Sydney in 1789, with officials, convicts and supplies for the newly established convict settlement. She loaded

cattle and horses at the Cape of Good Hope and to provide them with drinking water sent out boats to pick up loose ice when about 1300 miles from the Cape. Shortly afterwards, the *Guardian* hit an iceberg, severely damaging the ship and unshipping the rudder. Guns, cattle and cargo were thrown overboard. A number of the officers, seamen and convicts decided to gain courage from alcohol and became hopelessly drunk, but three boats got away and those in one of them were picked up after spending two weeks at sea. The captain remained on board with sixty-two people, including twenty-one convicts. They managed to bring the ship into False Bay where she went aground in a gale and was totally wrecked. On arrival in Australia, fourteen of the convicts were set free after the report given by the captain of the *Guardian* on their behaviour at sea.

Voyages within Europe

1707, 22 October. Isles of Scilly
The English fleet, led by the *Association*, the flagship of Admiral Sir Cloudesely Shovell, was sailing up the Channel on its return from the Mediterranean. The *Association* was carrying three million pounds in bullion and silver. Through a navigation error, the Admiral believed he was off Brittany, whereas in fact he was close to the Scillies. The *Association* and the four ships accompanying it were wrecked on the Scillies, with the loss of two thousand men. Islanders immediately got to work on the wrecks and Sir Cloudesely himself was probably strangled as he lay unconscious on the beach for the sake of his jewellery.

1743. Gunner Rock, Isles of Scilly
The Dutch East Indiaman *Hollandia* was on her maiden voyage from Texel to Batavia with three hundred people aboard and a valuable cargo. Off course, she struck Gunner Rock, and went down in 110 feet of water, with the loss of everyone on board.

1745, 27 February. Berry Head, Devon
The transport, *Tiger*, left Plymouth for the West Indies with troops for the islands. She was struck by a gale as soon as she reached the open sea, and was wrecked on the Devon coast. Most of those on board were drowned. The survivors tried to reach Plymouth, where they were confronted with posters offering a reward of one pound for every soldier caught.

1760, 15 February. Bolt Tail, Devon
When she was finally wrecked and lost, HMS *Ramillies* had been in service with the Navy for ninety-six years. She was launched at Woolwich in 1664 as the *Katherine*. Known after 1696 as the *Royal Katherine*, she was renamed the *Ramillies* after being completely rebuilt in 1702. She was rebuilt for the second time in 1749, when her tonnage was increased to 1698. During her incredibly long service with the navy, she took part in almost every major battle and acquired a proverbial reputation. In January 1760, she was on blockade duty in the Channel with six other ships. Caught in a gale, she was driven on to the rocks of Bolt Tail in thick fog. Seven hundred of the 720 on board died in the wreck, including the wives and children of some of the crew. The ship was completely broken up.

1772. Bigbury Bay, Devon
The *Chantiloupe*, returning from the West Indies, was wrecked off the Devon coast. The two survivors were a seaman and a woman passenger, who was

wearing valuable jewellery. A story, possibly legendary, says that while she was still alive, local people cut off her fingers and ear-lobes to get her rings, after which she was left to die and buried on the beach. A grave found by children in 1900 contained the skeleton of a Negro, who had probably been one of the crew.

1776, 16 April. Unst, Shetland Islands

The London whaler, *Syren*, bound for Greenland, was lost with all hands near the Wick of Hagdale during a severe storm. The ship was smashed to pieces.

1782, 29 August. Spithead, Portsmouth, England

The man-of-war, *Royal George*, was lying at anchor in sixty-five feet of water, with 1300 men, women and children on board. In order to repair a small leak below the water-line, the ship was heeled over by moving all the 108 guns to the side opposite the leak. Unfortunately, attempts were made to unload a cargo of rum on this side of the vessel, and the ship capsized, with the loss of more than a thousand people.

1795, 22 December. Tor Abbey Sands, Devon

The brig *Biscay* parted her cables and drove on to the Sands, where she went to pieces. The six survivors searched the coastline for their captain, who was reported to be wearing a money belt. The corpse was found, but no belt. Local wreckers quickly disposed of the ship's valuable cargo of food.

1796, 22 September. Plymouth, Devon

The 680-ton *Amphion* was launched at Chatham in 1780. In 1796 she was cruising in the North Sea, watching for signs of Napoleon's threatened invasion, when her foremast was damaged by a gale. Repairs were carried out at Plymouth. The work had been completed and a farewell party was being held when the ship blew up, killing three hundred out of the 312 people on board. The disaster was blamed on one of the *Amphion*'s gunners, who was stealing gunpowder. He contrived to drop a light on some spilt powder when he was drunk, causing the foreward magazine to explode.

1796. Plymouth, Devon

The East Indiaman, *Dutton*, sailed from Plymouth to the West Indies with troops on board. After seven weeks, she turned back, 'because of her condition'. She reached Plymouth but hit the Mount Batten bank, the warning buoy having disappeared, and was swept on to rocks just below the Hoe. Panic broke out among the crew, the officers abandoned the ship and nothing was done to help the men left on board until the captain of HMS *Indefatigable*, Sir Edward Pellew, got on board and took command of operations. Two boats from the *Indefatigable*, together with a third from another ship, rescued six hundred people from the wreck. Sir Edward was given the freedom of Plymouth and when he was made a baronet in the following year he included a stranded ship on his crest.

1798, December. Millbrook, Plymouth, Devon

The French warship, *La Coquille*, was captured by the British off the Irish coast. Taken to Plymouth, she blew up and caught on fire at anchor there. As she was being towed away from the anchorage to be beached on a mud-bank, she hit the Scarborough collier, *Endeavour* and set her on fire. Both ships were a total loss.

1798, 19 December. Southern Wells, Isles of Scilly. HMS *Colossus* was one of Nelson's men-o'-war and was making her way from the Mediterranean with sick and wounded from the Battle of the Nile when she dragged her anchors in St Mary's Roads during a gale and was wrecked on Southern Wells, south of the island of Samson. Only one crew member died, but most of the cargo was lost, including paintings, Etruscan vases and archaeological treasures belonging to Sir William Hamilton, British Ambassador in Naples.

1799, 9–10 October. Vlieland, Holland

HMS *Lutine* was a French ship, captured by the British. She contained a great quantity of bullion and coin, the property of various merchants, and was insured with Lloyd's. The Dutch government claimed the wreck and in 1801 granted a third of the salvage to a group of bullion divers. Pressed repeatedly by the British, the Dutch authorities eventually agreed in 1857 to allow Lloyd's half of what remained of the cargo. By 1859, Lloyd's had received about twenty-two thousand of an estimated one hundred thousand pounds recovered up to that date, with more than one million still lying somewhere on the seabed. The rudder was discovered in 1859 and Lloyds had a chair and table made from it to keep as souvenirs on their premises in London.

1799, 23 October. Plymouth, Devon

The *Washington*, a Liverpool-registered cotton ship was lost by fire under remarkable circumstances while anchored offshore. The crew saw a boat carrying a naval press gang approaching and disappeared into a specially prepared hiding-place deep in the hold. The ship's cook dropped his knife and while he was looking for it with a naked light accidentally set some cotton on fire. The ship burned for nearly twenty-four hours and, of the three thousand bales on board, only three hundred and fifty were salvaged.

Voyages off the North African Coast

1724, 19 November. Porto Santo, Madeira

The Dutch East Indiaman, *Slot Ter Hooge*, was wrecked here during a storm. All 224 people on board were lost and three and a half tons of silver bullion went to the bottom. Most of the silver was recovered soon afterwards by the English diver, John Lethbridge, working on behalf of the company. Lethbridge used a 'diving engine' of his own invention, a barrel through which he could push his arms. Most of the rest was salvaged two hundred and fifty years later by the Belgian diver and archaeologist, Robert Sténuit, who used the occasion to test a reconstruction of Lethbridge's equipment.

South America and the Caribbean

1706. Conil, Yucatán

The courier boat, *Nuestra Señora de la Concepción y San Joseph y Las Animas*, 68 tons, on its way from Spain to Veracruz, ran aground at Conil, while attempting to escape from a British privateer. The crew got ashore with the mail, and the ship was then looted by the British, who took the cargo, rigging, sails and fittings, before setting her on fire.

1708. Baru Island, Colombia

As a result of the War of the Spanish Succession, no treasure ships had gone from South America to Spain for six years. In 1708, seventeen ships arrived to transport the exceptionally large amount of cargo that had accumulated. Only four were armed and the gold and silver was consequently loaded on them, the less valuable commodities going on the other ships. Half of it, worth about eleven million pesos, was on the *San José*. The Spanish fleet was attacked by the British off Cartagena. The *San José* blew up and sank, another galleon was captured and a third set on fire by the Spaniards. All the others reached Cartagena safely.

1714. Grand Bahama Island
The galleon *San Juan Evangelista*, en route from Veracruz to Puerto Rico and Santo Domingo with money needed to pay the troops and royal officials at both places, was struck by a storm in the Bahama Channel and sank in four fathoms of water. All the treasure was recovered by salvage teams.

1715. Florida coast
A convoy of twelve ships left Havana for Spain. Their cargoes included gold and silver coins and bullion, cocoa, brazilwood, vanilla, tortoise-shells, hides, tobacco, pearls, jewellery, Chinese porcelain, indigo, sarsaparilla, balsam and snuff. The convoy made its way up the Bahama Channel and was then struck by a hurricane, which wrecked all but one of the ships on the Florida coast. More than a thousand people lost their lives and fifteen hundred reached shore. Salvage began immediately and within a year the officials in charge were able to report that they had recovered nearly all the king's treasure.

1724, 12 September. Samana Bay, Hispaniola
The Fleet of New Spain sailed from Veracruz on 25 August, but a hurricane forced it to head south and a number of ships, including the *Nuestra Señora de Guadeloupe*, the *Capitana* and *La Tolosa*, sank in deep water in the area of the Bay, after hitting reefs. All but one of the ships were salvaged.

1732, January. Veracruz, Mexico
A squadron carrying mercury from Cadiz to Veracruz had an unusually long and rough voyage. One of the largest ships in the squadron, the galleon *Nuestra Señora de la Concepción*, sank in the harbour of Veracruz, with the loss of five hundred men.

1740. Havana, Cuba
The galleon, *Invencible*, was struck by lightning as she lay at anchor in the harbour here. She exploded and was totally destroyed, causing a great deal of damage to the town. None of the four million pesos of treasure which the ship was carrying was recovered.

1741, 22 February. Off Yucatán
The Spanish ship, *El Matancero*, left Cadiz at the end of 1740 for the West Indies. In trying to escape from English warships, she went aground and was wrecked at what were then called the Yalcu Shoals, off Yucatán. In 1957, American archaeologists began to investigate the site and after initial difficulties with the Mexican authorities an arrangement was made whereby the Americans were to keep half of all the objects they found which were not considered by the Government to be of 'intrinsic archaeological value'. An enormous quantity of material was then raised, including crucifixes and shoe buckles, pins, needles and buttons. Everything was then declared to be 'of intrinsic archaeological value' and so the archaeologists got nothing for their pains.

1742, 20 March. Anegada, Virgin Islands
The Spanish armed merchant ship, *San Ignacio*, belonging to the newly formed Caracas Company, was wrecked on Anegada, with the loss of four hundred of the six hundred people on board.

1747. Basseterre, St Kitts, Leeward Islands
During hurricanes in September and October, twenty-four British ships were lost here, most of them fully loaded with sugar and waiting to sail for England.
1749, 28 August. Barbuda, Antilles
The English slave ship, *Pearl*, arriving from Africa with a cargo of slaves, was wrecked in a gale, with the loss of seventy slaves and eleven members of the crew.
1752, 17 September. Morant Keys, Jamaica
The English merchant ship, *Phoebe*, was wrecked here, bound from Liverpool to Jamaica with a cargo of trade goods and artillery for the Island's forts.
1755, 2 September. Barbuda, Antilles
The French slave ship, *Hazard*, bound for Hispaniola from Africa, was wrecked here. Eighty of the slaves on board were drowned.
1758, 23 August. Carlisle Bay, Barbados
A hurricane sank five ships. They illustrate the range of shipping trading with Barbados at this time – the American merchant ship, *Aurora*, from North Carolina; the *Jenny and Sally*, from South Carolina; the *Rose*, the *Good Intent* and the *David and Susanna*, all from England.
1762; 3 June. Havana, Cuba
Before the Spaniards surrendered Havana to the British they sank three large warships – the *Neptuno*, *Asia* and *Europa* – across the entrance to the harbour. A fourth ship, *La Victoria*, was destroyed during the attack on the city. After the English took the city, three small English ships, the *Providence*, *General Wolfe* and *Lion* were wrecked while leaving harbour with loot for England.
1766, 19 April. Kingston, Jamaica
The English merchant ship, *Minerva*, loading sugar and rum for London, caught fire in the harbour and was burnt out.
1767, 17 November. Barbados
The British slave ship, *Rebecca*, was wrecked on a reef near Long Bay on arrival from Africa. Her crew and slaves and a cargo of ivory and wax were saved.
1768, 22 January. Key West, Florida
The Spanish ship, *San Antonio*, bound from Havana to Spain, was wrecked on a reef near here. The passengers and crew spent twenty-two days on the reef before they were picked up by a turtling ship and taken back to Havana.
1768, 15 October. Havana, Cuba
Sixty-nine ships were destroyed here during a hurricane, which also destroyed a large part of the city of Havana.
1769, 19 June. Grand Roy Bay, Grenada
The English slave ship, *Sally*, bound from Africa with a cargo of slaves, was wrecked here. There were no casualties among either the slaves or the crew.
1770. Port Royal, Jamaica
The English merchant ship, *King David*, sank in harbour here after hitting a large anchor which was sticking up from the sea bed.
1772. Veracruz
The Spanish warship *Castilla* was lost in a gale here. The cargo consisted of seven hundred boxes of cochineal, none of which was recovered.
1772, 5 December. Chinchorro Reef, Mexico
The *Nuestra Señora de Guadeloupe* had sailed for Spain from Omoa, Honduras, with a cargo of silver and agricultural products, which included a large consignment of indigo. It was wrecked, but most of the silver was salvaged.

46

1773, 18 October. Florida coast
The British ship, *Dove*, nearing the end of her voyage from Africa to St Augustine with a cargo of a hundred slaves, went down in a hurricane off the coast of Florida. Eighty of the slaves and three of the crew were drowned.

1776, 6 September. Point Petre Bay, Martinique, Antilles
A convoy of more than a hundred French and Dutch merchant ships bound for Europe was annihilated by a hurricane. At least six thousand people drowned.

1780, 9 October. Dominica, Antilles
The new French frigate, *Juno*, was wrecked on the island with the loss of more than three hundred men on board.

1780, 12 October. Martinique
The October hurricane was the worst ever to hit the island. Forty French troopships and four large warships, together with four British ships belonging to Admiral Rodney's fleet, HMS *Andromeda*, HMS *Laurel*, HMS *Deal Castle* and a supply ship, the *Endymion*. The number of ships of different nationalities lost on the island during the hurricane has been put as high as one hundred and fifty.

1781, 1–2 August. Kingston and other ports, Jamaica
A hurricane which struck the island on these two days destroyed ninety ships in harbour at Kingston, thirty at Port Royal and seventy-three in other ports.

1782. Barbados
The British slave ship, *Lark*, was wrecked off the island, with the loss of everyone on board including three hundred and twenty slaves.

1784, 13 March. Jardines Reef, Cuba
The British ship, *Mercury*, was engaged on the classic run – slaves from Africa to Jamaica, sugar and rum from Jamaica to Bristol – when she was wrecked off the coast of Cuba.

1787, 17 May. Mona Passage, Puerto Rico
The British slave ship, *Sisters*, bound for Havana from Africa with a cargo of five hundred slaves, was overturned in a gale. Only five of those on board survived.

1792. Jardines Reef, Cuba
The cargoes of two British ships lost here illustrate the nature of the trade between Britain and the Caribbean at the time. The *Sarah*, sailing from Jamaica to Liverpool, carried sugar, rum and timber; the *Charming Mary*, Jamaica to Dublin, had sugar, rum, coffee, ginger and castor oil.

1797, 17 February. Chaguaramas, Trinidad
When a British fleet was approaching to capture the island, the Spaniards burnt five of their largest warships to prevent them from falling in to the hands of the enemy. They were the *San Vicente*, *Arrogante*, *Gallardo*, *San Damaco* and *Concha*.

Whalers and Liners: Nineteenth-century Wooden Ships

Great improvements in navigation took place during the latter part of the eighteenth century. The invention of the sextant, together with the development of more accurate chronometers, made it possible to calculate latitude more exactly, and charts were becoming considerably more comprehensive and reliable. By the end of the eighteenth century, the Pacific was no longer an unknown ocean. Voyages across it from South and North America to both Australasia and the East Indies were frequent, if not yet commonplace.

If one compares the world shipping routes in the nineteenth century with those which existed in the eighteenth, three differences are immediately apparent – the growth of the United States as one of the world's great maritime powers, with more and more voyages originating and finishing in North America; the British colonisation of Australia and New Zealand, with the increase in shipping tonnage that brought about; and the steadily increasing quantity of foodstuffs and raw materials brought from the New World to the old. In the second half of the century, emigration from Europe to the United States became an industry in its own right.

The construction of the Panama (1914) and Suez (1869) Canals shortened many long-distance sea journeys by thousands of miles and, by avoiding the dangerous and tedious stages around the Cape of Good Hope and Cape Horn, made journeys across the world safer and more pleasant. The beginnings of the northern route from west to east around Russia and Siberia were established by the Vikings, who travelled beyond the North Cape to the White Sea. In 1551, the English explorer, Chancelor, got as far as Archangel, and a little later the Dutch reached Novaya Zemlya. In 1728, Bering discovered the strait between Siberia and Alaska which carries his name. In 1878–79 the Swedish explorer, Nordenskjold, sailed round the whole coast from Norway to the Pacific.

From the 1860s onwards, a new pattern of oil routes was superimposed on the existing map of world trade. It has been extended and modified during the present century, but by 1900 three distinct routes had been developed. The first ran from the south and eastern United States and the Caribbean to the major ports and estuaries of Western Europe; the second, in operation from the mid-1880s, brought petroleum from the Caspian and Romania to the Mediterranean and Western Europe; the third, first used by a tanker in 1892, linked the oilfields

48

of Indonesia and Burma to Europe and provided the basis for the much more important oil exports from the Persian Gulf and the Arab states later on.

The Sailing Ships

It is easy to be hypnotised by the big ships – the clippers and the transatlantic steamers – which attracted so much publicity in the nineteenth century and to forget that throughout the nineteenth century the bulk of the world's trade was carried on by much more modest vessels. The average size of a ship in fact changed remarkably little between 1800 and 1900 and as a corollary of this most wrecks were of ships displacing considerably less than one thousand tons. An alphabetical list of the ships lost in the Atlantic during the great gale at the end of August 1873 (there are several hundred of them) gives the following as the tonnage of ten consecutive ships in the list, sailing ships and steamers being included together: 126, 267, 123, 1099, 218, 39, 32, 172, 57, 67. A similar list for the Caribbean, the Mediterranean or north-west Europe in, say, 1573 or 1673 would probably not be very different.

In some ways, the sailing ship reached its peak during the nineteenth century with the development of the clipper. This type of ship, with its long, slender lines and carrying an enormous area of sail, was first built during the American War of Independence. It proved its worth as a privateer and in the slave and opium trades before being transferred very profitably to the gold route between New York and San Francisco in the middle of the century. Some of the clippers were as big as three thousand tons – the *Great Republic*, which could sail at twenty knots, was 4555 tons – but their pinewood hulls were too fragile to withstand the strain to which they were subjected and it was the British ships, with their oak hulls, which brought the clipper design to perfection.

During the second half of the nineteenth century, clippers were used on the England–Australia run, transporting as many as a thousand passengers at a time. Those travelling first class went in considerable comfort and at unprecedented speed. One British clipper, the *Marco Polo*, sailed completely round the world in a little over five months. Mainly in order to bring wool from Australia to Europe, the European shipyards began to build much larger clippers, of up to six thousand tons, with steel hulls. Vessels of this size could carry ten thousand bales of wool, the fleeces of a million sheep, at a time.

Clippers apart, the years 1800–1860 represent a marking-time period in ship design. The average passenger carrier and the average warship continued to be a medium-sized wooden sailing vessel. With their massively built hulls and round bows, they were not fast, but, with a fully professional crew – not always obtainable – they were safe, providing they were well maintained and providing they did not meet really bad weather. They rode the waves, rather than cut through them, they needed constant pumping and they were very vulnerable to fire and to the loss of masts and rigging.

Australasia

1802, June. Tongabulu Island, Tonga group
The American whaler, *Duke of Portland*, was wrecked here soon after sailing from Norfolk Island. All her crew were massacred by natives, with the exception of a woman, Elizabeth Mosey, who was eventually rescued in 1804 by a ship which called at the island in search of sandalwood.

1805, 21 November. Reef at lat. 8.49N, 114.14E in the China Sea
The schooner, *Betsey*, of 75 tons, bound for Sydney from Calcutta with a crew of twelve, including three Portuguese, four Chinese and three Malays. After the ship had struck the reef, they got away in a boat and on a raft. The raft soon sank in the heavy seas, but the boat made land on Balambangan, an island near Borneo, where they were attacked by natives. During this and other confrontations with Malays, all but two of the crew were killed. These two were kept as slaves on another island for several months, until they were rescued.

1806, 25 August. Middleton Reef on Seringapatam Reef, Timor Sea
The London-registered whaler *Britannia*, of 301 tons, broke her back on the reef during darkness. Three boats got the crew away. One, containing eight men, was never seen again. The other two reached Port Jackson three weeks later.

1806, November. Haano Island, Tonga
The British warship, *Port-au-Prince*, (500 tons) sailed from London with instructions to attack Spanish settlements on the east and west coasts of America. Having looted churches, convents and seaports, the *Port-au-Prince* ran on to a reef off the coast of Haano Island. Seventy of the crew were killed by Tongans; the fate of the remainder is not known.

1816, September. Near Cardwell, New South Wales
The 353-ton *Lady Elliot*, built in Bengal and registered at Calcutta, sailed from Sydney bound for Batavia. Her cargo included hats, indigo, sealskins, turpentine, tar, and fifty tons of paving stones. She struck a rock and was wrecked.

1828, 17 April. Wreck Reef, north of Cato Island, Queensland
The brig, *Woodlark*, bound from Hobart, Tasmania to the Cape of Good Hope, was forced by bad weather to take the northerly passage through Torres Strait and struck Saumarez Reef, about a hundred and eighty miles from the mainland. Eighteen people, including two women and a baby, got away in the longboat, and six on a makeshift raft. At first the raft was towed by the boat, but tore away and was never seen again. The longboat made its way through reefs, looking for land. Seven days after the wreck they landed on a small island and gathered food and water. They sailed safely into Moreton Bay on 14 May.

1834, 15 August. Torres Strait, between Cape York and New Guinea
The 314-ton barque, *Charles Eaton*, bound from Sydney to Singapore with seven passengers and twenty-six crew, ran into a gale and was driven on to Detached Reef, at that time uncharted. Five crewmen eventually reached Timor in a cutter. Those remaining on the wreck made a raft, on which they drifted to Boydon Island, where islanders killed the adult members of the party, but spared four boys. Two were later killed, but the ship's boy and a baby were adopted by the natives and treated kindly. The boy later remembered seeing the decapitated heads of a woman passenger and the captain on poles outside village huts. The two boys were later bought by an island chief for a bunch of bananas and taken to Murray Island, where they remained until they were sighted by the *Mangles* when

it dropped anchor off Murray Island in 1835. A schooner was then sent from Sydney to take the two boys away, the islanders making no attempt to stop it.

1835, 12 April. Tasmania

The convict ship *George III*, struck a rock in D'Entrecasteaux Channel and sank rapidly. A hundred and thirty-four people drowned.

1835, 14 May. Near King's Island, Bass Strait

The convict ship, *Neva*, 837 tons, left Cork for Sydney carrying a company of two hundred and forty, of whom twenty-six were crew, one hundred and fifty female convicts and fifty-five children, as well as nine voluntary emigrants. As was customary, the prisoners were locked below decks. The voyage was uneventful until 14 May, when breakers were sighted and the ship struck the rocks twice, swinging broadside on to the reef. The prison doors burst open and panic-stricken convicts crowded into two boats, capsizing them. The ship was carried back into deep water and foundered. A total of two hundred and eighteen people drowned. Twenty-two survivors reached King's Island on floating wreckage, where they were found by another party of shipwrecked people, from the *Tartar*. They were helped by a sealer and lived on wallabies his dog killed until on 15 June the joint party's distress signals were seen, and they were brought to Tasmania.

1836, 21 May. The Swains, near Tropic of Capricon, Great Barrier Reef

The 351-ton brig, *Stirling Castle*, was bound from Sydney to Singapore with eighteen people on board, including the captain's pregnant wife. Captain Fraser was in poor health, never having recovered from his experiences when he was shipwrecked in the *Comet* on Boot Reef, east of Murray Island in 1829. The *Stirling Castle* crossed the Tropic of Capricon and went aground on a reef, the ship breaking up very quickly. Two boats were launched, with provisions and rum, but no water, and were damaged by reefs before one of the islands in the Cumberland Group was reached on 27 May. Two days later the survivors continued down the coast of the mainland but could not land because of bad weather. Eliza Fraser had lost her baby four days after the wreck, the captain was delirious and the crew drunk. The boats landed on Great Sandy Island after the captain's wife had heard the men planning to kill her husband. Aborigines surrounded the survivors and split them up, forcing them to work as slaves. Eventually the *Stirling Castle*'s Negro steward, Joseph, and three seamen managed to escape and reach Moreton and a relief expedition rescued Mrs Fraser and three crew members.

1837, 19 November. Foveaux Strait, South Island, New Zealand

The barque, *Lynx*, built in Java, had been charted to collect the season's crop of whale oil and whalebone from the various New Zealand whaling stations and then to take it to Sydney. She broke her anchor cable in a gale, became stranded at Invercargill in Foveaux Strait and broke up.

1840, 25 July. North Island, New Zealand

The sailing ship, *Buffalo*, was driven ashore near Whitianga, with a loss of two lives. She was used to carry convicts and cargo from England to Australia, Tasmania and New Zealand, and was bound from Mercury Bay, North Island, with a cargo of kauri wood and a detachment of the 80th Foot Regiment. All the soldiers and other passengers were saved. The vessel sank offshore, but in May 1960 it was washed to the surface, following a tidal wave set up by earthquakes in Chile. Some of her fittings were salvaged after 120 years under water.

1844. Morovo Island, Solomons

The Sydney whaler, *Cape Packet*, sent three boats ashore to Morovo Island to get water. The crews were all killed, after which the natives boarded the *Cape Packet* and killed the remaining men there. The flesh of all the white men was subsequently eaten at a cannibal feast. The ship, which was carrying sperm oil, was looted and set on fire.

1844, October. Endeavour Strait, off the Queensland coast of Australia

The cutter, *America*, was wrecked in a gale and stuck fast while searching for the wreck of an American whaler in the Torres Strait with a valuable cargo of whale oil. On board were a South Seas drifter, William Thompson, and his wife Barbara, who had been born in Aberdeen, emigrated to Sydney in the late 1830s and eloped when she was sixteen. The two men were swept away but Mrs Thompson, who could not swim, remained on the wreck and was found by three islanders who took her to Prince of Wales Island, where she was hailed as the ghost of the chief's dead daughter. She remained with the tribe for four years and was hidden whenever ships called at the island. In October 1849, the warship *Rattlesnake* was sighted and one of her rescuers, who had always promised to return her to her people, took her to the landing party. The natives were given rewards.

1845, 4 August. King Island, Bass Strait

The *Cataragui*, of about 800 tons, was carrying 369 emigrants from Liverpool to Melbourne. Nearing the end of her voyage, she struck the rocks on King Island. The boats were swept away as the ship broke up and only nine of those on board were able to get to shore. They were found by a sealer, but this ship had no boat in which to take them off, and they had to wait for nearly a month, with very little food, until another passing vessel responded to their signal.

1846, 8 March. Coral Sea

The 304-ton barque, *Peruvian*, was wrecked on a coral reef during a voyage to Peru and China. The boats were washed away and the twenty-one survivors made for the Australian coast on a raft. When the raft drifted ashore forty-two days later, there were only seven survivors, six of whom died soon after landing. The remaining man, James Murrell, lived with aborigines for seventeen years and was able to communicate with white men for the first time in January 1863.

1849, March. Queensland coast

The 12-ton cutter, *Psyche*, which belonged to the Bishop of Tasmania, had been taken from Hobart by four escaped convicts. Two of the convicts were discovered three months later on Percy Island. They were taken to Sydney, where one of the men escaped and was never found. There was no firm evidence as to the fate of the other two men, but the presence of a skeleton on Percy Island suggested that they had either been killed in a quarrel or deliberately murdered and their flesh eaten after the *Psyche*'s provisions had run out.

1853, 29 April. Tasmania

The sailing ship, *Rebecca*, left Gravesend for Sydney, New South Wales, in December 1852. Nearing the end of her voyage, she struck a reef between Arthur River and Sandy Cape, swinging broadside on to the shore with the force of the impact. Twenty were drowned, but eleven got ashore, in wild and desolate country. The survivors found a dog, and tied a message to his neck. His owner returned with a search party and rescued the shipwrecked men.

1850, 26 March. Honolulu Harbour, Hawaii

The 330-ton barque, *Caroline*, was carrying fifty-two Australians from Hobart to the Californian goldfields. The ship struck a reef outside the harbour, after a very protracted passage, during which water and provisions ran low. All the passengers, who included a number of women and children, were rescued.

1850, May. Off west coast of Tasmania

The 200-ton brig, *Lady Denison*, was totally wrecked here, during a voyage from Adelaide to Hobart. A rumour that she had been seized by a group of convicts among the passengers and sailed in the direction of California was never substantiated. One of her longboats was found, together with large quantities of wreckage scattered along the coast, and the body of the wife of one of the prisoners, a German, was washed up and identified. Those on board included sixteen passengers, eleven convicts, three constables and a crew of seven.

1857, 24 October. Sydney, New South Wales

The clipper ship, *Catherine Adamson*, 768 tons, was bound from Aberdeen to Sydney with a general cargo when she dragged her anchors during a storm and sank near the Inner North Head. A pilot was on board at the time. Twenty-one people drowned.

1862, October. Off south-east Australia

The wooden paddle steamship, *Citizen*, 146 tons, left Melbourne for Dunedin with an unknown number of gold diggers and was never heard of again.

1865, 23 April. Chatham Islands, New Zealand

The clipper ship, *Fiery Star*, left Moreton Bay for London, with a cargo of wool and ninety-six passengers and crew. Eighteen days after sailing her cargo was found to be on fire, and by 23 April it was clear the ship had to be abandoned. Only two boats were seaworthy, and seventy-eight people left in them, leaving eighteen volunteer crewmen to stay with the ship in case a passing vessel was sighted. On 12 May the sailing ship *Dauntless* took off the crew and soon afterwards the ship sank. The people in the boats were never seen again.

1866, 14 May. Disappointment Island, Auckland Islands, New Zealand

The wooden clipper ship, *General Grant*, 1200 tons, was en route from Melbourne to London, with eighty-three passengers and twenty-one crew and a cargo which included wool and, supposedly, nine tons of zinc ore. She lost her bearings in the voyage and having by mistake reached the Auckland Islands, went head on into the cliffs. Only twelve people got on shore. They survived for eighteen months on seals, goats and pigs and were eventually taken off by the whaler, *Amherst*, which arrived in response to an SOS message which had been carved on a miniature boat thrown into the sea by the survivors soon after they landed on the island. It was noted that zinc was not mined in Australia for twenty-two years after the *General Grant* was wrecked and it was considered that the mention of zinc ore – 'spelter' – on the ship's manifest was intended to defeat pirates and customs officers. The ship was certainly carrying gold.

1869, 9 March. Off Falkland Islands

The clipper ship, *Blue Jacket*, caught fire during a voyage from Lyttelton, New Zealand, to Liverpool with seventy-one passengers and crew. She was abandoned off the Falkland Islands, with the loss of thirty-two lives. Thirty-six survivors were picked up in a boat after a week at sea, and three others after three weeks. The ship's figurehead came ashore on Rottnest Island, West Australia, on

8 December 1871. The *Blue Jacket* was one of the fastest ships of the mid-nineteenth century.

1872, 26 February. Bramble Reef, east of Cardwell, Queensland
The 167-ton brig, *Maria*, set out from Sydney for New Guinea in search of gold. She had spent the last twenty years of her life carrying coal from Newcastle to Sydney and was unseaworthy when she was bought by the New Guinea Prospecting Association. Seventy-six men signed on as the *Maria*'s crew, because the Maritime Board would not clear the vessel for carrying passengers. The ship sailed northwards for three weeks, leaking badly and with rotten rigging. In a heavy sea the bottom of the ship was smashed in on a reef.

1876, 12 December. Waipapa Point, New Zealand
The wooden barque, *William Ackers*, 299 tons, on her way to Lyttelton with a cargo of 185,000 feet of sawn timber, hit the reef off Waipapa Point and broke in two. Some crewmen tried to swim the two hundred yards to shore, and others drifted in on planks. Eight drowned, but three survived.

1878, 1 June. Near Cape Otway, Victoria
The *Loch Ard* made three attempts to begin a voyage from England to Australia, but was dismasted twice before eventually sailing on 2 March. After about ninety days she went aground at Curdies Inlet. Only two people survived.

1887, 22nd April. North-east Australia
A pearl fishing fleet was destroyed in a hurricane, with a loss of life of about 550.

1890, c. 15 January. Off New Zealand coast
The full-rigged ship, *Marlborough*, bound from Lyttelton, New Zealand, to London with a cargo of frozen meat and wool, was sighted two days after leaving port but was never heard of again.

1890, 31 March. Off South Island, New Zealand
The wooden barque, *Emilie*, was bound from Bluff, South Island, for Port Pirie, South Australia, with a cargo of sawn timber when she began to leak during a hurricane, her boat was smashed and she drifted for five days before going ashore at Red Head, Stewart Island. Four survivors, one badly injured, reached shore, where they stayed for seven days eating shellfish and a dead seal. They were taken aboard the tug, *Awarua*, which landed them at Bluff on 14 April.

1893, c. 25 February. Off South Head, Kaipara, New Zealand
The wooden barque, *Northern Star*, was sunk in heavy storms on her voyage from Hokianga to Wellington with a cargo of timber. She was found floating bottom up off South Head on 15 March, with no sign of her crew of eight.

1909, c. 15 January. Off New Zealand coast
The auxiliary brigantine, *Rio Loge* was wrecked in gales during a voyage from Kaipara to Dunedin with a cargo of timber. A lifebuoy bearing her name was found outside Wellington Harbour, but her crew of twelve were drowned.

1909, 10 August. Cook Strait, New Zealand
The three-masted auxiliary schooner, *Toroa*, is believed to have foundered near Cape Farewell during a voyage from Greymouth to Wanganui with a cargo of coal and bricks. No trace was found of the ship or her crew.

North America

1802, 29 October. Cape May, New York
The Spanish warship, *Juno*, en route from Mexico to Spain, and with her hull

badly leaking, sank in a gale. All of the 425 people on board were drowned and her cargo, which included a large quantity of silver, was lost.

1811, 23–24 December. Long Island, New York
During a violent storm, more than fifty ships were wrecked on the south side of Long Island.

1817, 14 May. Portsmouth Beach, Maine
The American ship, *Commerce*, bound for New York from Jamaica with a cargo of rum, was wrecked here. All the crew and some of the cargo were saved.

1818, 12 September. Galveston, Texas
Four ships belonging to the French pirate, Jean Lafitte, were wrecked here during a hurricane.

1823, 2 November. Galantry Head, St. Pierre and Miquelon
During the nineteenth century the North American colonies had an important timber trade with Britain. The British three-masted schooner, *Saint Patrice*, left Antigonish, Nova Scotia, bound for London with a cargo of sawn spruce blocks. She was driven ashore on Galantry Head and totally wrecked.

1825. Somerset Island, Cresswell Bay
Attempts to discover a north-west passage from the Atlantic to the Pacific went on throughout the seventeenth and eighteenth centuries and continued into the nineteenth. In 1824, William Edward Parry made his third attempt, with the *Hecla* and the *Fury*, both of 375 tons. The *Fury* was so badly damaged in Cresswell Bay that she was abandoned, her stores being left behind as a cache for future expeditions. Both crews returned in the *Hecla*.

1828, 3 November. Dune of Langlade, St. Pierre and Miquelon
The schooner, *Fulwood*, was en route from Canada to England with a cargo of wooden chests filled with Spanish gold doubloons that were being shipped in payment for goods bought in England. The crew knew the nature of the cargo and soon after leaving Canada they mutinied and killed the Captain and officers. The ship was then left with no-one on board capable of navigating a course to England and the wreck inevitably followed. The chests were hidden on shore, but the mutineers were captured and eventually hanged.

1832, c. 12 April. Mississippi
The Mississippi river steamboat, *Brandywine* caught fire near Memphis on a voyage from New Orleans to Louisville. The fire was caused by sparks from the funnel igniting some straw packing, and the flames spread in the high wind. It is estimated that seventy-five passengers were saved out of the 230 or so on board.

1837, c. 9 May. Mississippi
The Mississippi river steamboat, *Ben Sherrod* was competing with another steamboat in a race up river to Louisville when she caught fire and sank. The boat was crowded with passengers and the firemen in the stokehold were encouraged by lavish supplies of whisky of which there was an open barrel. The stack of wood fuel near the furnaces caught fire and a hundred and fifty people died.

1837, 30 October. Mississippi
The Mississippi river steamboat, *Monmouth*, was grossly overloaded when she sank in a collision with the steamship, *Warren*, in darkness and torrential rain. She had been chartered by the US Government to transport the tribes of Cree Indians across the Mississippi, to a new settlement. Two hundred and thirty-five people lost their lives in the collision, which occurred at a bend in the river. The *Warren* had another vessel in tow at the time and could not take avoiding action.

1838, 21 April. Off Princeton, Mississippi
The American river steamboat, *Oronoko*, was lying off shore when her boilers exploded, killing over a hundred people on board. The casualties were either hurled overboard and drowned or were scalded to death by escaping steam.

1838, 25 April. Ohio River
The American river steamship, *Moselle*, left Cincinnati for Fulton with eighty-five first-class passengers, one hundred and fifty deck passengers and thirty crew. She had a reputation for speed and her captain's ambition was to make her the fastest vessel on the river. Not far from Cincinnati her boilers blew up, killing about 136 people. Bodies were blown on to the roofs of houses, and part of a boiler weighing 336 pounds was hurled 480 feet into a tanner's yard.

1841, 19 April. Off Newfoundland
The American sailing ship, *William Brown*, left Liverpool for Philadelphia with a crew of eighteen and sixty-five passengers, who were mostly Irish emigrants. In gale force conditions in the Atlantic the vessel hit two icebergs, and two boats got away before she sank with thirty-three people still on board. One of the boats with eight occupants was picked up by a French lugger six days later off Cape Breton and all on board survived. The other boat was overcrowded, containing forty-two people, and by the time it was picked up by the sailing ship, *Crescent*, sixteen dead or dying persons had been thrown overboard to give the remainder some chance of survival.

1841, 18 May. Red Island Reef, near Quebec
The emigrant sailing vessel, *Isabella*, left Limerick for Quebec with 156 people on board. In bad weather she went on the Red Island Reef and foundered suddenly, while the boats were still moored to the ship. There was no time to cut the ropes and the boats and their hundred occupants were drawn down with the ship.

1844, 3 January. Ohio River
The river steamboat, *Shepherdess*, struck a submerged object on her way from Cincinnati to St Louis and tore open the side of her hull. The boilers fell into the river, followed by the twin funnels, and the whole vessel disintegrated.

1844, 14 December. Lower Mississippi
The Mississippi River steamboat, *Belle of Clarksville*, was in collision with another steamboat here. Both vessels were in their correct positions, but just before the impact the *Belle of Clarksville* ran into shallow water, and trying to avoid this she steered across the bows of the oncoming vessel. She was badly holed and sank with the loss of thirty-six lives.

1847, 20 May. St. Lawrence Seaway
The brig, *Carrick*, left Sligo for Quebec with two hundred emigrants and had an uneventful voyage until she met a strong gale in the St. Lawrence and went ashore about sixty miles east of Cape Rosares, breaking up very quickly. Only twenty-two people were saved.

1849, 10 May. Fifty miles off St. Paul's Island, St. Lawrence river
The emigrant sailing ship, *Maria*, collided with an iceberg and sank with the loss of 109 lives, on her way from Limerick to Quebec. The following day three survivors were rescued from a boat by the barque, *Roslin Castle*, and the brig, *Falcon*, as well as nine found drifting on the ice.

1851, *c*. 29 January. Mississippi
The Mississippi river steamboat, *John Adams*, struck a submerged object about two hundred miles below Memphis where she was bound from New Orleans. She

broke in two with the force of the impact and went down very quickly, with the loss of 123 lives. About a hundred survivors reached the shore.

1853, 20 December. New York

The *Great Republic,* 4555 tons, was the largest sailing ship built in the nineteenth century and was intended for the Australian trade. She was lying in the harbour at New York, loading her first cargo, when a fire broke out in Front Street and spread to the East River quays and docks, where the ship was lying. The rigging caught first, then the burning yards fell to the deck and set fire to the hull and cargo. Two other ships were also totally destroyed.

1853, 23 December. Atlantic

The paddle steamship *San Francisco,* was chartered by the US Government to carry troops to California. She left New York with sixteen officers and 498 artillerymen on board, together with their wives and children, making a total with the crew of 750. Space was very cramped, and fever soon broke out. Two days out the ship was disabled in a gale and all the boats were washed away. She drifted helplessly for several days and on 28 December the barque, *Kilby,* took off about a hundred passengers. On 3 January the *Three Bells* took off 180-200 people, and the sailing ship *Antarctic* 176. The *San Francisco* was then abandoned and sank almost immediately.

1854, 2 January. Blonde Rock, Cape Sable

The sailing vessel, *Staffordshire* was carrying emigrants from Liverpool to Boston when she was damaged in a gale and her captain was injured. Under the command of the first officer, the ship then ran into a snowstorm and struck the Blonde Rock. Two of the four boats broke loose, but the other two were launched safely, carrying fifty survivors to the shore. The ship foundered soon afterwards, with the loss of 175 lives including the captain, who issued orders from his cabin and refused to be saved.

1854, c. 12 March. Mississippi

The Mississippi river steamboat, *John L. Avery,* left New Orleans with a heavy cargo and hundreds of passengers, and soon afterwards hit a submerged tree trunk with such violence that she capsized, throwing overboard a large number of people. Within five minutes the ship had broken in two and sunk with the loss of over eighty lives.

1854, 16 April. Off Barnegat, New Jersey

The American emigrant ship, *Powhattan,* struck the shoals twelve miles from the shore and became wedged finally on the bar a hundred yards out. She was on a voyage from Havre to New York with 250 people on board. The ship began to break up before the rocket apparatus could be brought to the scene and despite all efforts possible from the shore not a single person was saved from the wreck.

1854, 27 September. Sixty-five miles south-west of Cape Race, Newfoundland

The luxurious wooden-hulled paddle steamship, *Arctic,* was bound for New York from the Mersey with 246 passengers and 135 crew when she collided in dense fog with the steamship *Vesta.* The French vessel appeared to be worst off, but she was able to proceed to St. John's. The *Arctic* was holed in three places and her engines were swamped before she could reach Cape Race. Seventy-two men and four women got away on a makeshift raft, but only one person was still alive when it was sighted two days later.

After the disaster, a number of new regulations were introduced. They included water-tight bulkheads, better provision of lifeboats, and steam-whistles for use during fog. In addition, a plan was produced for separate North Atlantic shipping lanes for westbound and eastbound vessels.

1856, 20 February. Newfoundland Banks

The American sailing ship, *John Rutledge,* was in collision with an iceberg on a voyage from Liverpool to New York with 120 passengers and sixteen crew. The ship was badly holed and was abandoned. Five boats were launched, but they only had one compass between them, so when they became separated navigation became difficult for the other four. Eight days later the *Germania,* bound from Havre to New York, picked up one of the lifeboats containing several dead bodies and one youth, who proved to be the sole survivor from the ship.

1856, 30 May. St. Paul's Island, St. Lawrence River, Quebec

The barque, *Pallas* left Cork for Quebec with 136 emigrants on board and had an uneventful voyage until she reached the mouth of the St. Lawrence where she ran into fog and struck the rocks on St. Paul's Island. The panicking passengers crowded into the boats and capsized them and after this the captain persuaded the rest of those on board to remain there until daybreak, when they were all taken off safely. Eighty-two people died.

1860, 8 September. Off Waukegan, Lake Michigan

The American paddle steamer, *Lady Elgin,* was run down by the schooner, *Augusta,* about ten miles from land. The steamer continued for some distance, and the vessels lost sight of each other. The schooner reached port safely in a damaged condition, but the *Lady Elgin* foundered after thirty minutes with the loss of 279 lives, including the captain.

1861, 25 September. Near the Boston Light, Massachusetts

The sailing ship, *Maritana,* struck the Shag Rocks in bad weather on a voyage from Liverpool to Boston with a general cargo and thirty-nine passengers and crew. One of the crew tried to get a line to the shore, but fell and was critically injured. When the vessel broke in two as the tide fell, the captain was killed by falling from the deck into the wreckage. Twelve survivors were finally rescued, seven who swam ashore, and five seamen who swam to the Shag Rocks.

1865, 23 April. Mississippi

The American paddle steamer, *Sultana,* was in service on the river between New Orleans and St. Louis. On 21 April she left Vicksburg with a large number of Northern prisoners released at the end of the Civil War, and who were being returned to their homes. They were mostly in a poor state of health after long imprisonment in camps. It is not certain exactly how many were on board, but one estimate gives the number as seventy passengers, eighty-five crew, and 2239 soldiers, making a total of 2394. The *Sultana* was actually licensed to carry 276 passengers. The load was increased when the vessel called at Memphis and took on fifty pigs and one hundred barrels of sugar. Several halts were made on the journey to clear the boilers, which were of a new type and prone to clogging. On 23 April the steamer was off Tagleman's Landing, just above Memphis, when the boilers exploded and fire spread rapidly to all parts of the vessel. The decks collapsed and hundreds were thrown into the holds. There were 741 survivors.

1872, 26 December. Cape Cod

The iron-hulled Hamburg barque, *Frances,* on a voyage from the Far East to Boston with a cargo of sugar and tin iced up in a gale and was wrecked near the Highland Light on Cape Cod. All fourteen of the crew were saved.

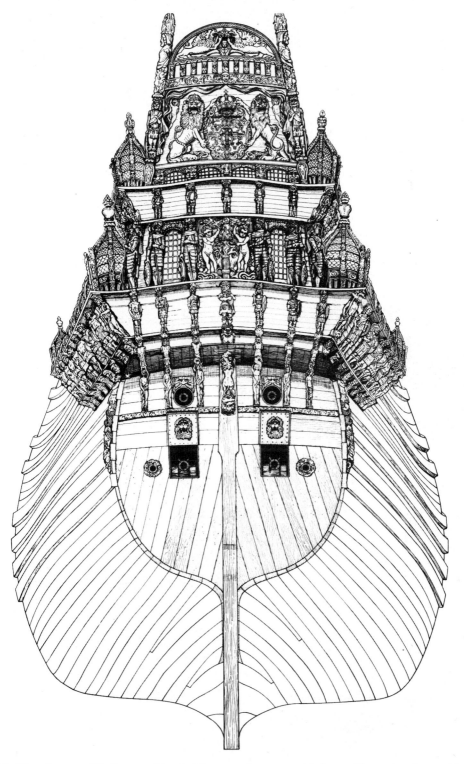

28 *King Gustavus II's first warship, the* Wasa, *as she appeared before setting out on her maiden voyage in 1628. The quantity of sculpture makes her one of the grandest and most absurd wooden ships ever built.*

29 *Articles from the Captain's table on the* Wasa, *which sank shortly after setting out on her maiden voyage, having keeled over in a gust of wind.*

30 *A seaman's chest and even a hat were recovered, remarkably well-preserved, from the ship after she was raised in 1959.*

31 *The* Wasa *in dry-dock, before a shelter was built over her to allow conservation to be carried out.*

32 *A seventeenth-century mariner's compass. The compass probably came to Europe via the Arabs who were great sailors and had learned of the properties of lodestone from the Chinese many years before. The stone magnetised a needle which would then be drawn automatically to the north.*

33 *The chiplog and line, used to reckon a ship's speed during the sixteenth, seventeenth and eighteenth centuries. The chiplog, on the left, scooped up water and remained stationary in the water. As the line slipped away the ship's speed was calculated in 'knots'.*

34 *A bizarre machine for raising wrecks. From Besson's* Théâtre des Instruments, *1594.*

35 *(Facing page) The title page of an early seventeenth-century pamphlet invoking support for colonisation in Virginia and showing one of the larger ships engaged in transatlantic voyages. Whole fleets were fitted out to colonise and explore the New World.*

Nova Britannia.

OFFERING MOST

Excellent fruites by Planting in VIRGINIA.

Exciting all such as be well affected to further the same.

LONDON
Printed for Samvel Macham, and are to be sold at
his Shop in Pauls Church-yard, at the
Signe ot the Bul-head.
1 6 0 9.

36 *The Board of Longitude, established by the British Admiralty in 1714, offered a prize of £20,000 to the first person who invented a reliable way of finding longitude. John Harrison's chronometer claimed the reward in 1735, and the unprecedented accuracy of Harrison's time-keepers provided the basis for navigation of a much higher order.*

37   *A vessel of the British East India Company in the Hooghly River, Calcutta, which was the base for commerce with China.*

38   *Eighteenth-century Spanish gold coins recovered from a wreck off the Scilly Isles.*

GOD save the KING.

Doublons.

SPANISH Dollar Bag
Consigned to Boney.

My LADS,
The rest of the GALLEONS with the TREASURE from LA PLATA, are waiting half loaded at CARTAGENA, for the arrival of those from PERU at PANAMA, as soon as that takes place, they are to sail for PORTOVELO, to take in the rest of their Cargo, with Provisions and Water for the Voyage to EUROPE. They stay at PORTO-VELO a few days only. Such a Chance perhaps will never occur again,

THE FLYING
PALLAS,
Of 36 GUNS,
At PLYMOUTH,

is a new and uncommonly fine Frigate. Built on purpose. And ready for an EXPEDITION, as soon as some more good Hands are on board;

Captain Lord Cochrane,
(who was not drowned in the ARAB as reported)
Commands her. The sooner you are on board the better.

None need apply, but SEAMEN, or Stout Hands, able to rouse about the Field Pieces, and carry an hundred weight of PEWTER, without stopping, at least three Miles.

COCHRANE.

To British Seamen.

BONEY's CORONATION
Is postponed for want of COBBS.

J. BARFIELD, Printer, Wardour-Street.

Rendezvous, at the White Flag,

39 *A recruiting poster of 1804 for collecting a crew to attack and, with luck, plunder the Spanish treasure fleet.*

40 *Slave traders were essentially gamblers and their ships were often old, ill-maintained, over-loaded and overcrowded. Sickness and starvation were common.*

41 *In 1791,* HMS Pandora *was sent from England to look for the mutineers of Captain Bligh's ship, the* Bounty. *On the return voyage, with fourteen prisoners on board, she struck the Great Barrier Reef and sank.*

42 *The wreck of the* Perseverance *bound from Batavia to Salem, Massachusetts, 31 January 1805.*

43 *The East Indiaman* Grosvenor, *wrecked on the Pondoland coast (Cape of Good Hope), in 1782.*

44 *'The wreck of Sir Cloudesley Shovel's flagship, the* Association, *and of other ships of the fleet in the Scillies, 1707. The* Association *was carrying £3 million in bullion and silver, and two thousand men lost their lives.*

45 *A contemporary illustration of a plan to raise the* Royal George *at Spithead, where she sank in 1782. No attempt was made, however, and she remained a hazard until blown up in 1839.*

46 *The frigate HMS* Guardian *which hit an iceberg about 1300 miles out from the Cape of Good Hope in December 1789.*

47 *The wreck of the* Dutton *East Indiaman – wrecked in Plymouth Sound, Devon, in 1781 – and the rescue of some of the crew.*

48 *The end of the* Anson *in Mount's Bay, Cornwall, 1825.*

49 *The American Ship* Belisarius, *'five days out under reefed Mizen Stay sail'. One of a series of watercolours painted by an unknown passenger, tracing the first few days of the ship's voyage.*

50 *Firing Captain Manby's mortar life-line, 1808. A mortar shell when accurately aimed would carry the line over the rigging.*

51   *The wreck of the troopship* Charlotte *in Algoa Bay, Port Elizabeth, 1854. When the vessel hit the rocks, Manby's life-saving apparatus was brought down, but although a rope reached the ship several times, it was impossible to secure it.*

52   *The frigate* Howadji, *built in 1852 and struck by lightning in mid-ocean in 1857.*

1879, 19 April. Columbia River
The paddle steamer, *Great Republic*, was built with her sister ships *America*, *China* and *Japan*, to establish a trans-Pacific service between San Francisco, Yokohama and Hong Kong. After a number of years on this run she was withdrawn and placed on the coastal trade, plying between San Francisco and Portland, Oregon. On 16 April she left San Francisco for Portland with nearly six hundred passengers and entering the Columbia River went aground in calm, clear weather. The passengers and crew got ashore safely, with the exception of fourteen crewmen who died when their boat capsized. The ship was a total wreck.

1883, 7 January. Smith Island, Virginia
The Maine schooner, *Albert Dailey*, with a cargo of coal, went aground here in fog. The crew and their belongings were taken off by a boat from the Smith Island life-saving station. A salvage ship began operations in a snowstorm, the crew having returned to the *Albert Dailey*. The ship was breaking up fast and the lifeboat brought the men off.

1883, 15 September. Lake Michigan
The lake schooner, *Arab*, went on the rocks in bad weather. The crew remained on board until the salvage steamer, *Protection*, arrived from Chicago. The hull was patched up and the ship was dragged off the rocks. Within a short time, however, she sank, the towline fouling the *Protection*'s propeller and disabling her. The steamer, *H. C. Akley*, took her in tow, but her engine stopped in a gale and her steering gear broke. Both ships then drifted to Saugatuck, Michigan, and anchored there. Beach apparatus had to be brought 60 miles by rail and then taken to the site by tug. The *Akeley* was towed into port and repaired. The *Protection* was a total loss.

1883, 4 December. Atlantic
The Canadian sailing ship, *Regina*, was bound from Philadelphia to London with a cargo of petroleum and a crew of eighteen when she ran into bad weather about eight hundred miles out and began to list badly. Three days later, most of the crew abandoned ship and one man was picked up by the barque, *Baroma*, soon after the *Regina* sank. Six men in a boat were found by the barque, *Helen Finlayson*, next day. There were no other survivors.

1884, 3 April. Newcomb's Hollow, Cape Cod
The schooner, *Viking*, on her way from Georges Bank to Boston with a cargo of fish, ran aground near here. The ship and its cargo were lost but the sails and rigging were salvaged. The crew were landed safely and sent home by rail.

1885, 26 August. Squam Head, Nantucket
The schooner, *Oregon*, 92 tons, ran on to the beach here when on a voyaae from Bay View to New Bedford with a cargo of granite blocks. The ship sank, but the cargo was salvaged.

1886, 9 March. Peaked Hill Bars, Cape Cod
The 398-ton schooner, *Hannah E. Schubert*, carrying coal to Boston from Perth Amboy, New Jersey, grounded five hundred yards offshore. Efforts to get her off failed and on the next flood tide she was swept over the shoals and on to the beach, where she was wrecked. The sails, anchors and part of the cargo were removed by wreckers from Provincetown.

1886, 14 December. Off Cape Flattery, Washington
The wooden sailing ship, *Harvey Mills*, ended her unfortunate career when she foundered in a gale with the loss of twenty-two lives. She caught fire on her

maiden voyage, was dismasted in a hurricane, ran down a barque and was again dismasted on another voyage.

1888, 12 January. Gray's Harbour, Oregon

The 1262-ton British barge, *Abercorn*, was carrying 2000 tons of railway track to Portland, Oregon. At the Columbia River, the pilot lost his bearings in thick fog and tugs sent out to bring her in failed to find her. She went ashore north of Gray's Harbour and her heavy cargo took her deep into the sand. The rails stayed there rusting for six years. They were then bought by two of the leading citizens of nearby Aberdeen and presented to the town to build a railway connection to its sawmill, an act which saved the town from bankruptcy.

1889, 27 January. Tuckernuck Island, Cape Cod

The British sailing ship, *Antoinette*, went ashore in dense fog. The crew of the nearest lifeboat station at Muskeget were unable to reach the ship, because of the very low tide. A surf boat was eventually pulled to the site by oxen, but by that time the wind had risen and made the surf too dangerous. All twenty of the people on board were eventually saved by a beach line and breeches buoy.

1890, 15 February. Nauset Inlet, Cape Cod

The four-masted schooner, *Katie J. Barrett*, left Bath, Maine with a cargo of ice. She was grounded between two lifesaving stations. A boat from the Nauset station took the crew off but the ship could not be refloated until six months later when she was towed to Boston. By then the cargo had melted.

1890, 3–12 October. Near Pictou, Nova Scotia

The Canadian wooden sailing ship, *Melmerby*, was dismasted on a voyage from Quebec to Greenock with a cargo of timber. The ship drifted for a week until she was driven on to a small island near Pictou, and in attempting to reach land fourteen men drowned.

1893, 5 December. Cape Cod

The full-rigged ship, *Jason*, 1512 tons, on her way from Calcutta to Boston with a cargo of ten thousand bales of jute, ran into bad weather off Cape Cod and lost her bearings. In gale-force winds and snow she struck the outer bar just off the Pamet River life-saving station. The ship broke up and twenty-three of the crew were drowned. The single survivor was found clinging to a bale of jute.

1894, 6 November. Cape Cod

The three-masted schooner, *Messenger*, on a voyage from Pensacola, Florida, with a cargo of timber, became stranded on the rocks opposite Peconic, Long Island. She was hauled off and towed to New London. Here she was taken in tow by a tug, but capsized fifteen miles from the Highland Light, Cape Cod. A fortnight later she was washed ashore at Wallfleet, a total loss.

1898, *c.* 22 March. Point Bonita, west coast

The American wooden barque, *Helen W. Almy*, bound from San Francisco to the Klondyke, was seen by a passing ship floating upside down off Point Bonita. Nothing was ever heard of the forty-one passengers and crew.

1899, 15 January. Off Tacoma, Washington

The four-masted sailing ship, *Andelana* was at anchor at Tacoma after a voyage in ballast from Shanghai. She had discharged her ballast and was preparing to take on board a cargo of grain for England. During the night she broke away from her moorings and sank in thirty fathoms, with the loss of nineteen lives.

1904, 15 June. Hudson River, New York

The paddle steamship, *General Slocum*, left the landing stage at Third Street,

East River with 1388 passengers and crew, including a large excursion party of mothers and children who were on a Lutheran Sunday school outing. As the ship approached Hell Gate channel, opposite the end of 138th Street, fire broke out in a small cabin which contained paint and other inflammable stores, and spread very rapidly. The captain made for North Brother Island about half a mile away, but in the general panic mothers began to throw their children overboard and jumped after them. A tug and fire-boats tried to assist, but without success. By the time the ship grounded on the island thirty minutes later, 957 people had died. At the enquiry it was said that no lifeboats had been lowered, no organised lifesaving attempts had been made by the crew, the fire hose was rotten and the lifebelts were stored at a level out of reach of the women and children.

1908, 20 September. Off Coronation Island
The American barque, *Star of Bengal*, left Fort Wrangel, Alaska with fifty thousand cases of salmon, a crew of thirty-six and a hundred and ten Chinese cannery hands. She dropped anchor in a gale off Coronation Island, and the tugs towing her steamed away. The anchors began to drag and heavy seas drove the vessel on to the rocks, where the masts collapsed and the decks were swept clear. Nine Europeans and a hundred and one Chinese were drowned.

Within Europe

1802, August. Brighton, Sussex
The clinker-built brig, *Adventure*, seventy-seven tons, foundered off the Sussex coast, the captain discouraging attempts to tow her into shallow water. Despite his protests, the vessel was brought into Shoreham harbour, where holes were found in her planking which had been made from the inside. She had been supposedly bound for the Mediterranean with a valuable cargo. Her owners, two London merchants named Easterby and Macfarlane, had planned the loss of their own ship, and had insured her for ten thousand pounds.

1803, 25 December. Plymouth, Devon
The brig, *Unity*, carrying coal and cask staves from Liverpool to Jersey, went down in a gale in Deadman's Bay. A sick member of the crew, who was in his bunk, floated to the surface after several minutes and was picked up alive.

1803, 25 December. Plymouth, Devon
The French brig, *Les Amis*, was en route from Martinique to Bordeaux with a cargo of sugar and coffee when she was captured by a British frigate, the HMS *Malta*, and brought to England. She was wrecked on the shore of Plymouth Sound. Troops mounted guard over the cargo all night, firing at looters coming in from the sea in small boats.

1804, 24 November. Paignton Ledges, Torbay, Devon
The British fleet blockading Brest had temporarily returned to Torbay and was at anchor there. The ships were suddenly ordered to set sail just before dark. While her anchors were being raised, several of the crew of HMS *Venerable* fell into the sea and while they were being picked up the ship lost her position and went ashore on Paignton Ledges in the darkness. The crew were taken off by boats from other warships and of the 555 men on board 547 were saved. Within twenty-four hours the ship had completely broken up and despite the presence of troops the local people from Brixham and Paignton had a field day with the wreckage.

1805, 21 December, Goodwin Sands

The transport ship, *Aurora*, foundered on the Goodwin Sands with a loss of over three hundred lives.

1809, 5 December. Seaford Bay, Sussex

A convoy of twenty-three merchant ships left Plymouth, with the sloop, *Harlequin*, to protect them against possible French attack. The *Harlequin* and six other ships ran aground in fog and with a heavy sea running. All of them broke up on the beach with heavy loss of life.

1811, 16 February. Mount Batten, Plymouth, Devon

HMS *Amethyst* was a 38-gun frigate built at Deptford in 1799. She dragged her anchors in a gale and went ashore at Mount Batten, where she filled with water so fast the crew had to take to the boats. All six boats were swamped and about thirty men drowned. Some of the survivors deserted on reaching shore.

1811, 24 December. Coast of Jutland

During a gale, three British warships, the *St. George*, *Defence* and *Hero*, went ashore on Jutland and were all wrecked, with the loss of two thousand men.

1816, 31 January. Kinsale, Ireland

The transport ships *Lord Melville* and *Boadicea* were lost in a storm near Kinsale, and two hundred soldiers with their wives and children were drowned.

1817, 18 January. Plymouth Sound, Devon

The warship, HMS *Telegraph*, formerly the American privateer, *Vengeance*, dragged her anchors across Plymouth Sound in a gale and went aground under the Hoe. The only casualty was a sailor who was crushed to death between decks when he tried to recover his possessions. The ship's surgeon saved his wife from drowning and got a line ashore, despite sustaining a broken leg.

1817, 18 January. Mount Batten, Plymouth, Devon

The brig o'war, HMS *Jasper*, with sixty-seven people on board, including fifteen women, was wrecked in a storm on Bears Head. Only two survivors managed to reach shore, one of them using a rope to swing out from the main yard. By chance he dropped straight into a small boat adrift in the Sound, which was then washed on to rocks from which he was able to wade to safety.

1820, 20 January. Lynmouth, Bristol Channel

The West Indiaman, *Picton*, of Bristol, came ashore in a storm and broke up eight hours later. Most of the crew and a woman passenger were saved, after being lashed to the rigging, but the cook and a boy were frozen to death.

1824, 1 January. Great Orme's Head, Llandudno, North Wales

The brig, *Hornby*, was driven close to the rocks under Great Orme in a fierce storm. A seaman was aloft in the rigging and the rolling of the ship brought him level with a ledge on the cliffs. He jumped to safety as the brig sheared away and foundered a few minutes later, with the loss of the remaining thirteen men on board. The survivor, John Williams, climbed the cliffs from ledge to ledge and reached part of the old coppermine workings on the Orme, where his sudden appearance among the miners caused quite a stir. He never went to sea again, but spent the rest of his life working in the Llandudno mines.

1824, 23 November. Near Eddystone lighthouse, Cornwall

The ketch *Coromandel* was returning to England from Portugal with a cargo of cork when she capsized in a hurricane near the Eddystone. The two men on deck were drowned, but the Captain and three others who had been in a cabin managed to get into the coal storage where they stayed for several hours with water up to their necks. The ship drifted towards Plymouth and became fixed to a breakwater, allowing the survivors to crawl out to safety.

1831, 3 March. Barnstaple Bay, Devon

The sloop, *Betsey*, returning to Devon from Wales with a cargo of coal, capsized in the bay while trying to cross the bar. The master, his brother and another sailor died, and the hull of the vessel came ashore at Appledore on the next tide.

1831, 18 August. Dutchman's Bank, Beaumaris Bay, North Wales

The wooden paddle-steamer, *Rothesay Castle*, on her daily service between Liverpool and Beaumaris went aground in bad weather and broke her back. Built in 1816 for work on the Clyde she was not designed to withstand the rougher waters of Liverpool Bay. Some passengers were swept away, and by morning only fifty of the hundred and forty people on board were still alive. Many were drowned when the mast fell, sweeping away those lashed to it. Rescuers picked up a total of twenty-three survivors.

As a result of this wreck, the Anglesey Lifesaving Association opened a station at Penmon the following year and a request was sent to the Government for the erection of a lighthouse on Trwyn Du, Penmon. The new lighthouse was completed in 1838.

The stranding of the *Rothesay Castle* was due to engine trouble, but it was discovered afterwards that her only boat had no signal gun, no oars, and had a hole in it. The unseaworthiness of the vessel was common knowledge and the officers were known to be quarrelsome and often drunk. At the time of the accident, many of the passengers were seasick, but they managed to man the pumps until these became choked with ash from the fires below.

1831, 28 August. Talacre, Point of Ayr, North Wales

The ship, *Burmese*, bound from St Petersburg with a cargo of tallow, was stranded not far from Point of Ayr. Four hours passed before the master, his wife and seventeen crew members were allowed ashore – a precautionary measure against cholera. During this time the master's wife had been lashed to the deck for safety as seas were breaking right over the vessel. When they eventually landed, the survivors were kept in quarantine for several days.

1833, 31 August. Off Boulogne, France

The convict ship *Amphitrite*, overloaded with 136 on board and undermanned, ran into a severe gale off Dungeness on her way from Woolwich to New South Wales and was run on to a sand spit by her captain. A crowd of onlookers made no attempt to give assistance and the captain refused the offer of a pilot because he was afraid some of the convicts would escape to the French shore. The female convicts were by this time on deck, and the seamen took to the rigging, but still the captain refused to launch the boats. Later that evening the ship broke in two and all on board drowned, with the exception of three seamen.

1835, 29 July. Cemaes Bay, Anglesey

The Belfast-owned smack, *Active*, was at anchor in Ramsey Bay, Isle of Man, when she dragged her anchors in a strong north-westerly gale. Drifting rapidly out to sea, she eventually grounded in Cemaes Bay some way from shore. Attempts were made to launch a boat, but then the Rev. James Williams rode a horse into the surf and threw a grappling hook and line over the bowsprit. The crew of five were found exhausted below decks, and were taken off safely.

1836, 11 October. Torbay, Devon

The *Duke of Marlborough* was a former post-office packet vessel stationed at Falmouth which had been brought out of government service and was fitted out for a trading expedition to West Africa. Shortly after leaving port in September she returned to put her sick master ashore and while she was still in Torbay she was caught in a severe storm and her main cable parted. Two men tried to get ashore by climbing the mainmast which was lodged against the cliff, but one was crushed to death when the wreck shifted. The other man climbed a second time and reached safety but the other men would not follow him and drowned.

1841, 20 February. Off Holyhead, Anglesey

The American sailing ship, *Governor Fenner*, left Liverpool for New York with a cargo of iron, but collided with the paddle steamer, *Nottingham*, in thick fog off Holyhead. The bows were smashed by the impact and the *Governor Fenner* sank with the loss of 123 lives. The *Nottingham*, which was carrying cattle and sheep, was badly damaged but got into dock safely. Most of the dead were emigrants.

1842, 12 November. Near Boulogne, France

The sailing ship, *Reliance*, was bound from Canton to London with 122 people on board and a cargo of twenty-seven thousand chests of tea. She ran ashore in a violent gale off Merlemont and was unable to launch her boats in the stormy conditions. A hundred and fifteen on board died, including the captain.

1843, 14–16 January. Near Saunton, Devon

The Liverpool-registered West African trading vessel, *John & Lilley*, was driven ashore at the northern end of Braunton Burrows after having battled against gales for eleven days and being blown between the English and Welsh coasts. The captain and crew, by this time very drunk, were all saved, but the valuable cargo of cotton goods, pots and pans, muskets, gunpowder and foodstuffs was looted by wreckers. Some of the cargo was found hidden in the Baptist church at Appledore.

1843, 16 January. Near Boscastle, Cornwall

The North American-built East Indiaman, *Jessie Logan*, was driven ashore here while running for shelter before a storm and became a total wreck. She was homeward bound from India with a cargo of rum, sugar and spices. Only a handful of survivors reached shore.

1843, 27 January. Crebawethan Rock, Isles of Scilly

The 400-ton Liverpool barque, *Duoro*, ran aground on the Western rocks here, with the loss of all her crew. Her manifest showed a cargo of 'bailed goods, armoury and brass stops', but when the wreck was located and excavated in 1973 the 'bailed goods' turned out to be aggries and manillas, the currency of slavery, evidence that the British slave trade was not ended by its official abolition in 1807.

1848, 31 March. Barricane Cove. Morte Bay, North Devon

The barque, *Princess Royal*, of London, bound from Mauritius to Bristol with a cargo of sugar, came ashore in dense fog. The crew were saved, but wreckers stripped the vessel very quickly and efficiently.

1848, 24 August. Off Abergele, North Wales

The American full-rigged ship, *Ocean Monarch*, 1500 tons, was bound from the Mersey to Boston with 354 passengers (mostly Irish emigrants) and a crew of forty-two. A fire broke out in the passenger accommodation and soon got out of control. A hundred and seventy-eight people died.

1848, 27 December. Lion Rock, Isles of Scilly

The *Polinarus*, bound from Demerara to London, was lost with all hands on Lion Rock. The first alarm was given by a herd of cows, frightened by the tearing and flapping of the ship's sails. Seventeen bodies were washed ashore and buried at St. Mary's. Seventy-one puncheons and fourteen hogsheads of rum were salvaged.

1850, 5 January. Ilfracombe, Devon

The Padstow schooner *Amelia* ran for shelter from strong gales and tried to enter Ilfracombe harbour at night, but struck a rock and sank. Her cargo of iron and coal was lost, and her master was reprimanded at a Board of Trade enquiry for not having gone up channel and anchored until daybreak.

1850, 12 November. West Coast of Ireland

The emigrant ship, *Edmund*, was bound from Limerick to New York when she was wrecked in a storm off the west coast. More than half of her two hundred passengers died.

1851, 9 November. Clovelly, Devon

The Finnish vessel, *Pollux*, left Dublin for Alexandria in ballast. Shortly after leaving Ireland she ran into a gale, the ballast shifted and she went over on her beam ends. The masts were cut away and she drifted into the Bristol Channel, where she was seen and boarded by pilots. The crew promptly abandoned ship, leaving the local men to get her into harbour as best they could. Next day the crew returned, but refused to help save the ship and when a tow line was taken on board it was cut by a member of the crew. The *Pollux* finally grounded on a beach near the pier at Clovelly. The Receiver of Wrecks ordered the stores and ballast to be unloaded and she floated on the next tide. Towed offshore and anchored, she broke her cables and was smashed on the shore in another gale.

1852, 13 April. Steeple Rock, Isles of Scilly

The *Mary Hay*, 250 tons, a London-registered barque, launched at Peterhead in 1837, struck Steeple Rock twice in a gale, finally being wrecked on Bream Ledges. She was bound for London from Jamaica with a cargo of rum, sugar, pimento, logwood, ebony, and coconuts.

1853, 28 September. Off Barra Island, Hebrides

The emigrant ship, *Annie Jane*, left Liverpool for Canada with over five hundred people on board but had to return with storm damage. When she set out again 450 passengers and crew were on board, and when she was struck by a huge wave off Barra Island two hundred people were instantly crushed to death by the collapse of the poop-deck. The ship went to pieces soon afterwards, and 102 people were washed safely ashore on a portion of the deck.

1854, 3 January. Dawlish, Devon

The 73-ton Exeter schooner, *Friends*, bound from Hartlepool with a cargo of coal, anchored off Exmouth and burnt flares for a pilot to come out. There was no response from the shore and being unwilling to enter harbour without assistance, in a strong north-east wind, the master tried to reach Torbay. The vessel struck a rock and beached between Dawlish and Langstone rock. The crew of five was saved, but the schooner went to pieces. At the Board of Trade Enquiry, the local pilots said they 'never went to sea at all on such occasions'.

1854, 21 January. Irish Sea

The sailing vessel, *Tayleur*, was the largest sailing ship ever built in Britain up to that time, and when she started on her maiden voyage from Liverpool to

Melbourne she had 652 people on board, many of them hopeful gold prospectors. She met bad weather as she entered the Irish Sea and it was found that her steering gear was defective and her compasses inaccurate. She dropped anchors in fog and gale force conditions, but when these gave way the vessel drifted on to the rocks, later sinking in deep water.

1854, 29 April. English Channel

The emigrant ship, *Favourite*, bound from Bremen to Baltimore in heavy seas, collided with the American ship, *Hesper*, off Start Point. The captain and five crew of the *Favourite* scrambled to safety on the *Hesper* before the two vessels drew apart. The 191 emigrants and ten crew members left on board the *Favourite* were left to their fate and drowned.

1854, 17 September. English Channel

The Norwegian barque, *Oceanus*, carrying five hundred tons of rice from Akyab to Kristiansand, was run down by an unidentified American schooner and cut to the waterline off Start Point, after calling at Queenstown and receiving instructions to discharge at Amsterdam. The colliding vessel refused to assist the *Oceanus* and the Brixham lugger *Hero*, took off the master and some of the crew, the remainder landing from their boat at Lyme Bay. The only casualty was a seaman killed when the foremast collapsed and struck him on the head.

1854, 14 November. Off Balaklava, Black Sea

The sailing ship, *Resolute*, formerly engaged in the Australian trade, had been chartered by the Government on the outbreak of the Crimean War and arrived at Balaklava in November with seven hundred tons of gunpowder and other war stores. She was ordered out of harbour when a Russian attack was feared, but was in a vulnerable position when an extremely violent gale struck the area, driving a large number of ships on to the rocks. The *Resolute* was lost with all hands.

1855, 3 May. Porthoustock, Cornwall

The three-masted Plymouth barque, *John*, 500 tons, was engaged in taking emigrants across the Atlantic and bringing back timber. She set sail for the New World, having been recently overhauled, with 268 passengers and a crew of eighteen. Although the weather was deteriorating, the captain was below when the ship struck the Manacle Rocks. At dawn the Porthoustock lifeboat fought its way through the surf and found about eighty exhausted people in the rigging. The boat made three journeys between shore and ship, rescuing ninety-one persons and hampered by drunken sailors, terrified passengers and heavy seas. The inquest revealed that the ship carried no distress flares or signal gun, and the crew was described as 'a drink-smelling rabble'. The captain was charged with manslaughter and received a prison sentence at the assizes, as did several St. Keverne men, who had looted the dead as they lay on the beach.

1856, January. Atlantic

The wooden paddle-steamer, *Pacific*, 2860 tons, vanished on a voyage from Liverpool to New York, with the loss of 186 people on board. No wreckage, messages or corpses were ever found. In May 1851, the *Pacific* had made the Atlantic crossing in a record of time of nine days, twenty hours, ten minutes.

1856, 3 February. Off Folkestone, Kent

The New Zealand packet, *Josephine Willis*, collided with the *Mangerton*, 363 tons, and sank, drowning sixty-nine passengers and crew. She had left St.

Katharine's Dock, London two days before, on her way to Auckland. In the confusion some lifeboats were sent away half empty, and other passengers used hen coops to help them reach shore.

1856, 21 February. St. Gowan's Head, near Milford Haven, Wales
The American sailing ship, *Great Duke*, was driven on to the rocks of St. Gowan's Head in a severe gale, on a voyage from New Orleans to Liverpool with a cargo of 4500 bales of cotton. The ship soon broke up and there were only three survivors.

1856, 5 September. Near Lizard Light, Cornwall
The American sailing ship, *Ocean Home*, 646 tons, collided with the American vessel, *Cherubim*, off the Cornish coast, while bound from Rotterdam to New York with 105 passengers and crew. Seventy-seven people drowned.

1859, 28 April. Near Ballyconigar, Ireland
The American emigrant ship, *Pomona*, was driven on to a sandbank here while off course on a voyage from Liverpool to New York. During the next day fruitless attempts were made to launch the boats, and before nightfall the ship slipped into deep water and began to sink. The crew began to abandon ship, a small number of them reaching the shore. 388 people died, including the captain.

1860, c. 31 March. Batten Reef, Plymouth, Devon
The 906-ton ship, *Havering*, left London for Hong Kong carrying government stores. When she was well out into the Atlantic, she was leaking badly and the crew's quarters and bedding were soaked. The men demanded the ship should return to England, so that she could be made watertight. Back in Plymouth, she was inspected by the Company's inspector, who said he could find nothing wrong with her. When the crew still refused to sail, the captain went ashore to get an order for their arrest. Meanwhile, the ship had dragged her anchors and gone on to the rocks; the men stood by and left her to become a total wreck.

1861. Gweal, west of Bryher, Isles of Scilly
The *Award*, an 846-ton ship launched in Quebec in 1859, was returning from Liverpool to New Orleans in ballast when she was wrecked on Gweal, in a severe gale. All the crew were saved by local people. Much of the ship's timber was used in the construction of the state room at Tresco Abbey.

1861, 1 January. Eddystone
The brig, *Aire*, of Goole, was carrying government stores from Woolwich to Malta, to replace the uniforms, cannon and shot lost on the Lizard when the steamer, *Czar*, was wrecked in 1859. The *Aire* foundered in a gale near the Eddystone lighthouse. The crew were saved by the American ship, *Bostonian*, but the majority died next day when this vessel hit the Le Hanios reef in the Channel Isles and went to pieces with only three survivors.

1863, 2 December. Taylor's Island, Isles of Scilly
The *Friar Tuck*, a 662-ton tea clipper of Liverpool, launched in Aberdeen six years previously, was bound for London from Foo Chow Foo, with a cargo of tea. Sheltering in St. Mary's harbour, she was driven on to Taylor's Island in one of the worst gales known in the area. The islanders 'acquired' most of the tea in spite of the efforts of coastguards and Preventive men. The Chinese geese at Tresco Abbey are descended from the geese carried on board this ship.

1866, 10 January. Brixham, Devon
The 340-ton sailing ship, *Monda*, was carrying a general cargo from London to Berbice when she ran ashore on rocks at Fishcombe Point near Brixham. She had

been making for Brixham harbour after her anchor cables parted, but in the dark and confusion missed her way. The ship was a total loss and five crewmen were killed, the captain and two others escaping by climbing the cliffs. Forty-six ships were lost in the same gale in Torbay and cargo and corpses were found along the coastline for a week.

1866, 30 March. Tinge Rock, Devon

The wooden paddle-steamer, *Queen*, left Bristol on her normal packet-service to Hayle with forty passengers and a hundred tons of general cargo, when she struck the Tinge Rock. Badly damaged, she headed for Ilfracombe, but was beached at Clovelly, near the pier head. During four thousand trips on the same route there had not been one accident and at the Board of Trade enquiry the captain, who had taken over command from his father the previous year, was found guilty of neglect in not using the lead and of having failed to keep and maintain a ship's log since he had assumed command of the vessel. The cargo was recovered, but the ship broke her back and went to pieces.

1867, 5 January. Entrance to River Exe, Devon

The Exmouth brigantine, *Julia*, 148 tons, was carrying 240 tons of coal when she was driven on to the bar at Pole Sand in a gale, almost opposite the lifeboat station. Because of a delay in launching the lifeboat only one man was found alive. At the Board of Trade enquiry the lifeboatmen were criticised, but it was also stated that the vessel was not in a fit condition to go to sea.

1867, 7 January. Mount's Bay, Cornwall

The 500-ton barque, *John Grey*, of Glasgow, drifted on to rocks in Mount's Bay after eight days' rough weather in the mouth of the Channel. She was bound for London from Demerara, with a cargo of rum, sugar and coconuts. The captain had lost half his crew through fever in the West Indies, and had been forced to take anyone he could get for the voyage home. The crew bolstered their courage with rum and tried to abandon ship, but the captain held them at gunpoint and threatened to shoot the first man who tried to launch a boat. The Penzance lifeboat, meanwhile, had been delayed by damage to the wheel of the carriage on which she was launched, caused during an earlier rescue. Eventually drawing alongside the wreck the coxwain urged the crew to jump into the lifeboat. Fifteen did so, but the remaining six, including the captain, both mates, the carpenter and a French passenger, refused and died.

1868, 10 December. Off Chivelstone, Devon

The 734-ton *Gossamer*, which had taken part in the annual tea-races from Shanghai to London, was on her way from London to Adelaide with twenty-four crew and five passengers. The voyage down the Channel was very rough. The pilot went too close to the Devon coast and the ship hit the rocks and broke into pieces. Wreckers got most of the cargo before soldiers and police arrived. At the Board of Trade enquiry, evidence was heard that the pilot had been drunk and he was found guilty of manslaughter.

1869, 11 December. Bigbury Bay, Devon

The 618-ton French brig, *Commerce de Paris*, was bound from Rio de Janeiro with a cargo of coffee, cotton, tapioca and dye wood. She anchored in Bigbury Bay in a gale, but dragged her anchors and at high water drifted beam on towards the beach. Several bales of cotton and a large number of hides were salvaged, but the wreckers were so persistent that police were brought in to guard the wreck.

1871, June. Seven Stones, Isles of Scilly

The Spanish barque *Primos*, 496 tons, was bound for Greenock from Havana with a cargo of sugar when she struck the Seven Stones in hazy weather and sank in twelve minutes. The only survivor, an Italian seaman, leapt into the sea with his arms round the ship's figurehead and drifted until he was picked up.

1872, 25 November. Chesil Beach, Dorset

The 1500-ton iron-clad sailing ship, *Royal Adelaide*, bound from London to Sydney, went aground with sixty-seven emigrants on board. Five people lost their lives and four of the rescuers drank themselves to death on the barrels of rum, gin and whisky washed ashore.

1872, c. 4 December. Between Portugal and the Azores

The *Marie Celeste* was found six hundred miles from Portugal by the British ship, *Dei Gratia*. She had nobody on board and the lifeboats, ship's papers, navigation books and navigation instruments were all missing. The ship was in perfect order and everything was intact, except for one of 1700 casks of industrial alcohol. At the Admiralty court of enquiry, the captain of the *Dei Gratia* and his crew were accused of piracy and murder. When the charge was abandoned, the Advocate General said the crew of the *Marie Celeste* had murdered the captain and his wife and child and the chief mate and then made off in the boat. The court refused to give an opinion on the matter and gave the *Dei Gratia* a salvage award. Another theory was that the captain of the *Marie Celeste* thought the cargo was about to explode and gave orders for the ship to be abandoned. The end of the ship was bizarre. In 1884, she was bought by an American, who loaded her with rubbish, insured her for twenty-seven thousand dollars, took on a down-at-heel crew and sailed her to the Caribbean where they ran her on to the Rochelois Bank and set her on fire. When they claimed the insurance money, they were arrested.

1872, 4 December. Near Start Point, Devon

The Italian brig, *Maria Theresa* was on a voyage from Newcastle to Genoa with a cargo of coal. Fifteen miles west off Start Point, she was in collision with an unidentified ship and had to be beached near the signal station, where she broke up. The crew spent the night at an inn ashore. One seaman went mad and stabbed a number of people, including three coastguards and their wives. He was eventually killed with a cutlass by another coastguard.

1873, 3 March. Prawle Point, Devon

The clipper, *Lalla Rookh*, was bound from Shanghai to London with 1200 tons of tea and twelve tons of tobacco. She met dense fog in the Channel and struck Prawle Point, where she was wrecked. Nineteen of the twenty crew were saved, most of them by breeches buoy. A stowaway, found dead in his bunk, was thought to have died of dysentery before the ship went aground.

1874, 18 January. St. Mary's, Isles of Scilly

The *Minnehaha* had called at Falmouth, after a voyage of fourteen months from South America with a cargo of guano, which she was to unload at Dublin. In a gale, the captain set a correct course, but the Channel pilot countermanded it without his knowledge. The ship struck the rocks under full sail and sank immediately. Nine of the crew were saved from the rigging. Ten others were drowned, including the pilot, whose body was washed up two months later.

1874, 14 February. Bigbury Bay, Devon

The German brigantine, *Theodor*, carrying timber and cotton from the West Indies, was blown off course and went aground on Thurlestone Sands, because the crew were unable to control the ship. She had met severe weather the previous three days, during which the master and mate had been swept overboard.

1874, 21 October. Off Ardrossan, Scotland
The paddle steamer, *Chusan*, bound from Glasgow to Shanghai, struck the Crinan Rock while running for shelter from a storm. Her peculiarly high superstructure was a great handicap and she broke in two very quickly, the forward portion being swept into the harbour and the after portion sinking. The captain drowned while saving his wife and child and others died trying to reach shore.

1875, 18 August. Solent
The yacht, *Mistletoe*, sank after a collision with HM steamship *Alberta*, which had Queen Victoria on board. Three people on the yacht were drowned. The coroner's inquest alleged error on the part of the *Alberta*'s navigating officers and the captain was reprimanded.

1877, 14-16 October. Plymouth, Devon
The Newport-registered barque, *R. H. Jones*, was sailing from Bremerhaven to Newport in ballast. In a gale, she was washed right over the breakwater at Plymouth and broke up, with her anchor cables draped across the breakwater.

1878, 24 March. Dunnose headland, Isle of Wight
The training frigate, HMS *Eurydice*, returning from Bermuda, was overturned and sank in a squall, with the loss of three hundred men. The ship was later raised.

1878, October. Barnstaple Bay, Devon
The brig, *Odin*, was bound for Llanelly with a cargo of cut timber. She missed the tide and was unable to enter port. The captain decided to move away from the Welsh coast and to wait for the next tide on the other side of the Bristol Channel. With little experience of the area, he put the ship on the rocks at Morte Point. Both the ship and the cargo provided welcome firewood for local people.

1879, 16 January. Salcombe, Devon
The Salcombe-owned and manned wooden brigantine, *Annie*, 242 tons, was attempting to enter her home port at the end of a voyage from Bahia with a cargo of sugar in bags, when she struck the bar and went to pieces. She was already damaged, having lost her bulwarks, topmast and longboat in a storm.

1879, 27 July. Off Annet, Isles of Scilly
The eleven-year-old barque, *River Lune*, struck the rocks at night and in fog. The ship sank aft within ten minutes. The crew got away in the boats, but returned in daylight to collect their possessions. The captain blamed the accident on a faulty chronometer, saying that he thought he had been fifteen miles further west.

1879, 20 October. Westdown Point, Bantham, Devon
The Quebec-built wooden barque, *Lady Young*, 598 tons, bound from Cardiff to Hamburg in ballast, was dismasted and driven on to the coast in a gale. The crew were taken off by breeches buoy. The following day the steward volunteered to return to collect the crew's belongings. He fell out of the bosun's chair as he was being hauled back to the shore and was killed on the rocks fifty feet below.

1881, January. Ramsgate, Kent
The three-masted barque, *Indian Chief*, went aground and broke her back on the Long Sand on a bitterly cold, foggy night. She was bound from Middlesborough to Yokohama with a crew of twenty-eight and a general cargo. The Ramsgate lifeboat was launched, with a crew of eleven, and towed by the paddle-steamer,

Vulcan, but could not find the wreck in the dark and lay-to until dawn in atrocious weather conditions. The crew of the *Indian Chief* had lashed themselves to the mizzen-mast and foretop, and sighted the lifeboat as daylight came, in seas 'like a boiling cauldron'. Twelve survivors were taken off, some having died during the night.

1881, 20 July. Shetland Isles
Ten fishing boats were sunk off the Shetlands in a storm, all fifty-eight of the men being drowned. This undramatic record is more typical of marine disasters than those of ships involving the loss of hundreds of people and of cargo worth thousands of pounds.

1883, 31 October. Irish Sea
The American sailing ship, *Alhambra*, collided with the London & North Western Railway's cattle steamer, *Holyhead*, on the Dublin–Holyhead route. Both vessels sank with the loss of fifteen lives.

1884, 7 December. Bishop Rock, Isles of Scilly
The brigantine, *Chalciope*, of Fleetwood, was inward bound from Corunna with a cargo of pitwood when she was forced to heave-to near the Bishop Rock in bad weather. After a steering error the vessel ran straight into the shore and the crew took to the rigging. All came ashore safely at low tide.

1884, 23 January. Saunton Sands, Devon
The brigantine, *Jonathan Weir*, of Monckton, New Brunswick, left Newport for Cuba with a cargo of coal. Meeting gales off the Scillies, she was blown into the bay and on to Saunton Sands, becoming a total wreck. The eight crew, one passenger and one stowaway got to shore safely at low water.

1886, 9 December. Southport, Lancashire
The German barque, *Mexico*, of Hamburg, bound for Guayaquil, Equador, from Liverpool, went aground in a gale. The Southport lifeboat was launched, but capsized drowning thirteen of the crew, and the St. Anne's lifeboat, asked to stand by with her crew of fourteen was never seen again. The twelve crewmen, who had lashed themselves to the rigging, were eventually rescued by the Lytham lifeboat.

1887, 17 January. Bolt Head, Devon
The *Halloween*, bound from Foochow to London with 1600 tons of tea, hit the rocks and became a total loss near Bolt Head. A considerable part of the cargo was taken off and, on this occasion, not stolen by local people. The owners received forty thousand pounds compensation for loss of cargo, but the ship itself was not insured.

1889, *c*. 29 January. Off Boulogne, France
The sailing ship, *Sir Walter Raleigh*, was on her way from Sydney, New South Wales, to London with a cargo of wool when she ran aground near Boulogne and was completely wrecked, with the loss of five lives.

1891, 9 March. Hallsands, Devon
The schooner, *Lizzie Ellen*, took on china clay at Charlestown and was on her way to London when gale-force winds drove her on to the foot of cliffs north of Hallsands. Three crewmen survived and owed their lives to local men who waded out to them with ropes. A terrified cabin boy refused to jump into the sea and the master drowned while trying to persuade him to leave.

1891, 10 March. Nare Point, Falmouth, Cornwall
The *Bay of Panama*, bringing jute from Calcutta went into the cliffs during a

blizzard. Nine people, including the captain and his wife, were swept overboard by a giant wave and drowned. Six men froze to death in the night and the boatswain went mad and jumped into the sea. Seventeen of the crew of forty were taken over by breeches buoy next morning. The horse-drawn omnibus taking them to Falmouth was caught in a snowdrift and the men had to finish the journey on foot, some without shoes.

1893, 4 April. St. Martin's, Isles of Scilly

The full-rigged ship, *Horsa*, homeward bound from New Zealand, was driven ashore in a cove here when she came too close inshore during a gale. She was pulled off the rocks by the Scilly packet, *Lyonesse*, and tried to make her own way to St. Mary's, but rolled over and sank. The *Lyonesse* saved all the crew.

1894, 29 January. Brandon Bay, Co. Kerry, Ireland

The Glasgow barque, *Port Yarrock*, left Cardiff for Mexico undercrewed and badly provisioned. The crew suffered great hardship on the return voyage and before the ship reached port she was driven ashore on the coast of Ireland. The Court of Enquiry censured the owner and fined him seventy-five pounds.

1895, 4 November. Land's End, Cornwall

The American windjammer, *Granite Slate*, struck the Runnel Stone rocks, near Land's End, probably as a result of a navigation error. She was hauled off and towed to Porthcurno Bay where she began to settle rapidly. The sodden cargo of wheat began to swell and the crew took to the boats. Soon afterwards she broke up completely in a gale.

1896, 26 October. Near Bude, Cornwall

The Danish barquentine, *Thyra*, was wrecked on the rocks at Cleave Strand, after her sails had been ripped to pieces in a gale. She was carrying a cargo of coal and bricks from Llanelly to Stockholm. The crew of nine were rescued by the Bude lifeboat.

1896, 14 December. North of Isles of Scilly

The 553-ton Norwegian barque, *Sophie*, was dismasted north of the Scillies, while she was bound from Cardiff to her home port of Fredrikstadt laden with anthracite. She was an old ship, which had been condemned and sold out of the British Merchant Service under the Act of 1888. The crew abandoned ship and were picked up by a steamer which landed them at Gibraltar. The *Sophie* was taken in tow with some difficulty and beached on Tresco, where her cargo was used for heating the island greenhouses and her timber for field fencing.

1900, 16 December. Off Malaga, Spain

The three-masted schooner and training corvette, *Gneisenau*, was lying off Malaga when severe weather caused her to drag her anchors. The ship headed for the open sea using her auxiliary engines, but insufficient steam was available for her to make any headway and she was driven on to the breakwater of the outer harbour, sinking in an upright position within a few minutes. She was carrying a crew of 460, of whom forty-nine were naval cadets and 230 were boys training as seamen. Thirty-eight drowned, and nearly a hundred were injured through being dashed against the rocks. The captain refused a line thrown to him, threw his sword to his would-be rescuer and went down with his ship.

1900, 28 December. Perran Bay, Cornwall

The French 'bounty clipper', *Seine* ran aground in Perran Bay in heavy seas. The 'bounty clippers' received the name because of a subsidy from the French government, which allowed exceptionally elegant ships to be built. The ship broke up on the beach and her remains were sold to a local man for forty-two pounds.

1901, 22 June. Bishop Rock Lighthouse, Isles of Scilly
The four-masted barque, *Falkland*, 2676 tons, bound for Falmouth from Tacoma with a cargo of wheat, a crew of twenty-eight and two passengers, struck the Bishop Rock Lighthouse while trying to manoeuvre. The captain and five crew were drowned, but the remainder were picked up by lifeboats. The marks where the yards struck are still visible on the masonry of the lighthouse.

South America and the Caribbean

1800, 7 November. Near Punta Santa Elena, Ecuador
The Spanish warship, *Leocadia*, was wrecked here with a large quantity of treasure on board. A hundred and forty of those on board died, including a number of English prisoners, but within a month salvage crews had recovered most of the valuable cargo.

1804, 4 September. Antigua, Antilles
A hurricane which struck the island sank the British warship, HMS *De Ruyter*, in Deep Bank. There were no casualties among her crew of 250.

1808, 24 February. Near Cabo de la Vela, Colombia
The British ship, *Chalmers*, carrying slaves from Africa to the West Indies, was wrecked here, but without loss of crew or slaves.

1811, 7 July. Antigua, Antilles
The British warship, HMS *Guachapin*, was wrecked here during a hurricane. A second warship, HMS *Gloire*, escaped being capsized by throwing all her guns overboard.

1813, 17 September. Amelia Island, Florida
The Spanish ship, *Flor de Guadiana*, on a voyage to Europe with a cargo of cotton, was driven on shore here during a severe storm and wrecked.

1815, 25 March. Pensacola, Florida
The armed Spanish merchant ship, *Volador*, with a cargo that included a large consignment of rifles, ran aground in a gale inside the port of Pensacola and broke up, with the loss of all its cargo.

1815, 24 April. Coche Island, Venezuela
On its way from Spain to put down the revolution in Venezuela, a large fleet of warships and transports anchored off Coche Island, near Margarita Island. One of the largest warships, the *San Pedro Alcantara*, caught fire and exploded. The cargo of silver, weapons and munitions was scattered over a wide area and salvage continued as late as 1871.

1816, 23 May. Anegada Reef, Virgin Islands
The British ship, *Dash*, bound from Puerto Rico to Barbados with a cargo of 120 oxen, was totally lost here. The crew and twenty oxen were saved.

1816, 11 November. Alacrán Reef, Mexico
The British warship, *Tay*, was wrecked here during a voyage from Campache to Jamaica. Her crew of 135 were all rescued, but treasure amounting to about two million pesos had to be abandoned.

1817, 3 March. Near Havana, Cuba

The English ship, *Prince Regent*, was wrecked during a gale, after arriving from the Bahamas with a cargo of salt.

1818, 17 May. Bermuda

The *Caesar*, from Newcastle, England, to Baltimore with a cargo of bricks, bottles and grindstones, was wrecked on a reef here.

1818, 10 August. Florida Keys

The British merchant ship, *Solway*, on a voyage from Jamaica to Withsharon, was wrecked on a reef here. Most of the cargo was recovered by an unusually large fleet of eighteen salvage vessels.

1819, 27 July. Grand Cayman Island

The English merchantman, *Constantine*, was wrecked shortly after beginning her voyage from Jamaica to London. Most of her cargo of coffee was saved.

1819, 3 September. Anegada Reef, Virgin Islands

The Portuguese slave ship, *Dona Paulo*, was wrecked and broke up here. The crew and 235 of the slaves were rescued.

1820, 14 December. Morant Keys, Jamaica

The English ship, *Martins*, sailed from Coro, Venezuela, to Kingston, with a cargo of mules. She was wrecked on the Keys, but most of the mules were saved.

1821, 7 April. Barbuda, Antilles

The 150-ton Spanish brig, *San Josef*, arriving from Spain with a cargo of olive oil, brandy, paper and almonds, went down in a storm.

1822, 20 July. Guadeloupe, Antilles

The British ship *Virginia* with several hundred soldiers on board, was on a passage from Dominica to Antigua, and was wrecked on the Isle de Su here, but without casualities.

1823, 4 March. Anegada Reef, Virgin Islands

The British ship, *Acadia*, bound for Trinidad from Puerto Rico with a cargo of cattle, went aground on the shoals and broke up. Some of the cattle were saved.

1828, 31 March. Imperial River, Chile

The 402-ton barque, *Saracen*, bound from Sydney to South America with six passengers and a crew of twenty-four, hit the rocks near the mouth of the Imperial River, as the result of a mistake on the part of the inexperienced helmsman. Those on board included a woman and her four children. They all reached the shore safely, but they were robbed by Indians of all their food and personal possessions. After walking for several weeks they reached a garrisoned village, from where they were able to get to Valparaiso by boat.

1830, 5 December. Cape Frio, Brazil

The British frigate, *Thetis*, with a crew of three hundred, left Rio for England carrying 810,000 dollars in coins. She went into the cliffs at Cape Frio under full sail, and sank, drowning nearly everyone on board. Using a diving bell, 600,000 dollars of the money was raised within two years of the ship's sinking, and a further 161,000 dollars soon afterwards.

1887, 29 March. Brazil

The emigrant ship, *Kapunda*, was bound for Australia when she sank after a collision with the *Ada Melmore* off the coast of Brazil. About 298 people drowned. At an enquiry the officers of the *Ada Melmore* were censured.

The African Coast

1822, April. Struys Bay, Cape of Good Hope
The *Grace*, of 245 tons, was on a voyage from Sydney to London with a cargo of wool and oil. Oil leaked on to the wool, and ignited through spontaneous combustion. The ship burst into flames in Struys Bay and it became a total loss. The crew escaped and, for saving Government despatches entrusted to him, the captain received a land grant of a thousand acres when he returned to settle in England in 1825.

1842, 27 August. Simon's Bay, Cape of Good Hope, South Africa
The convict ship, *Waterloo*, built at Bristol in the year of the famous battle (1815) left England for Sydney with 219 male convicts and fifty-one soldiers. The ship took on provisions at Simon's Bay and a gale sprang up while she was at anchor. She drifted ashore when her anchors parted, breaking in two almost at once. The convicts were released to save themselves, but huge waves swept them overboard. A hundred and ninety people were drowned, of a total of three hundred and thirty three on board.

1851, 25 July. Mauritius
The East India trading vessel, *Randolph*, was bound for Calcutta from Port Louis, Mauritius, when she ran on to a reef on the north-east end of the island and was totally wrecked. At daylight the survivors, who included about 220 Indian natives returning from a term of labour on the island, made for the shore in the boats.

1852, 7 September. Off the South African Coast
The wooden sailing ship, *Fairfield*, was bound from Calcutta to England, when she ran into bad weather and was driven ashore south of Port Natal. Twenty men were drowned, but the seven survivors who reached land were found by Kaffirs and guided safely to a white settlement.

1884, 13 December. About 1600 miles from the Cape
The yacht, *Mignonette* sailing from Southampton to Australia, foundered in a storm and three men and a boy took to the boat without provisions. On the twentieth day the boy was killed and eaten by two of the men. The survivors were picked up by the German barque *Montezuma*, on the twenty-fourth day and taken to Falmouth. The two men were tried for murder at Exeter and the death sentence was passed; they were later reprieved and sentenced to six months imprisonment.

India and the Far East

1842, c. July. Strong's Island, Caroline Group, South Pacific
The whaler, *Harriet*, 350 tons, called at the island for water and the crew were set upon and killed by the natives, who had seemed friendly at first. The ship itself, with five men on board, was attacked next and the men took to the boat, never to be seen again. The ship was plundered and set on fire by the natives.

1850, 30 October. Macao Harbour
The Portuguese frigate, *Donna Maria II* was at anchor here preparing for a party to celebrate the birthday of Don Fernando, consort of the Queen of Portugal, when she blew up without warning, killing everyone on board with the exception

of nine men rescued by the US ship, *Marion*. Five of these later died of their injuries.

1852, 8 October. Madras, India
The British barque, *Successor*, was chartered by the Indian Government to transport troops, camp-followers, horses and cattle from Madras to Rangoon. The monsoon, expected during the next few days, broke suddenly while the ship was still at anchor and she broke from her moorings and drifted ashore. The captain and second officer were not on board at the time, and the first officer did his best to evacuate the ship, dying in the attempt. With him went sixty-three other casualties, another 220 being saved.

1853, 7 April. Near Hubshee Jungeera, India
The sailing ship, *Nessree*, was a British-owned vessel on the India-Arabia trade route. On a voyage from Arabia to Bombay with 400 Indian pilgrims she ran into bad weather and the ship became unmanageable. There was panic among the passengers, who rushed the boats and swamped them. The *Nessree* finally went ashore about thirty-five miles south of Bombay and was totally wrecked. Of the 450 on board, only ninety-four people survived.

1854, c. 24 May. Bay of Bengal
The wooden ship, *Lady Nugent*, was presumed lost in this area during a typhoon on her way from Madras to Rangoon with the 25th Regiment of Madras (Native) Light Infantry aboard. The 409 officers and men, women and children and crew were presumed drowned.

1857, 29 June. Off Karachi, West Pakistan
The sailing vessel, *Julia*, struck the bar as she was being towed out of harbour at Karachi, carrying part of the 4th troop of Horse Artillery to Bombay. The ship drifted on to the rocks near Clifton, where she became a total wreck. Fourteen men lost their lives.

1860, 9 September. Pacific Ocean
The sloop, Camilla, 549 tons, left Hakodate, Japan for Kanagawa and was never heard of again. She carried a crew of 121 and her loss was attributed to a typhoon which swept the coast of Japan that day.

1864, 22 February. Pacific
The Australian vessel, *All Serene*, sank during a gale in the Pacific, with the loss of thirty lives. The survivors endured much hardship before they reached the Fiji Islands in a small boat.

1866, 16 April. Straits of Sunda
The sailing ship, *Jeddo*, was bound for British Guiana from Amoy with a large number of Chinese coolies. At the start of the voyage trouble broke out and a number of men were severely flogged. On 16 April the ship caught fire, the cause being unknown, and 146 coolies and four crew members lost their lives.

1868. Leuconna Reef, Shanghai
The wooden sailing ship, *Hamilla Mitchell*, went down with a general cargo and 50,000 pounds in coins. Lloyds met the owner's claim and their surveyor reported the vessel to be lying twenty fathoms below the surface, a depth which few divers were willing to consider at that time. Two of Siebe Gorman's most experienced divers reached the strong-room, however, and recovered 40,000 pounds of the treasure. Despite the attempts of Chinese junks to hijack their ship, they got the money safely to Shanghai and afterwards returned to bring up the rest.

1870, January. China Sea
The tea clipper, *Caliph*, left Foochow for New York early in January, one of the last of the tea fleet to sail. She was never heard of again and was presumed to have gone down somewhere in the China Sea. No bad weather was reported in the area.

1872, 2 November. Paracel Islands, near Hong Kong
The China tea clipper, *Serica*, was wrecked here on her homeward journey from Hong Kong. One member of the crew survived, nine died from exposure and starvation, and the remainder were killed when their raft was smashed to pieces.

1874, 17 March. East China Sea
The wooden steamship, *Manchu*, was bound from Nagasaki to Shanghai when she ran into bad weather and the engines became choked with coal as the ship rolled. She was abandoned on 17 March and the captain, second mate and a Chinese fireman were the only survivors of the crew of fifty-seven.

1875, 1 July. Crozet Islands, South Indian Ocean
The sailing ship, *Strathmore*, left Gravesend for New Zealand with fifty-one emigrants and thirty-eight crew, and a cargo of railway iron and gunpowder. She ran on to the Twelve Apostles Rocks in thick fog and was badly holed. Forty-nine people managed to reach the islands, where they endured great hardship for seven months until they were rescued by the American whaler *Young Phoenix*.

1884, 11 May. Nasilai Reef, Fiji, South Pacific
The sailing ship, *Syria*, was bound from Calcutta to Fiji with 494 Chinese coolies on board. She was wrecked on the reef in a gale with the loss of fifty-nine lives.

1890, 22 September. Rynkyn Islands, Japan
The sailing ship, *Lizzie C. Troop*, 1391 tons, was driven ashore here during a cyclone while on a voyage from Nagasaki to Puget Sound. The captain, his son and ten crewmen died, but the captain's wife and twelve others reached shore and were kindly treated by the islanders, who took them to an island a hundred miles away, from where they went by ship to Japan.

Iron Ships: into the Twentieth Century

The first practical steam boat was the *Charlotte Dundas*, built in Scotland at Grangemouth Dockyard in 1801 and used successfully as a tug on the Forth and Clyde Canal. In America, Robert Fulton's paddle-steamer, *Clermont*, began operating on the Hudson River between New York and Albany and gave good service for many years. The first steamer to run commercially in Europe was Henry Bell's Glasgow-built *Comet*, which began carrying passengers on the Clyde in 1812. In 1820, she went ashore at Graignish Point, the first steamship to be wrecked on regular service. By then steam ships were well established for river and coastal traffic, but not for ocean-going ships. There were two reasons for this: marine steam engines were still unreliable and they had to be stopped at frequent intervals in order that the accumulation of salt could be cleared from the

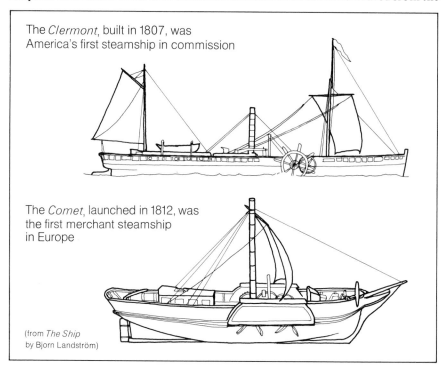

The *Clermont*, built in 1807, was America's first steamship in commission

The *Comet*, launched in 1812, was the first merchant steamship in Europe

(from *The Ship* by Bjorn Landström)

78

boilers, an operation which necessitated the use of a lot of coal. In the 1830s, however, a practical surface condenser was developed, which allowed the boilers to be supplied with fresh water. This greatly cut down the amount of coal needed for a long ocean voyage. Before this improvement, the American ship, *Savannah*, a 320-ton wooden sailing ship, had an auxiliary engine fitted to drive paddle-wheels. She crossed the Atlantic in this way in 1819, taking just over twenty-seven days for the voyage, but her engine was used for a total of only about eighty-five hours.

The first vessel to cross the Atlantic under continuous steam power was the *Sirius* built in 1837 for sailings between London and Cork. She had a surface condenser, patented in 1834, and could reach a speed of about nine knots. In 1838, she was chartered to sail from Cork to New York, which she accomplished in eighteen days. She did this double crossing twice and then returned to her original service. The first steamship built especially for the Atlantic was the *Great Western*. Designed by Brunel and built in Bristol, she could carry 240 passengers and had a crew of sixty. Between 1838 and 1846, she made sixty-four crossings of the Atlantic. She was then transferred to service on the Southampton—West Indies route.

All the ships mentioned so far had wooden hulls. The first iron steamship, the *Aaron Manby*, was built in 1821. In 1838, iron ships were admitted to Lloyd's A1 classification and by the early 1850s more than a hundred and fifty iron ships were registered. Two-thirds of them were steamships. In the 1840s the propeller began to take the place of the paddle-wheel. The *Great Britain*, the first screw-propelled iron vessel to cross the Atlantic, accomplished her maiden voyage from Liverpool to New York in just under fifteen days.

Ships constructed of steel, rather than iron, were available in the 1860s. The first steel ship to cross an ocean was the *Colonel Lamb*, built in Britain for the Confederate forces during the American Civil War. She sailed from Liverpool in 1864. It was not until the 1880s, however, that steel came into general use for ship construction and by 1890 nearly all new ships were being built in steel.

From the end of the 1880s, twin-screw propulsion was giving the larger liners higher speeds, but the introduction of the steam turbine in the 1890s greatly improved the performance of large ships. The Cunarders, *Lusitania* and *Mauretania*, launched in 1906, were each of 40,000 tons, with four propeller shafts, and were able to reach a speed of twenty-six knots. Oil fuel was being extensively used by the 1930s and marine diesel engines were being installed in oil tankers and cargo ships during the first decade of the present century.

With the development of competing air services, the day of the very large passenger ship came to an end. The *France*, 66,000 tons, and the *Queen Elizabeth*, 58,000 tons, were the last of them. Oil tankers, on the other hand, have grown steadily larger. The average tanker in the 1920s was of about 10,000 tons deadweight. By the end of the 1960s tankers of over 310,000 tons were in service.

Radio transformed the situation of ships at sea, but most ship-owners were slow to see its advantages, especially in cases of disaster. In 1897, Marconi had formed a company for sending wireless messages for short distances between ship and shore. One of his first customers was the East Goodwin lightship, equipped with radio at the end of 1898. Three months afterwards it was rammed by a steamship. The first distress call in history was picked up at the South Foreland, tugs were sent out and the lightship, damaged but still afloat, was towed to safety.

What really made an impression on the shipping world, however, was the case of the 15,378-ton White Star liner *Republic*. On 24 January 1909, in fog, she was rammed twenty-six miles off Nantucket by the emigrant ship, *Florida*. The *Republic's* radio operator sent out a distress call, a flotilla of ships arrived on the scene and all the passengers were saved.

By the time steamships became commonplace, all the main shipping routes had been established and charted by sailing ships. What happened from the mid-nineteenth century onwards was that the volume of shipping on these routes increased enormously. More goods and more people were being moved about the world, faster and in bigger ships. Accidents increased in proportion. The typical wreck of the late nineteenth and early twentieth century was not, however, a large transatlantic liner hitting an iceberg. It was of the run-of-the-mill kind indicated by such bald entries in the records as:

25 June 1890   Channel near Portland. Barque, *Ethel*, bound for Brisbane, sank after collision with the screw steamer, *Umbilo*. Loss of life: four.

This is the bread-and-butter, repeated hundreds of times around the world each year, with nothing sensational to catch the attention of journalists or the world of marine insurance, yet each with small-scale drama, danger and misery of its own. In one way or another the examples which follow rise above the general tide of disaster.

Australasia

1847, 17 March. Moreton Bay, Queensland
The Australian paddle steamer, *Sovereign*, foundered here with a loss of forty-four lives. She was one of the pioneer Australian coastal steamships and was employed between Manning River and Moreton Bay. Her engines had been salvaged from the wreck of the *King William IV*, lost on Oyster Bank in 1839.

1853, 15 May. New South Wales
The *Monumental City* was the first steamship to cross the Pacific from San Francisco to Sydney, taking over two months to make the voyage. She arrived in Australia on 17 February 1853 and was put on the Melbourne to Sydney run. She left Melbourne under sail and an Australian captain travelling as a passenger warned the officer of the watch that the ship was travelling too close to the shoreline. This advice was ignored, and early next morning the vessel ran on to a small rocky island near Gabo, still under sail.

1859. Carpenter Rocks, South Australia
The screw-driven *Admella*, 395 tons, was built in Scotland in 1857 to operate between Adelaide and Melbourne. The Carpenter Rocks form part of a reef running for a hundred miles off the South Australian coast. The Carpenter Rocks had a bad record for wrecks and the Government erected a lighthouse there which began to operate on 1 January 1859, a few months before the *Admella* was wrecked. On this particular voyage she had 113 people on board, with a cargo of copper. There were only twenty-four survivors.

1870, 23 July. Hauraki Gulf, New Zealand
The steamship, *Tauranga*, was in collision with the schooner, *Enterprise* between Point Rodney and Sail Rock. Both vessels sank within a short time because of the violence of the impact. The crew of the schooner escaped in a boat without rowlocks, and so did not reach shore for some time. The only sign of the *Tauranga* was the finding of the ship's dog on Sail Rock.

1875, 24 February. Great Barrier Reef
The steamship, *Gothenburg*, was on a voyage from Port Darwin to Adelaide when she ran into one of the worst cyclones known in the area. She had a small engine and was blown helplessly on to the Reef, sinking twenty-four miles off Cape Upstart with the loss of ninety-eight lives. Twenty-two people survived. The ship was carrying a gold consignment worth 43,000 pounds, all of which was recovered before she broke up. The *Gothenburg* was operating at the height of the gold rush, and during her voyages on the Australian coastal service she had been known to carry up to a thousand passengers.

1881, October. Off Gabo Island, New South Wales
The Australian steamship, *Balclutha*, was sunk off Gabo Island in a severe gale while carrying a heavy cargo of blue stone from Melbourne to Sydney. She went down with all hands. The *Balclutha* was one of four small vessels forming a steamer service between Australia and San Francisco in the early 1860s.

1884, 6 November. Near Akaroa, New Zealand
The 562-ton barque, *Clyde*, struck rocks near Horseshoe Bay in fog and heavy seas and went to pieces soon afterwards. The only survivor was a young apprentice. The eighteen dead included the captain's wife and three children.

1886, 11 April. Mouth of Clarence River, New Zealand
The steamship, *Taiaroa*, left Wellington for Lyttelton, Akaroa and Dunedin after putting back to port three times to take on late comers. She carried a general cargo and forty-eight passengers and crew. In bad weather she ran aground at the mouth of the Clarence River and the ship was abandoned. One boat arrived at Blenheim on 12 April with eleven survivors.

1886, 25 April. North of Green Island, Queensland
The iron schooner, *Upolu*, bound for the South Seas with stores for a copra plantation, hit a reef to the north of Green Island. The captain and three crew reached Port Douglas in a whaleboat two days later. Five more men were picked up off Cape Grafton by the British India Steam Navigation Company's SS *Bulimba* and were taken to Townsville. All that was officially salvaged was the ship's cat and a pig left on board, but rum, tobacco and other supplies found their way into local larders.

1886, 30 May. Green Cape, New South Wales
The *Ly-ee-Moon* was built as a paddle steamship and later converted to screw propulsion. On a voyage from Melbourne to Sydney the ship hit the rocks at the foot of the Cape, breaking in two shortly afterwards. The captain was unfamiliar with the coast, and was below deck when the accident happened. The after part sank in deep water and only fifteen survivors managed to reach shore from the forward portion. Eighty people drowned.

1886, 8 December. Off New South Wales
The Australian coastal service vessel, *Keilawarra*, was bound from Sydney to Brisbane with a full cargo, two racehorses and a full complement of passengers when she was in collision with the steamship, *Helen Nicoll*, in clear weather. The

Keilawarra sank very quickly, the 41 casualties including six people from the *Helen Nicoll* who had jumped on to her deck in the mistaken impression their own ship was sinking.

1887, 20 March. Auckland Islands

The iron barque, *Derry Castle*, bound from Geelong, Australia, to Falmouth, struck a reef off Enderby Island in foggy conditions. She was in full sail and broke in two with the violence of the collision. Fifteen people died and the eight survivors lived for ninety-two days on shellfish while in sight of a New Zealand Government food depot at Port Ross, which they could not reach. After a time they made a rough boat and managed to get supplies from the depot. They were eventually found by the sealing steamship, *Awaruna*, which took them to Melbourne. The wreck was attributed to faulty charts.

1890, 28 February. Adolphus Channel, Torres, Strait, Queensland

The British India Steamship Company's 3484-ton iron screw steamer, *Quetta*, struck a rock in the narrow Adolphus Channel while bound for India and England from Queensland ports. The ship sank within three minutes and there was no time to lower more than two lifeboats. Of the 291 on board, 133 were drowned. Seventy survivors got to Cape York by raft and boat, and the remainder reached nearby islands.

1891, *c.* 4 January. Off Macquarie Island, South Pacific

The steamship, *Kakanui*, disappeared on the return leg of a voyage to Macquarie Island to relieve a small sealing expedition known to be there. It was feared their food supplies were running low, and the New Zealand Government chartered the ship to take the sealers off, if they wished. In the event the sealers were found in good health and eight of them returned in the *Kakanui*.

1891, May. Magnetic Island, Flinders Passage, Queensland

The three-masted iron sailing ship, *Moltke*, 827 tons, with a cargo of fencing wire, lager and other items, sailed for Cape Upstart from Hamburg after discharging some cargo at Townsville and Rockhampton. The captain was ignorant of local tides and reefs, and the badly stowed cargo meant the ship did not respond as she should have done. She struck the coral reef at the north-eastern end of Flinders Passage and held fast, her back broken. Most of the cargo was taken to Townsville and the wreck put up for auction.

1894, 28 October. Great Barrier Island

The steamship, *Wairarapa*, was bound from Sydney to Auckland when she struck the cliffs in thick fog, heeling over and flinging those on deck into the sea. Sixteen horses being transported added to the confusion on board, and it was not until daybreak that a line was run ashore. Ninety-seven people died.

1895, 8 August. Off New South Wales

The Eastern & Australian Steamship Company's liner *Catterthun*, left Sydney for Hong Kong with eighty-seven people on board. In gale force winds off Sugarloaf Point she struck the rocks and listed heavily. The Chinese crew panicked, and the Captain and first officer were washed off the bridge. Twenty-two people reached shore in the one serviceable lifeboat. Salvage work was carried out to recover eleven thousand pounds in sovereigns on board, and using special gear from England divers recovered nine thousand before the wreck went to pieces.

1897, 29 July. Off Gisbourne, New Zealand

The Australian steamship, *Tasmania*, 2252 tons, was on her usual run from

Sydney to Gisbourne when she grounded in thick fog, having failed to call at Gisbourne and continued on her way to Napier. Six boats were launched, of which two capsized in the surf. Twelve crew members and one passenger were drowned, the remainder landing safely near Gisbourne. The *Tasmania* was one of the finest vessels engaged in the Australia–New Zealand trade.

1898, 5 May. Off Sydney, New South Wales

The paddle steamship, *Maitland*, was damaged in a gale on her way from Sydney to Newcastle, New South Wales with a heavy deck cargo of machinery. It was decided to put back to Sydney, but the engine room became flooded and the ship went on the rocks off Barrenjoey Lighthouse, near Broken Bay, and broke in two. The twenty-one people who died were mainly in the bow section.

1899, 24 April. Gulf of St Vincent, South Australia

The barque, *Loch Sloy*, bound from Glasgow to Adelaide and Melbourne with a general cargo, came too close inshore and ran on to the Brothers Rocks, Kangaroo Island, about three hundred yards from shore. Four out of the thirty on board managed to reach land, but found themselves far from a settlement and forced to live off shellfish and dead penguins. One died from exposure, but three managed to walk to May's Settlement and Cape Borda Lighthouse.

1899, c. 14 May. Off Cape Campbell, New Zealand

The steamship, *Ohau*, 740 tons, ran into a gale on her journey from Greymouth, to Dunedin. She carried a cargo of eight hundred tons of coal and 13,000 feet of timber, and a crew of twenty-two. The last sighting of her put her in the Cape Campbell area, and a search was made after she had not arrived in reasonable time. On 28 May wreckage and lifebuoys were washed ashore between Cape Turnagain and Castlepoint.

1902, 27 October. Cape Egmont, New Zealand

The steamship, *Ventnor*, left Wellington for Hong Kong with a cargo of 499 coffins containing the bodies of Chinese who had died in New Zealand. The Chong Shing Society of China was responsible for collecting the bodies, some of which had rested in New Zealand for twenty years, and arranging their conveyance to China. Nine Chinese accompanied the coffins as 'body attendants'. In fine weather and a smooth sea the ship ran on to a reef south of Cape Egmont, but the pumps proved inadequate and she sank by the bows next day.

1902, 9 November. Tasman Sea

The steamship, *Elingamite*, struck rocks off the Three Kings during a voyage from Sydney to Auckland. She had reduced speed during thick fog, but the engines did not respond to a command to reverse when the first impact was felt. Of the 136 passengers and 59 crew, 150 survived. At a Court of Enquiry the captain's certificate was suspended for twelve months and he was fined fifty pounds. Years later an error in the charts was discovered and the court decision was reversed.

1904, 5 November. South-west Tasmania

The iron barque, *Brier Holme*, was wrecked off Elliott Cove on a voyage from London to Hobart, with a general cargo which included dynamite. There was a large explosion after she struck the reef and the vessel sank immediately.

1905, c. 25 September. Kangaroo Island, South Australia

The iron sailing ship, *Loch Vennachar*, was reported missing on a voyage from Glasgow to Adelaide with a general cargo. A reel of blue printing paper from the ship was picked up by another vessel on 29 September, and after a search wreckage was found near Backstairs Passage.

1907, 12 March. Western Australia

The Australian steamship, *Mildura*, was on a voyage from Wyndham to Fremantle, carrying a cargo of bullocks, when she was wrecked at the North-West Cape.

1907, c. 16 September. North Island, New Zealand

The barque, *Loch Lomond*, is believed to have foundered off North Island at the end of a voyage from the Clyde to Lyttleton, New Zealand, with the loss of all hands. Wreckage from the ship was found as far away as the Great Barrier Reef and the New Hebrides.

1909, 12 February. Cape Terawhiti, near Wellington, New Zealand

The steamship, *Penguin*, was on a voyage from Picton to Wellington when she struck on Tom's Rock in Cook Strait in fog. One boat capsized and drowned its occupants, and hastily constructed rafts proved no safer. Only twenty-six out of the hundred on board reached land.

1909, 18 June. Tasman Sea

The Norwegian barque, *Errol*, 1446 tons, was wrecked on the Middleton Reef during a voyage from Peru to Newcastle, New South Wales. Three weeks later five survivors were rescued by the steamer, *Jofua*. Seventeen had died from exposure and privation.

1911, 23 March. Great Barrier Reef, Queensland

The Adelaide Steamship Company's *Yongala* was lost in a cyclone on a voyage from Brisbane to Townsville with forty-eight passengers and a crew of seventy-two. A cyclone warning was given shortly after her departure from port, but unknown to the *Yongala*, which did not carry wireless, although the first Australian shore wireless station capable of communicating with ships had been established in Sydney the previous year. The ship was sighted off Dent Island and Cannonvale Beach, but an intensive search revealed nothing. Wreckage began to come ashore over a wide area a week later, but the only body to be found was that of a racehorse called Moonshine, which was being shipped north to run in Townsville. A Marine Board of Enquiry found that the ship was equal in construction, stability and seaworthiness to any in her class, but was unable to come to any further conclusions. In 1958, two divers located the wreck after a report in 1947 by the survey ship, HMAS *Lachlan*, of a large vessel about ten miles east of Cape Bowling Green. They recovered a large steel safe which was identified by its number as having been supplied for the purser's cabin of the *Yongala* during her construction in England in 1903. The cause of the disaster remains unknown.

North America

1841, 13 March. Mid-Atlantic

The steamer, *President*, was bound from New York to Liverpool with a large number of passengers and was two days out of port when she ran into a severe storm. Those who died in the disaster included the Duke of Richmond.

1852, 24 December. In the North Atlantic

The steamship, *St. George*, bound from Liverpool to New York with 121 passengers, mostly Irish emigrants on board, was destroyed by fire at sea. The crew and seventy of the passengers were saved by an American ship and taken to Le Havre.

1854, 17 July. Off Montauk Point, New York
The early American steamship, *Franklin*, was wrecked here while on her normal trans-Atlantic run. No casualties were reported. Her sister ship, *Humbolt*, was wrecked in the previous year, and this double blow meant the end of the New York & Havre Steam Navigation Company, although it struggled on until the outbreak of the Civil War in 1861, when it stopped operating.

1859, 21 November. Off Cape Race, Newfoundland
The barque-rigged screw steamship, *Indian*, bound from Liverpool to Portland, Maine with 157 passengers and crew, crashed into rocks in bad weather and broke in two. Some boats capsized as they were launched, but in all 130 people were rescued by various means. The mails were saved, but many survivors complained of being plundered by people along the shore.

1860, 8 September. Lake Michigan
The American steamer, *Lady Elgin*, sank after a collision with the schooner, *Augusta*. Of the 385 people on board, 287 were lost, including Herbert Ingram, MP, founder of the *Illustrated London News*, and his son.

1860, 20 February. Off Cape Sable Island, Nova Scotia
The steamship, *Hungarian*, left Liverpool for Portland, Maine, and was seen off Cape Sable Island before she vanished. Later that day when the tide ebbed, the wreck could be seen lying in twenty-five feet of water. Fragments of boats were found, mailbags and many bodies, but no survivors of the 205 people on board. At an enquiry it was established that no light had been burning at Barrington, on the mainland of Nova Scotia, and this was undoubtedly a contributory cause of the disaster.

1863, 27 April. Off Cape Race, Newfoundland
The Allan liner, *Anglo Saxon*, struck the rocks at Clam Cove in thick fog on a voyage from Liverpool to Quebec, with 445 passengers and crew on board, most of the passengers being emigrants bound for the Canadian West. The *Anglo Saxon* was due to rendezvous with the Associated Press News boat at Cape Race to hand over mails and despatches. Two hundred and eighteen survivors got ashore in four boats, a basket, and by dropping from the jib-boom on to the rocks below. After less than an hour the ship slipped off the rocks into deep water and remaining 227 people on board drowned.

1865. Near De Soto, Nebraska
Between 1819 and 1897, more than 250 steamboats were wrecked on the Missouri. One of them was the sternwheeler, *Bertrand*, which was holed on a journey from St Louis to Fort Benton and went down in ten minutes. She was soon covered with silt and sand, which protected the cargo wonderfully well. The hull was located in 1968, buried thirty feet deep in what had once been the river channel. The cargo provides a remarkable picture of the supplies required by a frontier fort of the period. The items range from champagne to hob-nailed boots, and from candles and ploughs to canned oysters and peaches.

1875, 4 November. Forty miles off Cape Flattery, Washington
The paddle steamer, *Pacific*, collided with the sailing ship, *Orpheus*, on a voyage from Victoria, British Columbia to San Francisco. The inexperienced crew did not know how to launch the boats and there was panic on board as the ship

listed heavily to port, and sank within an hour of the collision. On 8 November one survivor was picked up by the US revenue steamship, *Oliver Wolcott* — the rest of the crew and all the passengers had been washed away or had died from exposure.

1880, *c.* 13 February. Atlantic

The steamship, *Hindoo*, left New York with a cargo of grain and a large number of cattle. During the voyage the cargo shifted and the vessel became unmanageable. Her funnel was carried away and the decks swept clear. Six men were swept overboard before the ship was sighted by the steamship, *Alexandria*, which took off the remaining fifty-three passengers and crew.

1881, 24 May. Ontario, Canada

The steamer, *Victoria*, grossly overloaded, sank in the river Thames. It was estimated that between six and seven hundred people had been on board at the time and of these several hundreds drowned.

1882, 28 February. Near San Francisco, California

The iron clipper ship, *Norval*, was bound from Hull to San Francisco with a cargo of coal when fire broke out in the hold. Four days later she was burning from end to end and the crew took to the boats. One boat with eight men in it was never seen again, but two more reached Honolulu on 26 March.

1883, 14 February. Atlantic

The steamship, *Glamorgan*, bound from Liverpool to Boston, was damaged in bad weather and lost her captain and seven men, who were swept overboard. On 16 February the ship was sighted by the steamship, *Republic*, which took off forty-four survivors before she sank.

1884, 18 January. Off Martha's Vineyard, Massachusetts

The Steamship, *City of Columbus*, left Boston with eighty-seven passengers and forty-five crew and a pilot aboard. Most of the passengers were New Englanders going south for the winter season. The ship struck a rock off Gay Head, Vineyard Sound, was backed off and sank very quickly. Twelve passengers and seventeen crew survived, being picked up by other vessels in the area.

1885, 9 July. Scatterie Island, Cape Breton

The British cargo ship, *Colombo*, was wrecked here on a voyage from Bull River, South Carolina, to Dublin with a cargo of phosphate rock.

1886, 12 August. Off Cape Pine, Newfoundland

The *Acton* was wrecked three miles from the cape while on a voyage from Montreal to London with a cargo of timber and copper phosphate.

1887, 1 May. Near St John's, Newfoundland

The steamship, *John Knox*, was bound from Glasgow to Quebec when she stranded on her way through the South-West Island channel. She went aground in a bad gale at a place where it was impossible to give assistance to her and onlookers saw the vessel break up and go down with the loss of all twenty-nine on board.

1888, 28 March. Nantucket Shoal, Massachusetts

The British cargo ship, *Canonbury*, was wrecked here while on her way from Matanzas to Boston with a cargo of sugar.

1890, 9 January. Wood End Light, Cape Cod

The British brig, *Matilda Buck*, went ashore near here en route from Gonaives to Boston with a cargo of logwood. The crew were rescued by a line from the shore

1891, 29 August. Two hundred and fifty miles from Halifax, Nova Scotia
The British steamship, *Dunmurry*, capsized and sank during a hurricane with the loss of eight lives. She was bound from New York with a cargo of grain. Twenty-one survivors, including the captain, were picked up by the German tanker, *Hans von Kurt* after three days with no food or water.

1892, 25 July. Pollock Rip Slue, Cape Cod
The steam-yacht, *Aloa*, was built in 1886 for William K. Vanderbilt, at a cost of half a million dollars. She was named after Mr Vanderbilt's wife. On her way to Newport, Rhode Island, the *Aloa* became fogbound east of Chatham, Cape Cod. She anchored, and the next morning the Boston-New York steamer, *H. F. Dimock*, collided with her. Mr. Vanderbilt and his guests were in bed at the time. They were hurried into the boats and transferred to the *H. F. Dimock* which, although damaged, took them to Boston. Mr. Vanderbilt's first act on landing was to telephone to order himself a new yacht. Four days after the accident, the *Everett Webster*, loaded with coal, hit the underwater wreck and had to be towed into Salem, with water in her hold. At that point, the *Aloa* was judged to be a danger to navigation, and was blown up.

1893, c. 19 February. Atlantic
The cargo liner, *Naronic*, was bound for New York from Liverpool and failed to arrive at her destination. On 3 March a message was picked up in an inlet of New York Bay, saying the ship was sinking with all hands, and another picked up on the beach at Ocean View, Virginia, was dated 19 February and said the ship had struck an iceberg in a snowstorm and was sinking, and that it was impossible to survive in the open boats.

1896, May. Near St John, New Brunswick
The British iron steamship, *Belgravia*, was wrecked at Mispeck Point on her way to Liverpool with a cargo of timber.

1898, 8 June. Newfoundland
The British cargo ship, *Para*, hit an iceberg near Tilt Cove and sank. She was on her way from Swansea to Tilt Cove in ballast.

1898, 26 November. Near Highland Lighthouse, Maine
The steamer, *Portland*, was lost with all hands after being caught in a hurricane. Between 150 and 200 people were on board, the passengers mostly returning to Portland after a Thanksgiving holiday outing. Most of the wreckage and sixty bodies were washed ashore on the beaches between Provincetown and Chatham.

1899, 23 April. Fifty miles east of Cape Canaveral (Cape Kennedy), Florida
The American steamship, *General Whitney*, foundered in heavy seas after taking in water through a defective seacock. The crew took to the boats, one of which capsized with the loss of twelve men, including the captain. Nineteen survivors reached shore.

1900, 30 June. Hoboken, New York
Five liners belonging to Norddeutscher Lloyd were involved in a fire which broke out. They were the *Saale, Bremen, Main, Phoenicia* and *Kaiser Wilhelm der Grosse*. The fire started in a bale of cotton which was being handled by stevedores and soon set fire to a stack of whisky barrels, which in turn ignited the nearby wooden warehouses. Despite efforts to tow the ships into midstream the *Main* and *Bremen* caught fire and the *Saale* grounded on Communipaw Flats. Within nine minutes the frontage of the wharf was on fire and to prevent it spreading the

officials of the Hamburg-Amerika Company at the next wharf blew up their pier. Many people were trapped between decks and died.

1901, 22 February. Pacific

The steamship, *City of Rio de Janeiro*, bound from Yokohama to San Francisco, tried to navigate the passage of the Golden Gate in thick fog and struck a rock. She sank in fifteen minutes, with the loss of seventy-two passengers and thirty-two crew, including the captain. The dead included the US Consul-General at Hong Kong and his wife and children.

1901, 20 August. Pacific

The steamship, *Islander*, struck an iceberg and sank on a voyage from Alaska to Vancouver, about one mile from Juneau. A hundred and seven survivors reached land in calm weather, but sixty-five passengers and crew died, including the captain.

1904, 9 September. Near Highland Lighthouse, Maine

The wooden-hulled steamer, *Longfellow*, was carrying explosives from Wilmington, Delaware to Portsmouth Navy Dockyard when she sprang a leak. She was abandoned four miles off the Highland Lighthouse and sank, the crew being saved by lifeboats. Two months afterwards, the hull of the *Longfellow* was knocked againt the sea bottom during a gale. Explosions left a long stretch of the Cape Cod shore littered with wreckage and dead fish.

1905, 21 July. San Diego, California

The United States gunboat, *Bennington*, was lying in the harbour here when the top of the lower furnace of one of the boilers exploded, causing a chain reaction. Thirty men died and about eighty were injured in the explosion.

1907, 13 January. Near Old Harbor, Cape Cod

The American ship, *Onandaga*, left Boston for Jacksonville, Florida, with a mixed cargo, which included shoes, wrapping paper and doors. In thick fog, she ran aground in the middle of the night—the ship remained safely on the beach for three months until she was pulled off by tugs. In order to lighten her and make refloating possible, the cargo was taken from the *Onandaga* to the railway at Orleans. During its transfer from ship to rail, about a third of the cargo mysteriously disappeared. Eleven years later, on 28 June 1918, the *Onandaga*, bound this time for France, hit the rocks off Sugar Reef, Rhode Island, and sank in fifty feet of water.

Europe to the Far East

1852, 26 February. Simon's Bay, South Africa

The 2000-ton troopship, *Birkenhead*, an iron vessel driven by paddle-wheels, was on a voyage from Queenstown to the Cape with 638 people on board. She struck a concealed rock off Simon's Bay, broke in two and sank. Of the soldiers and crew 454 were lost, many being eaten by sharks. It was learned afterwards that the boats and tackle were in poor condition.

1857, 11 November. In the Indian Ocean

The iron screw steamer, *Sarah Hands*, sailed from Portsmouth to Calcutta in August 1857 with three hundred soldiers on board. On 11 November the cargo of government stores caught fire. By tremendous efforts the flames were got under control, but an exploding barrel of gunpowder had blown a hole in the ship and during a gale a great deal of water got into the hold. The soldiers and crew somehow kept the *Sarah Hands* afloat and she reached Mauritius without the loss of a single life.

1859, 12 June. Near Aden, Red Sea
The British steamer, *Alma*, was grounded on a reef about thirty-five miles from Mocha. Everyone on board was saved by HMS *Cyclops*, after three days' exposure to the sun without water.

1871, 17 March. Klipstrand Reef, Struys Point, South Africa
The steamship, *Queen of the Thames*, was on the return run of a new service from England to Australia via the Cape, with two hundred passengers. With coal supplies running low, it was planned to call at Cape Town instead of St Helena. The light of a bush fire was mistakenly thought to be the lighthouse at Cape Agulhas, and in altering course the ship ran on to the Klipstrand Reef.

1871, 3 September. St. Paul's Island, Indian Ocean
The *Megoera*, a screw-driven iron steamship owned by the British government, was on a voyage from England to Australia with about four hundred people on board. After making slow progress for four months, she sprang a leak. It was discovered that her bottom was almost eaten away by corrosion. To prevent a disaster, she was beached on St Paul's Island. Huts were built and stores landed, and further provisions were brought two months later by another ship. All the passengers and crew were taken off safely eventually. At an enquiry held in 1872 the captain was acquitted of all blame. It was revealed that the *Megoera* had been reported unfit for service in 1867 and a number of Admiralty officials were censured by a Government Commission.

1881, 30 August. Near Cape Agulhas, Cape of Good Hope
The screw steamer, *Teuton*, hit a rock and sank within a few hours. Nearly all of the two hundred on board, including the captain and most of the officers were lost. The official enquiry gave as the cause of the accident the captain's 'imprudent navigation'.

1890, 16 May. Indian Ocean
The steamer, *Dacca*, belonging to the British East India Company, hit a reef four hundred miles from Suez and sank. The passengers, mostly emigrants to Queensland were all picked up within a short time. At an enquiry, the accident was attributed to unskilful navigation.

1896, 7 March. Boma, West Africa
The British cargo ship, *Matadi*, on a voyage from Liverpool to Luanda with a general cargo, was destroyed by an explosion of gunpowder.

1898, 16 February. Teneriffe, Canary Islands
The French liner, *Flachat*, 2175 tons, was driven on to Anaga Point in heavy seas and dense fog. Three lifeboats were swamped and only twenty-five people survived in the two remaining boats, after great difficulties in launching them.

1900, 5 April. Off the South African coast
The Union Castle steamship, *Mexican*, bound for Southampton with 104 passengers and the mail, ran into dense fog off Cape Town and collided with the steamship, *Winkfield*, going dead slow. The *Mexican* began to sink slowly and her passengers and crew, and the mail, were transferred to the *Winkfield*, which was only slightly damaged. The *Mexican* sank some hours later.

1901, 16 January. Lambert's Bay, South Africa
During the Boer War the light cruiser, *Sybille*, was off Saldanha Bay, where she

had landed her captain and some ratings to help in the organisation of the colonists. The weather worsened and she made for open waters, but was driven ashore in Lambert's Bay, striking rocks three hundred yards from the shore. She soon became a total wreck. One seaman was drowned, the remainder of the crew being taken off by the supply ship, *City of Cambridge*.

1908, 9 January. Cesstown, Kroo Coast
The British steamship, *Sansu*, 2495 tons struck rocks here and sank, during a voyage from West Africa to Hamburg. She was carrying a cargo of palm kernels and cocoa.

1908, 12 March. East African coast
The Union Castle liner, *Newark Castle*, 6224 tons, left Durban for Delagoa Bay and Mauritius with forty-six passengers and sixty-nine crew. Most of the passengers were soldiers drafted to the garrison at Mauritius. Six hours after leaving port she ran ashore in Richard's Bay near the Umhlatuzi River. The boats were launched in calm seas, some of the crew remaining on board to be picked up later by a Government tug. The boats intended to make for Durban, but the weather worsened and after distress signals were sent up, the survivors were picked up by the trawler, *Elelyn*. Three people drowned when one of the boats capsized. The *Newark Castle* grounded on another sandbank after drifting free and became a total wreck.

1909, c. 28 July. South Africa
The Blue Anchor Line's *Waratah* disappeared while bound from Sydney to London on only her second voyage. The vessel had put into Durban on 25 July and while in port one of the passengers had booked a passage on another vessel as he had been alarmed by the ship's sluggish recovery from rolling. On leaving Durban with 211 passengers and crew, the *Waratah* made for Cape Town. Very bad weather was reported in the area, with squalls of hurricane force. None of the ships in the area was equipped with wireless.

1909, 4 August. Table Bay, South Africa
The Shaw Savill steamship, *Maori*, left Table Bay for New Zealand with a cargo of explosives. In bad weather she was driven inshore against the rocks near Duiker Point. As she lay with her stern in the air and her bows beneath the water it was impossible to launch the boats, and in the attempt several men drowned. A fisherman saw the wreck in its remote spot next day, and walked to Cape Town to report it, but because he could only speak broken English and his story was garbled, help did not reach the *Maori* for some time. When it did arrive, twelve survivors were taken off by rocket line, twenty-four having died in the previous days.

Within Europe

1838, 6 September. The Farne Islands, Northumberland
The brigantine-rigged paddle-steamer, *Forfarshire*, bound from Hull to Dundee with about forty passengers and a crew of twenty-five, had to stop her engines because of renewed boiler trouble and in a storm mistook the Longstone light for the Inner Farne. The ship split in two on the rocks, the afterend being swept away with most of the passengers, the captain and a few crew, and was never seen again. The forward half was jammed on the rocks with twelve people still

53 *The stern wheelers* Memphis 1872 *and* James Howard *in a midnight race on the Mississippi in 1875. Overdriven in this way, the river steamers were liable to blow up.*

54 *The American brig* Somers, *lost in a storm in 1847 off Vera Cruz, where she was maintaining the blockade off the harbour. She sank in less than ten minutes.*

55 *Passengers fighting to get clear of the American paddle-steamer* General Slocum, *on fire in the Hudson River in 1904.*

56 *The wreck of the East Indiaman the* Assaye *on the south coast of Ireland in 1865.*

57 *In the Bay of Biscay in 1825 the East Indiaman* Kent *ran into heavy weather. Fire broke out on board, and in an attempt to put it out, the sea was allowed to flood the ship's fore-section, with disastrous results.*

58 *The deserted* Marie Celeste *as she appeared when first sighted by the* Dei Gratia, *1872. A painting by Rudolph Ruzieka.*

59 *Divers at work on the wreck of the training frigate HMS* Eurydice, *lost in a squall off Ventnor, Isle of Wight, in 1878.*

60 *The wreck of the* Bay of Panama *near Falmouth, Cornwall, during a gale and snowstorm in 1891. Nine people were swept overboard and drowned, and six men froze to death.*

61 *On 4 November 1895 the American windjammer,* Granite State, *struck the Runnel Stone rocks near Land's End.*

62 *The Liverpool barque* Alexander Yeats, *wrecked at Gurnard's Head, St Ives, Cornwall, in 1896. The crew were rescued by breeches buoy.*

63 *In 1900 the elegant French 'bounty clipper'* Seine *ran aground off the Cornish coast and broke up on the beach.*

64 *The wooden three-masted barque* Minerva, *which foundered near Jaedern, Norway, in 1896. Six men were saved, some by mortar life-line, others by swimming ashore.*

65 *The first really big steamship was the* Great Eastern, *692 feet long and 18,914 tons, and propelled both by paddle-wheels and a screw.*

66 *The capsizing of the grossly overloaded steamer* Victoria *in 1881. Several hundred people were drowned.*

67 *The American river steamer* Isaac Newton *whose engines blew up, probably due to being overdriven, on her way from New York to Albany in 1864.*

68 *The foundering of the Australian screw steamer* London *in a hurricane in the Bay of Biscay, 11 January 1866.*

69 *The wreck of the 2000-ton troopship, HMS* Birkenhead, *off the Cape of Good Hope, 1852. From the painting by Thomas M. Henry.*

70 *HMS* Captain. '*This ill fated Ship designed by Captn. Cowper Coles . . . turned bottom upwards in a Gale, and sank in three minutes in the Bay of Biscay on the 7th of Septr. 1870. 500 Officers and Crew, together with Captn. Coles perished, and 18 only survived this fearful catastrophe.*'

71 *In 1852, off Northfleet Point in the Thames, the steamer* Duchess of Kent *was run down by the* Ravensbourne, *bound for Antwerp with nearly 200 passengers and a full cargo.*

72 *Henry Freeman, the sole survivor of the Whitby lifeboat disaster of 1861 in which twelve men drowned. He was the only one wearing a newly designed Ministry lifejacket.*

73 *The German screw-driven steamer* Schiller *left New York in April 1875, with 355 passengers and 250 bags of Australian and New Zealand mail on board. She had been ten days at sea when she hit the Retarrier Ledges off the Scilly Isles in thick fog and a storm.*

74 *The iron clipper* Eastminster, *after capsizing in London Docks, 1878.*

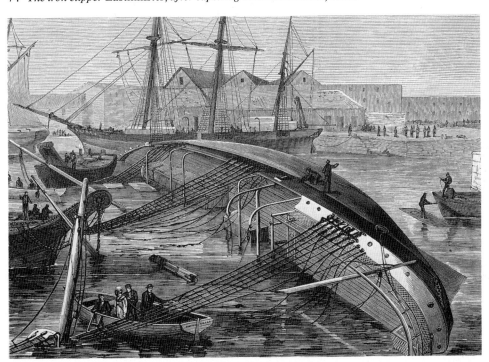

"Then rose from stream to sky a wild farewell,
Then shrieked the timid, and stood still the brave."

THE LOSS
OF THE
PRINCESS ALICE
SALOON STEAMER in the THAMES, Sept. 3rd, 1878.

AN AUTHENTIC NARRATIVE by a SURVIVOR, not hitherto published.

HEARTRENDING DETAILS—FACTS NOT MADE PUBLIC—NOBLE EFFORTS TO SAVE LIFE—ROBBING THE DEAD—PARTICULARS AS TO LOST, SAVED, AND MISSING—PLAN OF THE LOCALITY.

SKETCHES BY AN EYE WITNESS.

BEAUTIFUL POEM, specially written on the event,
NOW FIRST PUBLISHED.

/ MEMORIAL FOR ALL TIME OF THIS FEARFUL CALAMITY.

WHOLESALE OF J. F. NASH, 75, FLEET STREET, E.C.

75 *(Above and facing page above) The great Thames disaster: the collision of the* Princess Alice *and the* Bywell Castle *on the Thames at Woolwich in 1878. Between six and seven hundred people lost their lives.*

76 (Below) The wreck of the Stella, 1899. 'Immediately after the vessel had struck, Captain Reeks called out, "Lower away the boats," and then, when all was ready, "Women and children first." . . . they were passed down in so speedy and workmanlike a manner that within ten minutes all had been taken off.'

77 *The* Noisiel, *wrecked off the Cornish coast in 1905. She was on her way from Cherbourg to Italy loaded with armour plate, which shifted during a gale. All but two of the crew were saved.*

78 *Crew members being rescued from the* City of Cardiff *by breeches buoy at Land's End, Cornwall, in 1908.*

aboard. The lighthouse-keeper of the Longstone, William Darling, and his daughter, Grace, aged twenty-two, rowed across half a mile of wild sea to the reef and managed to get its survivors safely back to the lighthouse. The one boat that had got away from the *Forfarshire* before she broke in two had been picked up by a sloop and its nine occupants landed at Tynemouth. The coroner's inquest at Bamburgh attributed the loss of life to the negligence of the captain in not putting back to port and to the greed of the owners in allowing the ship to sail in an unseaworthy condition. The shipwreck and rescue were headline news for some time, and Grace Darling received the silver medal of the Glasgow Humane Society and of the Leith Humane Society, as well as more than seven hundred pounds in money from wellwishers.

1850, 22 July. Hotwells Wharf, Bristol
The iron screw steamship, *Red Rover*, 80 tons, used for passenger service on the River Avon, was lying at the wharf embarking passengers when her boilers exploded. Nine people were killed and six died later.

1852, 24th December. Atlantic
The emigrant steamship, *St George*, caught fire in mid-Atlantic and sank on a voyage from Liverpool to New York. The crew and seventy passengers were rescued by the American ship, *Orlando*. Fifty-one passengers died.

1853, 15 February. Dublin
The Liverpool-registered steamship, *Queen Victoria*, mistook her course in a snowstorm and grounded near the Bailey lighthouse. Sixty-seven people lost their lives.

1853, 1 April. Aberdeen
The steamer, *Duke of Sutherland*, was docking after a voyage from London, when she struck the pier and was severely damaged. Seventeen people died.

1854, 13 October. Little Mewstone Rock, Plymouth
The London steamer, *Ajax*, with a general cargo and three hundred passengers, hit the Little Mewstone Rock in a calm sea and with perfect visibility. At the enquiry, the coastguard duty officer said that 'it was either done purposely or from sheer culpable negligence'.

1854, 14 November. Black Sea coast, off Balaklava
A violent hurricane struck the coast near Balaklava on 14 November, when thirty sailing and steamships supplying the British forces in the Crimea were anchored there. An American ship, the *Progress*, went on to the rocks first. Then came the *Resolute*, which had a valuable Government cargo on board. After that a second American ship, the *Wanderer* was wrecked, to be followed by the *Kenilworth*. The *Kenilworth* was particularly unfortunate. She had lost her masts and was holding on with her anchor, when she was fouled by the India Mail steamer, *Avon*, and immediately drove on to the rocks. The *Prince*, a screwsteamer, hit the rocks, broke her back and was torn into fragments, with a loss of 314 lives and a cargo of military stores and equipment valued at half a million pounds.

1857, 5 January. Goodwin Sands, Kent
The cross-channel paddle steamer, *Violet*, left Ostend with nineteen people on board. In gale-force conditions she struck the Goodwins and was smashed to pieces with the loss of all hands. The mail was thrown overboard and later recovered.

1859, 26 October. Near Moelfre, Anglesey
The 2719-ton steamer, *Royal Charter*, left Melbourne in August with 388

passengers, a crew of 112 and a cargo which included three hundred thousand pounds in gold. After fifty-eight days she called at Queenstown in Ireland and landed thirteen of the passengers, then continued towards Liverpool in worsening weather. The wind increased to hurricane force and the ship dropped anchor east of Point Lynas. Early next morning the anchor cables parted and the vessel grounded, broke in two and disintegrated. Only twenty passengers and eighteen crew survived, bodies being washed ashore all along the coast. At the Board of Trade enquiry the captain was exonerated from all blame. Salvage operations recovered all but thirty thousand pounds of the gold.

1860, c. 28 February. Off St David's Head, Ireland

The paddle steamer, *Nimrod*, broke down in the Irish Sea on a voyage from Liverpool to Cork. The steamship, *City of Paris*, offered a tow, but a price could not be agreed on, and finally the captain of the *City of Paris* said he would tow the vessel into port and leave the question of cost to the respective owners. This offer was declined and the *Nimrod* drove on to St. David's Head with the loss of all forty-five on board.

1861, 2 January. Wilderness Point, Cornwall

The steamship, *Queen Victoria*, 1434 tons, was carrying telegraph cable from London to Rangoon for use by the Post Office authority there. After taking on coal at Keyham dockyard, a pilot was taken on board, but a few hours later the ship failed to answer his helm and went aground at Wilderness Point. All attempts to move her were unsuccessful and, when her hull was found to be holed, she was abandoned and broken up, after her cargo had been removed.

1864, 24 November. Tyne estuary, Northumberland

The steamship, *Stanley*, left London for Aberdeen with fifty-six passengers and crew, and forty head of cattle, as well as sheep and pigs on board. After an error of navigation she went on the Black Middens in the estuary while running for shelter, as did the schooner, *Friendship*, whose crew of six were drowned when their vessel broke up. Twenty survivors were taken off by the Cullercoats rocket brigade, but two crewmen from the lifeboat at Tynemouth were drowned.

1865, 4 January. Bay of Biscay

The *London* was a full-rigged steamship of 1428 tons. She left London for Melbourne and ran into a hurricane in the Bay of Biscay. A huge wave carried away the engine-room skylight and put the boiler-fires out. The exceptional height of the bulwarks prevented the decks from draining quickly and, once the skylight had gone, water flooded down into the hull and sank the ship.

1865, 25 January. Arklow Bank, Wicklow, Ireland

The steam barque, *Armenian*, was bound from Liverpool to West Africa with the monthly mails when she hit the Arklow Bank in foggy weather, catching fire shortly afterwards. The ship broke in two, and twenty-four survivors were picked up by the steamship, *Montague*, which was in the area.

1866, 30 March. Clovelly, Devon

The wooden paddle-ship, *Queen*, had been on the regular Bristol to Hayle service for 14 years. She had made this 150-mile journey more than four thousand times without the slightest accident of any kind. After leaving Ilfracombe at ten thirty at night, the mate for some reason set a new course, which caused the ship to run into Tinge Rock. Heading back towards Ilfracombe in a seriously damaged condition, the *Queen* was beached near Clovelly, where she went to pieces. At the Board of Trade enquiry, the captain was found guilty of neglect, in not having used the lead to take proper soundings and of failing to keep a ship's log.

1867, 28 September. Start Point, Devon

The 501-ton Sunderland-registered steamer, *Hiogo*, bound from London to Japan, struck the reef at Start Point and became a total loss. The captain had refused to alter course when the Eddystone light had been sighted, and the second mate would not take the responsibility of altering course himself. At the Board of Trade enquiry they both had their certificates suspended for twelve months, for having 'by joint default' contributed to the loss of the ship.

1870, 11 February. Atlantic

The *City of Boston* sailed from New York in early February and was never seen again. A wooden board with a message on it saying she was sinking was washed up on the Cornish coast.

1870, 18 March. Off the Isle of Wight

The paddle steamship, *Normandy*, was bound for Jersey from Southampton when she was in collision with the steamship, *Mary*, of Grimsby, in thick fog. Two boats were launched before the *Normandy* sank thirty minutes later, and thirty-one survivors were picked up by the other ship.

1871, 26 May. Morvah Cliffs, Cornwall

The *Gannet*, a three-masted schooner-rigged steamship, registered at Cork, was on a voyage from Liverpool to Antwerp, with a very mixed cargo of rock salt, cotton wool, palm oil and mahogany. In darkness, but in clear weather she ran into the cliffs about a mile east of Pendeen Watch. The crew and passengers took to the boats and arrived at St Ives in time for breakfast. The *Gannet* broke up on the rocks, but much of her cargo was salvaged.

1872, 16 July. St Martin's Neck, Isles of Scilly

The paddle-steamer, *Earl of Arran*, had been built in 1860 and was originally used for excursion trips on the Clyde. She then became one of the two mailboats operating between Penzance and Scilly. One of the passengers, who worked on a pilot boat, persuaded the captain to try a shortcut. The ship struck a rock in St Martin's Neck and was then deliberately grounded on Nornour. The *Earl of Arran* was a total loss, but her cargo and passengers were saved. The captain had his certificate suspended for four months. The other Scilly steamer, the *Little Western*, was wrecked three months later.

1873, 6 January. Paignton, Devon

The *Wallace*, of Boston, discharged her cargo of petroleum at Antwerp and was on her return journey to Key West when a gale sprang up and she had to shelter in Torbay. Four days later, a fire broke out in one of her holds. Attempts to put it out were unsuccessful and so were efforts to beach her. Drifting, she was blown against the sea front of the town. There was a serious danger that the town itself would catch fire, but the situation was kept under control by putting a fire engine on a barge, so that water could be played on the blazing ship from both sides. Even so, the *Wallace* burned for forty-eight hours, before the flames were finally extinguished.

1873, 18 April. Meagher Rock, near Sambro Head

The liner, *Atlantic*, belonging to the White Star Company, was on a voyage from Liverpool to Halifax when she ran short of coal and was unable to raise sufficient steam. About 560 people were lost and 442, including the captain, were saved. The captain was suspended from duty for two years.

1874, 12 March. Bay of Gibraltar

The steamship, *Queen Elizabeth*, ran aground here on her way from Calcutta to England, via Suez and the Mediterranean. A heavy sea and her position broadside on to the shore prevented all but one of the boats being launched, and this made three trips to the shore before it capsized the fourth time, being overloaded. The British Consul at Algeciras organised the rescue from the shore but the rocket apparatus did not arrive for two days, as it had to be carried by mule over rocky country.

1874, 13 April. Isles of Scilly

The British and African Steamship Company's *Liberia* and the steamer, *Barton*, were in collision off the Isles of Scilly with the loss of everyone on board both vessels.

1874, 14 November. Bay of Biscay

The cable ship, *La Plata*, an iron-hulled screw steamer of 1218 tons, was bound from Gravesend to South America with two hundred miles of deep-sea cable on board. The great weight of the cable, together with 218 tons of coal, made her difficult to steer. She went down in a gale, with the loss of sixty-eight of her crew.

1875, 7 May. Retarrier Ledges, Isles of Scilly

The German liner, *Schiller*, left New York with 372 people on board, and with valuable cargo. She was creeping towards Scilly through a very thick fog and in a heavy sea. She was within half a mile of the Bishop Light, when, at 10 p.m. without any warning having been seen or heard, she struck the Retarrier Ledges. She pulled herself clear, but then three huge waves swept her sideways on to the rocks. During the night the ship's lifeboats were smashed and passengers were washed overboard. In the morning a fleet of local vessels attempted rescue work, but only thirty-seven people were saved. Many of the bodies were recovered and were buried in mass graves at Old Town. A surprisingly high proportion of the mailbags were picked up and the mail was delivered in due course, mostly to Australia and New Zealand. By May 1876, a considerable part of the gold had been recovered for the owners and some, it is rumoured, for the inhabitants of Scilly. A row of houses in Hugh Town, known as Schiller Row, is supposed to have been built from the proceeds of money found in the wreck.

1875, 6 December. Off The Kent coast

The Norddeutscher Lloyd liner, *Deutschland*, 2898 tons, struck the Kentish Knock sands, breaking a propeller. She was on a voyage from Bremen to New York, but had been thrown off course by snowstorms. The wreck was not seen until the morning of 7 December, when the paddle tug, *Liverpool*, took off 173 persons. Fifty-seven people died, many frozen to death in the rigging.

1876, 17 February. Dover Bay, Kent

The Glasgow steamer, *Strathclyde*, was in collision with the Hamburg-registered *Franconia* in broad daylight. About seventeen people on board the Glasgow vessel died, and the captain of the *Franconia* was convicted of manslaughter. This verdict was later quashed on appeal.

1877, 9 May. Near East Mouse, Anglesey

The liner, *Dakota*, of the Liverpool-based Gunion Line, left the Mersey bound for New York with 580 passengers and crew and a general cargo. Near Anglesey she met dense fog and although speed was reduced and her course re-checked, she stranded on a ledge of rocks between the East Mouse and the mainland.

1877, 11–12 May. Near Braila, Romania
The Turkish ironclad, *Lutfi Djelil*, was serving in the Turkish navy prior to the outbreak of the Russo-Turkish War of 1877–78 and was blown up by Russian gunfire as she was preparing to bombard the town of Braila on the Danube. Nearly all the two hundred officers and men died as the warship exploded.

1878, 3 September. River Thames, London
The *Princess Alice* was rammed by the screw steamer, *Bywell Castle*, near Woolwich and sank rapidly. It is estimated that between six and seven hundred people lost their lives.

1878, 25 November. Off Dover, Kent
The Hamburg-Amerika Line vessel, *Pomerania*, was in collision with the iron barque, *Moel Eilian*, when travelling at fourteen knots. She was bound from New York to Hamburg with mail and a large number of passengers. Many passengers were drowned when they went below to collect their possessions and the vessel sank suddenly. Forty-eight lost their lives; survivors were picked up by the SS *Glengarry*.

1879, 7 September. Rickham Sands, Devon
The full-rigged iron ship, *Meirion*, was bound from Rangoon to London with a cargo of rice. She had been seriously damaged while rounding the Cape of Good Hope. Having passed the Eddystone, she went ashore to the east of Salcombe. The crew were all saved by a line got on to the ship by rocket apparatus.

1881, 27 January. Near Bolt Head, Devon
The *Rupera*, of Cardiff, was carrying 1529 tons of cotton seed from Alexandria to Hull. She went ashore between Bolt Head and Tail in the early hours of the morning. The ship was completely wrecked, her loss being attributed to a remarkable and inexplicable deviation in the master compass.

1883, 1 February. Bay of Biscay
During a voyage from London to Shanghai the iron steamship, *Kenmure Castle*, met bad weather, which destroyed her steering gear and washed away her superstructure. One boat was launched before the ship sank with thirty-two still on board. The boat was nearly two hundred miles from land and in a desperate situation as the seven Chinese seamen on board were drugged with opium and the women passengers were dressed only in nightdresses with coats over them. The officer in charge managed to keep the boat afloat until they were sighted by the French steamship, *Montataire*, three days later.

1883, 3 July. River Clyde, Scotland
The coastal steamer, *Daphne*, heeled over during her launching and 124 people died.

1883, 31 October. Irish Sea, between Dublin and Holyhead
At midnight, on the Irish Sea route, the German sailing barque, *Alhambra* and the London and North Western Railway's cattle steamship, *Holyhead*, were in collision. Both sank, with the loss of fifteen men and all the cattle.

1884, 28 October. Near Lamorna Cove, Cornwall
The 738-ton Sunderland steamer, *Avebury*, bound from Lisbon to Cardiff with a cargo of iron ore and esparto grass, ran aground in thick fog. She had taken a course too far east while trying to find her way round Land's End. The crew of sixteen were brought ashore by breeches buoy. The ship herself was a total loss.

1885, 8 June. St Agnes, Isles of Scilly

The schooner-rigged steamer *Earl of Lonsdale*, carrying a cargo of cotton from Alexandria to Portishead, was steaming at full speed in thick fog. She mistook her position and crashed into the rocks. All twenty-two of the crew were saved.

1885, 5 October. West Mouse, Anglesey

The iron-built ship, *Earl of Chatham*, being towed from Liverpool as far as Holyhead, a normal practice at that time in bad weather, broke free and drifted on to rocks east of the West Mouse. Bound for India with a cargo of salt, she was eventually abandoned as a total loss. The crew were taken off by a tug.

1885, 6 December. Mudstone Beach, Devon

The Liverpool steamer, *Bretton Hall*, on a voyage from Antwerp to Newport, had a cargo which included 450 tons of Belgian iron of a quality used in sword-making; packs of playing-cards; and boxes of eau-de-cologne. Off course and steaming through thick fog at eleven knots, the ship went ashore near Sharkham Point. Despite the efforts of customs officers, local people stocked up with playing-cards and eau-de-cologne from the beach.

1886, 21 March. Higher Sharpnose Point, Cornwall

The West Hartlepool steamer, *Newton*, launched by Swan Hunter at Newcastle in 1883, was wrecked in thick fog bound from Bremerhaven to Newport in ballast. The crew got ashore and the wreck was later sold for thirty pounds.

1886, 28 September. Lizard Head, Cornwall

The three-masted schooner-rigged steamer, *Suffolk*, broke her back under Lizard Head after hitting the rocks at speed in dense fog. Forty-three crew and two passengers were rescued by local lifeboats, and about fifty head of cattle were hauled up the cliffs to safety, the remainder of the livestock taken on at Baltimore being washed overboard.

1887, 18 April. Mykonos, Greece

The British steamship, *Volta*, was wrecked here on a voyage from London to Syracuse with telegraph cables and stores. Eleven crewmen lost their lives.

1887, 8 June. Crebawethan, Isles of Scilly

The cattleship, *Castleford*, ran ashore in thick fog here. The 450 head of cattle on board were mostly saved. Salvage money ran as high as five pounds a head for cattleship wrecks and even burying the drowned carcasses was profitable. The islanders refused to bury those from the *Castleford* for less than thirty shillings each.

1887, 27 June. Salcombe, Devon

The 844-ton French steamer, *Soudan*, with a cargo of pig nuts from Senegal, was bound for Dunkirk when she struck the Hamstone Rock and foundered. Two Belgian salvage steamers tried to raise her but she became a total loss.

1889, 2 February. Ilfracombe, Devon

The steamer, *Lymington*, got into difficulties near Bull Point. Lifeboatmen manhandled the rocket apparatus to the clifftops, but by the time they arrived the ship had gone to pieces and the crew had drowned. The bow section was seen drifting offshore and the stern was washed up in a nearby bathing cove.

1889, 15 October. Near Cape Cornwall, Cornwall

The 2244-ton Cunard liner, *Malta*, the second Cunarder to be wrecked on the Cornish coast within five years, ran aground on the headland known as Kenidjack Castle, near Cape Cornwall, in thick fog. She was bound from Liverpool to Genoa with a general cargo and nineteen passengers, all of whom were saved. A flotilla of small boats, manned by local fishermen and miners, hovered around the sinking ship to pick up rugs and carpets, kegs of spirits and bottles of wine and beer as they floated to the surface.

1890, 19 January. Baggy Point, Devon

The iron, full-rigged ship, *Penthesilea*, went ashore here in a gale. Large quantities of coal were thrown on to the beach and removed by local residents.

1890, 23 June. Pendeen Watch, Cornwall

The Cardiff ship, *Scheldt*, 1090 tons, was steaming from Newport to Bordeaux with a cargo of coal. She was wrecked on the headland here in dense fog. The crew of seventeen got to safety in the ship's boats. The area had produced many disasters of this kind before the lighthouse was installed in 1900. The captain had his master's certificate suspended for six months, after he had been found guilty of failing to use the lead and of failing to verify his course in an area known to be dangerous.

1890, 6 September. Off Ushant, at the entrance to the English Channel

The British cargo ship, *Royal Crown*, on a voyage from Fiume to Leith with a cargo of wheat, foundered after striking a wreck.

1890, 23 November. Hartland Quay, Cornwall

The Cardiff steamer, *Uppingham* was bound for Port Said with a cargo of coal when she developed engine trouble, and struck the rocks. Eight crewmen drowned. One of the survivors was on board another steamship, the *Welbury*, which was wrecked almost on top of the *Uppingham*'s rusting remains on 24 April 1900.

1891, 8 March. Blackstone Rock, Devon

The *Marana*, 2177 tons, left London for Colombo with a cargo of railway sleepers. Off the Dorset coast, she was caught in a hurricane and blizzard. Despite the weather, however, she continued at full speed and went straight into the Blackstone Rock, tearing off her rudder and propeller. The crew got away in two boats and then both capsized. There were only three survivors.

1891, 17 March. Bay of Gibraltar

The British steamer, *Utopia*, was taking 830 Italian emigrants from Naples to New York. During a gale she collided with HMS *Anson*, which was at anchor, and sank. Twenty-six of the fifty crew died and 538 of the passengers. For the relief of the survivors, £1,150 was subscribed including £200 from the Italian government.

1891, 12 September. Off Cape Sounion, Greece

The Italian steamship, *Taormina*, collided with the Greek steamship, *Thessalia*, off the Cape, with the loss of forty passengers and crew.

1891, December. Off Cape Finistere, Spain

The *Skyro* was on her way from Cartagena to London, with twelve thousand pounds worth of silver bars among her cargo. She struck Mexiddo Reef in fog and sank in twenty minutes, coming to rest on the bottom at a depth of thirty fathoms. In 1894, a British company got the salvage contract and engaged a Spanish diver to try to recover the silver, a very difficult task in view of the great depth at which he would have to work. It took him two years to blast his way into the strongroom, from which he took out fifty-nine bars, worth ten thousand pounds. His reward was five hundred pounds, which seems hardly adequate, since his health was permanently damaged and he was never able to dive again.

1892, 22 April. Baggy Point, Devon

The *Maria*, of Gloucester, en route from Cork to Llanelly with a cargo of pitprops went aground near Baggy Point. The crew reached Ilfracombe in their own boat, but when they returned next day to salvage their possessions, they found the ship had refloated herself and drifted out to sea, never to be seen again.

1892, 14 June. Blaye, near Bordeaux, France

The British petroleum tanker, *Petrolea*, was blown up in harbour here.

1892, 27 June. Prawle Point, South Devon

The Greek steamship, *Maria*, ran into Langler Rocks in thick fog and at high tide. She was well off course, being bound for Rotterdam with a cargo of wheat and barley. The passengers and crew were saved, but the ship was a total loss.

1892, 1 July. Old Head of Kinsale, Ireland

The Inman transatlantic liner, *City of Chicago*, went aground here during a fog. The passengers were all landed safely, but the ship was completely wrecked. The captain had his master's certificate suspended for nine months.

1892, 21 July. Kinsale, Ireland

The Inman Atlantic liner, *City of Chicago*, ran ashore near the Old Head of Kinsale during fog. Passengers were landed on 1 July and the liner went to pieces on 7 July. The master's certificate was suspended for nine months.

1893, *c.* 20 September. Gulf of Finland

The Russian monitor, *Roosalka*, built in 1867, was in an unseaworthy condition when she sank in the Gulf in a storm. She was on a voyage from Tallinn to Helsingfors on the orders of the Russian Admiralty, despite protests from the *Roosalka*'s officers. The only clue to her fate was a bottle picked up by fishermen at Riga saying there was no hope for the vessel and giving the time as 9.45 p.m.

1895, 25 January. Portreath, Cornwall

The Glasgow-registered steamer, *Escurial*, was driven ashore on Portreath beach after a leak had put out her stokehold fires. She was bound from Cardiff to Fiume with a cargo of coal. Heavy seas made it impossible to get a line aboard and the crew were swept overboard one by one, seven of the eighteen on board being saved by onlookers.

1895, 21 July. Gulf of Spezia, Italy

The Italian steamship, *Maria P.*, was bound from Naples to Genoa when she collided with the Italian steamship, *Ortigia*, at the entrance to the Gulf, off Isola del Tino, and sank in three minutes. The *Ortigia* stood by until daylight and picked up forty-two survivors. A hundred and forty-eight people were drowned.

1896, 1 December. Graystone Rock, Devon

The Russian oil-tanker, *Blesk*, was on her way from Odessa to Hamburg with a cargo of petroleum. In fog, she struck the Graystone Rock and sank until the sea was over her upper deck. Oil from her tanks spread over the coastline and up into Kingsbridge estuary.

1897, 8 May. Off Heligoland

The Dutch steamship, *Firdene*, was sunk in collision with the Norwegian barque, *Bödvar*, while on her way from Cagliari to Stockholm with a cargo of salt. Eight crewmen died. The *Bödvar* also sank, but without loss of life.

1898, 7 March. Giampilieri, Sicily

The British cargo ship, *Orsino*, was wrecked here on a voyage from Stratoni to Philadelphia, with a cargo of manganese ore.

1898, 14 October. Porthoustock, Cornwall

The liner, *Mohegan*, 7000 tons, on only her second voyage to New York, sailed from Tilbury with fifty-three passengers, ninety-six crew, six cattlemen to attend to the animals carried on deck, and one stowaway. She was carrying a very mixed cargo of artificial flowers, lead, antimony, glassware and church ornaments. She dropped her pilot off Dover and next day she hit the Manacles at her full cruising speed of fourteen knots. An enormous hole was torn in the starboard side and water flooded in. Ten minutes later the vessel was three-parts underwater and only two boats had been launched, the chaos being added to by the failure of the generators, plunging the ship into darkness. The lifeboat saved the lives of forty-four people, and another seven were rescued by other boats. A hundred and six people died, including the captain and all his deck officers. At a Court of Enquiry they were unable to reach any conclusion, although a theory with strong local support was that the *Mohegan's* compasses had been affected by magnetism from the rocks.

1898, 9 December. Off Land's End, Cornwall

The tramp steamer, *Blue Jacket*, in ballast from Plymouth to Cardiff, struck the Longships lighthouse rocks off Land's End. The captain, who had been resting in his bunk, came on deck to find his ship illuminated by the lighthouse only a few yards away. The crew took to the boats and were picked up by the Sennen lifeboat. The cause of the wreck is a mystery.

1899, 30 March. Near Alderney, Channel Islands

The Channel steamship, *Stella*, left Southampton bound for Guernsey with 174 passengers and forty-three crew. The vessel was particularly crowded as it was the first run of the season and the day before Good Friday. Running into fog after leaving the English mainland, the *Stella* reduced speed but hit the Black Rock, eight miles from Alderney and sank after eight minutes. There was little panic on board and four lifeboats were launched safely, the occupants being picked up next day by the steamship, *Vera*, and the Great Western Railway Company's steamship, *Lynx*. The total number drowned was 112, including the captain.

1899, 20 October. Off Vigten Island, Norway

The British steamship, *Zurich*, bound from Archangel to London with a cargo of timber, was disabled in a violent storm and the crew were forced to abandon ship on two improvised rafts, the ship's boats having been damaged. One raft was picked up four days later, the only occupant being the captain, who was suffering from exposure. The other was washed ashore on 25 October with the body of a dead Negro on board.

1900, 18 September. Off Andros Island, Aegean Sea

The steamship, *Charkieh*, 1533 tons, was bound from Piracus to Constantinople with a cargo of wood, rice and provisions and a number of passengers when her propeller shaft broke in strong winds and heavy seas. She was driven on the rocks at the entrance to the Doro Channel and sank immediately. Two boats with women and children got away and reached shore safely.

1900, 28 December. Moelfre, Anglesey

The ship, *Pass of Balmaha*, of Glasgow, sheltering from gale-force winds off Moelfre, sent a distress signal because her anchors were dragging. A lifeboat took off twenty-six men and when a rollcall revealed two missing, returned to find the men asleep in their bunks. They, too, were taken off safely. The *Pass of Balmaha* rode out the gale and went on to become notorious in the First World War, when the Germans converted her into a commerce raider. As the *Seedler*, she caused havoc among Allied shipping before she was finally wrecked on a South Seas island after a chase by naval vessels.

1901, 8 August. St George's Channel, between Wales and Ireland

The steamship, *Kincora*, bound from Limerick to Liverpool, was run down off the Tuskar Rock by the White Star liner, *Oceanic*, in thick fog. The *Kincora* had reduced speed and was sounding her fog horn, but knew nothing of the liner's presence until the collision. She sank in seven minutes, with the loss of seven lives.

1902, 4 January. Off Aveiro, Portugal

The steamship, *Alfonso*, bound from Cartagena to Maryport with a cargo of ore was in collision off the Portuguese coast with the Spanish collier, *Hullera Española*, bound from Aviles to Barcelona. The collision took place in thick fog and the British vessel sank with the loss of eighteen lives, only the captain surviving. The Spanish ship sank later, with the loss of one man.

1903, 1 October. North Sea

The Dundee steamship, *Loch Maree*, was bound from Odessa with a cargo of grain when the cargo shifted in a storm and she sank. Two boats got clear before the vessel heeled over, but one was swamped by a large wave and the ten men on board were drowned. The other boat with sixteen survivors was picked up by the Dutch steamship, *Olanda*.

1904, 28 June. Rockall, North Atlantic

The Danish steamship, *Norge*, went on the rocks here during a voyage from Copenhagen to New York carrying seven hundred emigrants and eighty crew. She sank rapidly, with a loss of 651 lives.

1905, 3 June. Off Dungeness, Kent

The four-masted iron barque, *Afghanistan*, 2286 tons, was bound from Hamburg to San Diego when she dropped anchor off the Kent coast in dense fog. At the same time, the Channel Fleet, steaming at twelve knots, ran into the fog, and the battleship, *Caesar*, collided with the *Afghanistan* as she lay at anchor and sank her immediately. Eighteen seamen, mostly Dutch and Scandinavian, died, and fourteen were picked up by other ships in the fleet.

1905, 8 June. Plymouth Sound, Devon

The submarines A7 and A8, both of 320 tons, had begun exercises in the Sound, when the breakwater lighthouse reported that A8 had sunk, apparently in distress. A fishing boat rescued three of the crew of nineteen, who said that an explosion had occurred when the submarine was cruising on the surface. The three survivors were on deck at the time and had been blown into the sea. Tugs sent to the scene succeeded in attaching sweep-wires to the hull of the submarine, but as they were raising her another explosion occurred. Three days later A8 was brought to the surface and moved into dock for examination. An Admiralty enquiry showed there was a loose rivet in the hull. Tests showed that a defect of this kind could let in a ton of water in ten minutes. A8 was subsequently overhauled and refitted, and survived continuous service throughout the First World War.

1905, 7 August. Praa Sands, Mount's Bay, Cornwall

The *Noisel* was on her way from Cherbourg to Italy loaded with armour plate. The cargo shifted during a gale off Ushant and, listing badly, the ship made for Plymouth. She was driven into Mount's Bay, where attempts were made to anchor her, but these failed. Eventually the breakers took her broadside on to the beach, where she broke her back. All but two of the crew were saved. The first that people on land knew about the wreck was when an old lady saw the face of the *Noisel*'s Negro cook peering through her window.

1906, 31 July. Near Cadgwith, Lizard peninsula
The *Socoa*, of Bayonne, was on her way from Stettin to San Francisco with a cargo of cement, which was urgently needed for the rebuilding of the city after the great earthquake earlier in the year. She ran aground on the Cornish coast in a gale. Fifty thousand barrels of cement were thrown overboard and the ship was then refloated. She was later renamed the *Thiers* and remained in service until 1927.

1906, 4 August. Off Spanish coast
The Italian liner, *Sirio*, was on a voyage from Genoa to Montevideo and Buenos Aires with 695 passengers and 127 crew, when she struck the rocks off the Hormigas Islands, heeled over and sank with the loss of 442 lives.

1907, January. Off Agger, Denmark
The British cargo ship, *Cabral*, was wrecked here during a voyage from Novorossisk to Nyborg with a cargo of grain and oilcake.

1907, 17 March. Maenheere Rock, Lizard Head
The 12,500-ton liner, *Suevic*, was on the last stage of her voyage from Australia with 456 passengers and crew when she hit the rocks off the Lizard in poor visibility. The navigator was almost certainly at fault. Lifeboats from Stations in Cornwall saved everyone on board. The *Suevic* was so badly damaged that she had to be cut in half with explosives. The aft section was towed to Southampton and a new bow section built on to it there.

1907, 18 March. Whitechurch, Devon
The 3813-ton Elder Dempster liner, *Jebba*, homeward bound from Sierra Leone, ran aground on the rocks here in dense fog and darkness. The Hope Cove lifeboat was unable to reach the ship, but two local men climbed down the two hundred foot cliffs and rigged up the bosun's chair which allowed all the 155 passengers and crew to be saved. The mail being carried by the *Jebba* was salvaged together with most of her cargo of rubber and ivory.

1908, 27 April. North Sea
The steamship, *Yarmouth*, left Rotterdam for Harwich with 443 tons of cargo, of which 192 tons was meat. Her deck cargo included three pantechnicon vans, weighing three tons, filled with furniture. She was seen rolling heavily later that day, and then disappeared.

1908, 25 November. Mediterranean, near Malta
The steamship, *Sardinia*, left Malta for Alexandria carrying 152 pilgrims bound for Mecca, as well as a nitrate cargo. Soon after the ship had left port fire broke out in the hold and an attempt was made to return to Malta, but the engine room was abandoned, leaving the *Sardinia* steaming at full speed in circles. Eventually the ship ran on to the Ricasoli rocks and was wrecked. About 121 people died in the disaster, which is believed to have been caused by embers from the pilgrims' cooking braziers falling from the deck through the hatch cover into the hold.

1909, 11 June. Azores
The liner, *Slavonia*, 10,606 tons, left New York for Gibraltar and the Mediterranean and ran aground near Velos. Passengers were taken off by the

Princess Irene and the *Batavia* and there was no loss of life among the 598 people on board. The liner became a total wreck.

1909, 31 July. West coast of France
The British cargo ship, *Melrose Abbey*, was wrecked on Les Fourches Rock while bound from Arcachon to Cardiff with a cargo of pit props.

1909, 2 December. Hartland Point, Devon
The Sunderland steamer, *Thistlemor*, 4008 tons, was bound for Australia from Cardiff with a cargo of coal when a hurricane-force wind forced her to seek shelter in Lundy Roads where she became completely unmanageable with water breaking over her and her screw and rudder seldom totally immersed. The crew took to the boats, one of which capsized, and nine survivors from this were picked up by the steamship, *Arndale*. Next day the second ship's boat was found capsized near the South Tail and twenty-one bodies were recovered.

South America and the Caribbean

1862, 27 July. Off Manzanillo, Mexico
The paddle steamship, *Golden Gate* 2850 tons, caught fire off the Mexican coast and burnt rapidly. The captain headed for the beach, but before he reached shore the upper deck collapsed on the passengers. Of the 337 people on board, only eighty reached shore, where they endured great hardship before being rescued. The ship was carrying 1,400,000 dollars' worth of gold, some of which was salvaged later by divers.

1864, 14 December. Off Montevideo
HMS *Bombay* was built at Bombay in 1827, of Indian teak. She was originally a sailing ship, but in 1860, when the Navy had at last decided to go over to steam, she was lengthened and converted to screw-propulsion. Particular pains were taken during the conversion to improve the through ventilation of the ship and this, together with the fact that the timbers had by this time become very dry, produced a serious fire risk. At the end of 1864, the *Bombay* was on exercises off South America with 655 men on board. She caught fire fifteen miles off Montevideo. Ninety of the crew were drowned, mainly because they were unable to swim.

1867, 29 October. Off Virgin Islands
The Royal Mail Steam Packet Company's liner, *Rhone*, 2738 tons, was caught in a hurricane and went aground on rocks near Salt Island, where she broke in two and sank. Of the 145 people on board, only one passenger and twenty-one crewmen survived. Sixty ships in the area tried to ride out the hurricane, but only two did so successfully.

1867, 29 October. St. Thomas, Virgin Islands
The Royal Mail Steam Packet Company's steamship, *Wye* was caught in the hurricane which struck the harbour. In trying to get out of the crowded port the ship was badly damaged and crashed into the rocks of Buck Island, becoming a total wreck. Forty-one officers and men drowned.

1874, 7 March. Off Los Vilos, Chile
The *Tacna*, left Valparaiso with a general cargo, ten head of cattle and 250 bundles of hay, and was nearing her first port of call at Los Vilos when a gust of wind caught her and made her heel over. The captain tried to trim the vessel by

throwing the hay overboard and cutting away the foremast, but before this could be completed the ship foundered. Nineteen people died, and many survivors owed their lives to the floating bales of hay which brought them to shore.

1880, 12–16 February. Off Bermuda
The training ship, *Atalanta*, was a converted frigate and on 7 November 1879 she left Portsmouth with 265 men and boys on board, and fifteen officers. When yellow fever broke out on board the ship made for Bermuda, arriving on 29 January 1880. Two days later she left the port, and was never heard of again.

1884, 11 September. São Sebastião, Brazil
The British cargo ship, *Dart*, was wrecked here while on a voyage from Santos to New York with a cargo of coffee.

1889, 5 September. Bahamas
The Newcastle steamer, *Earnmore*, sank in a cyclone off the Bahamas. One boat was picked up, the seven men in it nearly starving, and taken to Nassau, New Providence, on 30 September.

1890, c. 25 March. Cape Horn area
The iron ship, *Dunedin*, was bound from Oamaru, New Zealand, to London with a cargo of frozen meat. Nothing was heard from her after a passing ship had sighted her some days from port, and she is thought to have foundered in a storm off Cape Horn, or perhaps struck an iceberg. The *Dunedin* was the first ship to have refrigerating machinery fitted on board.

1892, 21 May. Off Cape Polonio, Uraguay
The Brazilian ironclad, *Solimões*, foundered here in a gale, with the loss of 125 officers and men. She was on her way to help suppress an insurrection which had broken out in the province of Matto Grosso and is believed to have become caught up in the dangerous currents and shoals in the area.

1895, 5 February. Abrolhos, Brazil
The British cargo ship, *Elmete*, was carrying a cargo of grain, wool and sheep when she was wrecked here on her way from Buenos Aires to Antwerp.

1895, 27 May. Fifty miles off Manzanillo, Mexico
The Pacific Mail ship, *Colima*, was on a voyage from San Francisco to Panama when her boilers exploded and she began to sink rapidly. There was panic among the passengers, aggravated by the fact that the captain, chief engineer and pilot had been killed in the explosion. In the fight for the boats only nineteen people out of 192 on board managed to escape.

1896, 16 March. Off Cape São Thome, South Brazil
The British cargo ship, *Egglestone Abbey*, 2401 tons, was wrecked here while bound from Cardiff to Buenos Aires with coal.

1898, 15 February. Havana, Cuba
The US battleship, *Maine*, 6682 tons, was in harbour at Havana, officially on a courtesy visit. An explosion in one of the magazines killed 266 of the crew. The Spanish and American authorities disagreed as to whether the cause was a mine outside the ship or deliberate action inside the magazine. The wreck remained in the harbour until 1909, when she was pumped out, refloated and towed into deep water for re-sinking. An examination showed that the plates were buckled inwards, which could only have been caused by an explosion outside the ship.

1898. Near Puerto Bello, Venezuela
The 1500-ton steamer, *Orinoco*, collided in darkness with an abandoned derelict when she was a few hours out of Puerto Bello, and sank. She was carrying, among

other items of cargo, a hundred tons of silver. The underwriters in New York paid the owners for the loss and then tried to recover the silver, hiring two divers for the purpose. In order to get at the silver, which was in a special strongroom, the divers had to pump several tons of sodden coffee-beans out of the hold.

1902, 2 May. St. Pierre, West Indies

The volcano of Mount Pelee on St. Pierre erupted suddenly, destroying the town and all but one of the ships in the harbour. The *Roddam*, an old British tramp steamer, had almost finished unloading her cargo and had steam up. Although she was badly damaged and partly on fire, and many of the crew had been killed, the captain managed to get her out to sea and eventually to St. Lucia. Only six of the dockers who had been on board survived, together with thirteen of the crew of twenty-three.

1903, c. 30 May. Pacific Ocean

The clipper ship, *Aristides*, was lost on a voyage from Caleta Buena, Chile to San Francisco with a cargo of nitrate of soda. No trace of her was ever found. She had a famous career as a fast clipper on the Australian run, and on her maiden voyage from London to Port Phillip, Australia her time of seventy-four days beat the existing record.

1903, 3 June. Off Valparaiso, Chile

The PSN Company's ship, *Arequipa*, was anchored off Valparaiso during a storm, when her cable fouled the propeller after striking her stern buoy and she sank in fifteen minutes with the loss of eleven lives.

1906, 21 January. Off Jacarepaguá, Brazil

The Brazilian ironclad, *Aquidaban*, blew up at anchor here, south of Rio de Janeiro, and sank within three minutes, with the loss of 212 men. Ninety-eight survivors were rescued and thirty-six were injured. She had been accompanying the cruiser, *Barroso*, which had the Minister of the Marine on board, the object of the cruise being the selection of a suitable site for a naval dockyard.

1907, 12 November. Smyth Channel, Chile

The British cargo ship, *Hazel Branch*, 2623 tons, was wrecked here while carrying a cargo of copper ore from the west coast of South America to Liverpool.

Far East

1845, 30 September. Off Hainan Head, China

The British steamship, *Charterhouse*, bound from Hai-k'ow to Hong Kong, foundered here in a storm, with the loss of sixty-six lives. Twenty-six survivors were picked up from a raft by the German steamship, *Koh-si-Chang*.

1851, 21 July. Straits of Malacca

The paddle-steamer, *Pasha*, was bound for Penang and Calcutta when she collided with the *Erin* and sank in seven minutes, with the loss of sixteen lives. Both vessels were owned by the P&O Steam Navigation Company.

1860, 22 May. Point de Galle, Ceylon

The iron ship, *Malabar*, was wrecked here on her way to China. Among the passengers were two ambassadors, Lord Elgin and Baron Gras, who were reported to have shown great heroism during the wreck.

1864, 4 November. Off Yen-t'ai, China

The gunboat, *Racehorse*, left Portsmouth for the China Station with 108 officers and men aboard. Off Chefoo Cape the ship struck on the rocks in calm but foggy conditions. A gale sprang up and it was impossible to launch the boats in the huge seas. Ninety-nine men drowned and the commander and eight men were later rescued from a small boat by a Chinese junk.

1870, 24 January. Yokohama Harbour, Japan
The corvette, *Oneida*, was leaving harbour for Hong Kong when she collided with the P&O liner, *Bombay*, and foundered off Saratoga Spit, five miles from shore. The *Bombay* continued on her way to Yokohama, unaware of the severity of the damage she had inflicted on the other vessel, but later returned to the scene to pick up survivors. A hundred and fifteen officers and men out of a total complement of 176 were drowned.

1879, 28 February. Seventy miles north of Bombay
The British India steamship, *Vingorla*, sprang a leak and sank with the loss of sixty-eight lives. She was bound from Bombay to Karachi, with 190 people on board.

1879, 22 May. Mouth of Hooghly River, India
The British India liner, *Ava*, 2600 tons, left Calcutta for Madras, Colombo and London and had just dropped her pilot at the mouth of the Hooghly when she was run down by the sailing ship, *Brenhilda*. The *Ava* was almost cut in two by the impact and sank rapidly. Three boats were launched safely, with fifty-three persons on board. Seventy people drowned.

1883, 9 August. Yen-t'ai, China
The British cargo ship, *Foochow* was wrecked here on a voyage from Newchwang to Chefoo with a cargo of beans.

1884, 23 September. Off Wenchou, China
The British cargo ship, *Miramar*, foundered here while on a voyage from Nagasaki to Hong Kong with a cargo of coal. The only survivors were two Chinese who swam to the shore.

1885, 2 March. Off Java
The British iron steamship, *Bengal*, was wrecked on Bawean Island while on a voyage from Saigon to Java with a cargo of rice.

1887, 3 December. Hainan Island, China
The British cargo ship, *Lorne*, was carrying rice and paddy from Saigon to Hong Kong when she was wrecked here with the loss of five lives. There were sixty-nine survivors.

1890, 25 December. River Yangtze, China
The British paddle steamship, *Shanghai*, caught fire six miles below Mud Fort on a voyage from Shanghai to Hankow, with a general cargo. Two hundred lives were lost. The vessel was later salvaged and re-registered as a sailing vessel at Shanghai in 1893.

1892, 10 January. Cupchi Point, China
The Chinese steamship, *Namchow*, foundered here after her propeller shaft had broken. Only a small number of those on board could get away by boat, and it was estimated that 414 people died, including all the Europeans in the crew.

1892, 24 August. Mouth of Hooghly River, India
The Anchor liner, *Anglia*, with forty-seven people on board, left Calcutta for England, but hit a sandbank in the Jellingham Channel between Mud Point and Sangor, heeling over and sinking within a short time. Survivors were picked up by the British India steamship, *Goa*, but several men were trapped inside the ship.

1892, 10 October. Sand Island, Pescadores Group, China

The P&O liner, *Bokhara*, was wrecked here, west of Formosa, during a typhoon. She was on her way from Shanghai to Hong Kong. A hundred and twenty-six people, including the captain, drowned, and twenty-three survived.

1892, November. Tokushima Straits, Japan

The Japanese cruiser, *Chishima*, was sunk by collision here with the P&O steamer, *Ravenna*. Seventy-five people lost their lives.

1893, 4 September. Off Antipodes Island, South Pacific

The iron barque, *Spirit of the Dawn*, 716 tons, ran on to a reef on a voyage from Rangoon to Talcahuano, Chile with a cargo of rice. The vessel became a total wreck. Eleven survivors lived on the island for eighty-seven days, living on birds, roots and mussels. A makeshift flag they erected was seen around 1 December by the Government steamship, *Hinemoa*, which took the men to New Zealand.

1898, 24 May. Bay of Bengal

The British steamship, *Mecca*, was on a voyage from Calcutta to Rangoon when she took in tow the British India steamship, *Lindula*, which had a broken propeller shaft. Next day the tow rope broke during a manoeuvre and the *Mecca* was sunk during the following collision. Fifty-three passengers and crew died.

1898, 30 December. Linting Rock, Sa Mun Group, China

The British cargo ship, *Glenavon*, was bound from Japan to Hong Kong with a cargo which included tea and rice when she was wrecked here. Five men lost their lives.

1902, *c.* 6 May. Off coast of India

The British steamship, *Camorta*, left Madras with eighty-nine crew and 650 passengers, bound for Rangoon, but it is thought to have been sunk during a cyclone in the area with the loss of all on board.

1904, 10 March. Off Port Arthur, China

The Russian destroyer, *Steregushchi*, 240 tons, was one of a number of ships of the same design which were sent out to Port Arthur in sections and assembled at the dockyard there. During the Russo-Japanese War the ship patrolled off the fortress and she was attacked by the Japanese 3rd Flotilla and disabled just outside harbour. In the face of heavy odds the ship surrendered. She was taken in tow but later sank, with the loss of forty-seven of her crew.

1904, 11 March. Catalan Bank, near Guam

The British steamship, *Scotia*, 4676 tons, was wrecked here while on a voyage from Hong Kong to Guam with a cargo of cable fittings.

1904, 16 July. Off Chinese coast

The British cargo ship, *Hip Sang*, bound from Newchwang to Chefoo, was torpedoed by a Russian boat in Pigeon Bay. The European officers swam to safety, and the Chinese crew and passengers crowded into the boats. Twenty-one survivors were picked up by the Russians and kept prisoner until 2 August, when they were set adrift in a captured Chinese junk. They were later taken off by the German steamship, *Sullberg*.

1904, 13 November. Port Arthur, (Lü-shun) China

The Russian destroyer, *Stroini*, was struck by a mine when she was at anchor under Golden Hill. She sank quickly, with the loss of two men. The survivors were taken off by the destroyer, *Silni*, which also struck a mine and was badly damaged.

1905, 27 April. T'ung-chou, Yangtze River

The British steamship, *Yuen Wo*, was burnt out at the start of a voyage from Tungchow to Shanghai with a general cargo. Thirty Chinese were drowned.

1905, 5 June. Off Hong Kong

The British steamship, *Saint Kilda*, 3518 tons, was sunk by Russian warships while on her way from Hong Kong to Yokohama with a cargo of jute, rice and cotton. The Russians alleged that the ship was carrying contraband.

1908, 27 September. Brennus Shoal, Ceylon (Sri Lanka)

The British steamship, *Sir John Jackson* was wrecked here on a voyage from Saigon to Bordeaux with a cargo of rice and maize.

1909, 17 November. Bombay Reef, India

The British cargo ship, *Shrewsbury*, was wrecked here. She was on a voyage from Penarth, via Singapore, to Hong Kong, carrying coal.

Radio and Radar: Wrecks since 1914

A random sample of ships wrecked around the coasts of Britain during the years 1910–12 includes a Russian wooden barque; an American schooner; a Brixham sailing trawler; a 2660-ton steamer loaded with Swedish pitprops: a forty-two year-old Cardiff steam collier; a French brigantine with a cargo of coal and bricks; a P&O liner sunk after a collision; a full-rigged ship built in Scotland in 1886; a Norwegian full-rigged ship bringing nitrate from South America; and a small Italian steamer bound from Genoa to Barry in ballast. It is a fair cross-section of the world's ocean-going shipping at the time. To complete the picture, one would have to add perhaps a hundred fishing vessels and small coasters, the normal year-by-year casualties of inland waters. Whether the area is the coasts of Britain, New England, the Caribbean or Australia, the mix of wrecks is much the same. The number of ships wrecked each year, however, varies very much with the part of the world. The western tip of England, the counties of Devon and Cornwall and the Scillies have always had an exceptional number of wrecks, simply because so many shipping routes come together at this point. Ships travelling between Western European ports and the Mediterranean, Africa, the Far East, and North and South America all have to pass close to Land's End. From a shipping point of view, it is the most densely populated in the world and the number of wrecks reflects this.

Equally, there are a number of parts of the world where there is a considerable amount of shipping but very few wrecks. The Baltic is a case in point, as is the Mediterranean. Both these areas were full of perils to mariners in the days of small sailing ships, but present few difficulties to modern steamships. The same is true of the Norwegian coast, which to the layman appears dangerous in the extreme, but which in fact produces very few accidents indeed nowadays, mainly because its hazards are of a type to which sailing ships are particularly vulnerable. With sailing ships, the main risks were fire, hurricanes and hidden reefs. These are still, of course, to be feared, but, despite radar, the major problem for big modern ships is collision.

There is a dreadful democracy about wrecks. Little ships and big ships are both just as likely now as fifty or a hundred years ago to meet an unpleasant end on rocks or the bottom of the ocean. What has fortunately changed very much during the present century has been the proportion of survivors to casualties among both passengers and crew, and for this one must certainly thank radio and better equipped and maintained ships' boats. Radio has not prevented wrecks from happening, but it has made it much more likely that the people on board a wrecked ship will be picked up quickly.

In the list which follows, it will be noticed how the proportion of oil tankers increases decade by decade. In one sense, this is inevitable, because oil tankers of one size and another now make up a very large part of all the ships at sea. Because there are more tankers afloat now than there were fifty years ago, one would expect the number of wrecked tankers to have increased too. A tanker wreck is unlike all other kinds of wreck in one important respect, however. Its cargo does not remain where the vessel came to grief, it can spread for hundreds of miles, fouling coasts and beaches and causing immense destruction to fish and sea birds. A wrecked tanker presents much more serious problems than a wrecked cargo ship carrying any other commodity.

Another important difference to observe is the remarkable reduction in the number of passengers travelling any great distance by sea. A disaster such as that which befell the *Titanic* could not happen now, not because ships are safer or because fog and icebergs have ceased to exist, but because the days of the large passenger liner are over. Developments during the remainder of the present century are difficult to forecast. If the most pessimistic forecasts of the speed with which the world's resources of oil are being exhausted turn out to be correct, it may well be that by the year 2000 oil tankers will be a thing of the past and what is now a major hazard will have been removed from the world's shipping lanes. If the developing countries industrialise quickly, a large proportion of the manufactured goods which they import at present will no longer have to be transported to them. If such tropical and sub-tropical luxuries as bananas, cocoa, tea and coffee price themselves out of the world markets, ships will no longer be required to carry them.

But, in all these cases, one has to say 'if'. Forecasts and imponderables are constantly changing and the only fact one can be sure of is that for the past century ships have been becoming steadily larger, more specialised, more complex and more expensive. A high proportion of the wrecks that take place today represents the loss of a large investment and there is consequently every incentive to make sure that wrecks do not happen, except in those cases – and they are regrettably numerous – where the owners have reasons of their own for preferring the insurance money to the ship.

The size to which ships have grown during the past ten years is indicated by the following select list of major tanker disasters between 1967 and 1976.

Date	Ship	Weight (dead weight tons)	Hull Value ($ millions)
March 1967	*Torrey Canyon*	123,000	16.5
December 1969	*Marpessa*	207,000	16*
December 1969	*Mactra*	205,000	16*
December 1969	*King Haakon VII*	209,000	16
September 1970	*Aquarius*	214,000	23
January 1971	*Universe Patriot*	157,602	15.6
December 1971	*Elisabeth Knudsen*	216,187	28
March 1973	*Igara*	145,000*	22.5*
June 1973	*Conoco Britannia*	117,000*	21
November 1973	*Golar Patricia*	217,000*	24
December 1973	*Elwood Mead*	119,000*	25

February 1974	*Nai Giovanna*	133,850	24*
April 1975	*Cactus Queen*	158,000*	16*
October 1975	*Kriti Sun*	123,000	30
January 1976	*Berge Istra*	223,913	18.2

approximately

Australasia

1911, *c.* 9 September. Tasman Sea
The barquentine, *Mary Isabel*, 339 tons, left Whangape, New Zealand, bound for Sydney with a cargo of kauri wood, but she never arrived. Bad weather was reported in the area, and one of her lifeboats was picked up by the Norwegian barque, *Este*. Eleven crewmen were presumed drowned.

1912, 21 March. Western Australia
The steamship, *Koombana*, was presumed lost in a typhoon which swept the coast. She left Port Headland for Broome, and nothing more was heard of her until wreckage came ashore and was identified as belonging to her.

1914, *c.* 25 September. Near Greymouth, New Zealand
The New Zealand coastal steamship, *Kairaki*, 462 tons, was bound from Wellington to Greymouth with a crew of seventeen and a general cargo, when she was reported overdue. Wreckage and lifebuoys were found along the shore, and the ship was located five miles from Greymouth with her derricks visible above the water. No survivors were found.

1918, 26 June. Off New Zealand coast
The *Wimmera* was bound for Sydney from Auckland with 152 people on board when she struck two mines and began to sink. Five lifeboats were lowered, but there was great confusion in the total darkness. The wireless operator repaired damaged equipment and sent out an SOS at the cost of his own life. Twenty-six lives were lost, including the captain, the first officer and the chief steward.

1919, 17 September. Off Gore Bay, New Zealand
The wooden steamship, *Tainui*, 128 tons, blew up and caught fire during a voyage from Lyttelton to Wanganui with a cargo of 1808 cases of petroleum. The crew of nine took to one lifeboat, which capsized, and only the cook managed to reach the shore. The remains of the wreck drifted ashore near Shag Rock, Gore Bay.

1924, 7 August. Off Cape Palliser, New Zealand
The coastal steamship, *Ripple*, 413 tons, was reported in distress in gale-force winds off Cape Palliser while on a voyage from Wellington to Napier with a cargo of wool and general stores. The vessel was never seen again, and next day the coast was strewn with wreckage.

1926, 5 April. East coast of Australia
The Australian steamship, *Dorrigo*, foundered in heavy weather off Double Island Point on a voyage from Brisbane to Thursday Island, Queensland, with a loss of twenty-two lives. Two survivors were picked up from a raft.

1935, 24 December. Gippsland, South-East Australia
The Chinese ship, *Paringa*, was towing the *Vincas* from Melbourne to Hong Kong for breaking up, but during a storm off Lakes Entrance she cast off the tow and disappeared. A message was heard from her two days later, but nothing

further. The *Vincas*, with four men on board, drifted inshore and anchored off the coast of Victoria.

1940, 19 June. Hauraki Gulf, New Zealand
The liner, *Niagara*, ran into a minefield laid by a German raider a few days before, was holed and later sank in seventy-three fathoms. She was on a voyage from Auckland to Suva, Honolulu and Vancouver with 136 passengers and about 200 crew. Her valuable cargo included two and a half million pounds in gold and half the New Zealand stock of small arms ammunition for trans-shipment to England. All the passengers and crew were taken off by the *Wanganella* and the *Kapiti*, in answer to distress signals. By February 1942, bullion to the value of £2,379,000 had been recovered.

1940, 20 August. Tasman Sea
The steamship, *Turakina* was bound from Sydney to Wellington with a cargo of frozen meat for England, part of which was to be put on board at Wellington, when she was intercepted by the German raider, *Orion*, and so badly damaged by her gunfire that she sank within two minutes. During the battle about half her crew of fifty-six were killed or wounded and twenty-one survivors, one of whom died later, were picked up by the enemy.

1940, 26 November. Three hundred and twenty miles off East Cape, New Zealand
The liner, *Rangitane*, 16,712 tons was sunk by a German commerce raider, which then picked up survivors and took them to Emirau, landing them after several weeks at sea. Sixteen died in the attack.

1942, 19 February. Darwin, Northern Territory
The Philippine motorship, *Don Isidro*, was on her way from Batavia to Darwin when she was bombed by Japanese aircraft. The vessel was run aground near Darwin and wrecked. Eleven people died.

1942, 2 March. Two hundred and fifty miles west of North-West Cape, Western Australia
The Dutch motorship, *Siantar*, was torpedoed, shelled and sunk by a Japanese submarine with the loss of twenty-one of her crew of sixty-one.

1942, 5 May. One hundred and twenty miles south-west of Amadee Lighthouse
The steamship *John Adams*, 7180 tons, was carrying aviation spirit from Noumea to Brisbane when she was torpedoed by a Japanese submarine, caught fire and blew up.

1943, 14 May. Off Brisbane, Queensland
The hospital ship, *Centaur*, on her way from Sydney to New Guinea was torpedoed by a Japanese submarine forty-three miles east of Brisbane. She was clearly marked with a red cross and brightly illuminated at the time. Of the 363 people on board, only sixty-four survived. The submarine surfaced and watched the ship sink in three minutes, before boats could be launched.

1944, 27 March. Four hundred miles east of Diego Garcia Island
The Australian motorship, *Tulagi*, was bound from Sydney, New South Wales to Colombo with flour when she was torpedoed and sunk by a Japanese submarine. Seven survivors on a raft landed on a small island in the Seychelles on 25 May, having drifted 1500 miles in fifty-nine days.

1956, 2 August. Sydney, New South Wales
The Australian ship, *Birchgrove Park*, bound from Newcastle, New South Wales, to Sydney with a cargo of coal, when the cargo shifted in a gale and she sank north of Sydney Heads. Ten crewmen drowned and four were saved.

1959, 24 November. Off South Island, New Zealand

The motorship, *Holmglen*, with a general cargo, left Dunedin for Wanganui. She called at Oamaru and on the 24 November a distress signal was received at Taiaroa Head and Wellington, saying she was listing to port and about to launch her boats. The wreck was located by a large patch of oil. Divers examined her, but could find no reason for the sinking.

1962, 30 January. Two hundred and thirty miles north-west of Fremantle, Western Australia

The tanker, *Bridgewater*, broke in two during rough weather. The crew were rescued by another tanker. A salvage tug found half the ship drifting forty miles from its original position, with its generators still running. At the second attempt, the tug managed to get the derelict to Fremantle, where 7840 tons of oil were rescued from the tanks. What remained of the wreck was then sold for scrap.

1964, 10 February. Off Sydney, New South Wales

The Australian Navy destroyer, *Voyager*, was struck by the aircraft carrier, *Melbourne*, during an exercise off the coast of New South Wales. The destroyer was cut in half by the violence of the impact, the forward portion remaining afloat for ten minutes and the after portion for three hours. Seventy-nine men were missing, presumed drowned, and three were killed, out of a total complement of 319.

1970, 3 March. Prince of Wales Channel, Great Barrier Reef, Queensland

The 58,000-ton tanker, *Ocean Grandeur*, sailing from Dumi in Sumatra for Brisbane with a cargo of 55,000 tons of crude oil, tore open her bottom on an uncharted rock. Eight of the fifteen oil tanks were punctured. The vessel was refloated and the spillage contained, the slick being dispersed with detergent. It was claimed that the detergent killed large areas of pearl shell in Torres Strait.

North America

1910, 12 January. Coos Bay, Oregon

The American steamship, *Czarina*, was driven on to the jetty here in bad weather. She was refloated, but dragged her anchors and stranded close to the shore. There were no passengers on board at the time, but the crew of thirty-one was unable to launch a boat and only one man survived.

1912, 14 April. Five hundred miles off Cape Race, Newfoundland

The White Star liner, *Titanic*, the largest liner afloat, hit an iceberg on her maiden voyage from Southampton to New York, with the loss of 1500 people. The enquiry showed that the provision of lifeboats was inadequate, that the captain had ignored warnings of ice, that organisation after the collision had been poor, and that the liner, *Californian*, only a few miles away, had failed to go to the assistance of the *Titanic*. The *Olympic*, after hearing the radio call for help, covered four hundred miles at twenty-four knots, the highest speed the liner had ever attained. The survivors had, however, been picked up by the *Carpathia* when the *Olympic* arrived on the scene. The passengers who died included ten American millionaires, among them Colonel Astor and Benjamin Guggenheim.

1913, 13 February. Near Nehalem River, Oregon

The 2400-ton *Mimi* went aground in heavy seas. The salvage company instructed by the insurers to refloat the ship removed most of the ballast and gradually worked her down to deeper water. When she was eventually pulled off, there was not enough ballast in her to keep her upright and she capsized, drowning a number of the crew and leaving others clinging to the rigging. Few of the survivors could be rescued in time to prevent them dying of exposure in the bitter weather. The ship broke up and became a total loss.

1913, 9 November. Lake Huron
The Canadian steamship, *James Carruthers*, foundered in a storm while carrying wheat from Fort William, Ontario, to Port Colborne. There were no survivors among the crew of twenty-two.

1914, *c.* 31 March. Off Cape Race, Newfoundland
The Newfoundland sealer, *Southern Cross*, foundered during a blizzard off the Cape on her way home to St. John's with the season's catch. A hundred and seventy-three men on board lost their lives. A search was made of the area, and wreckage was reported off Cape Race, as well as a number of seal pelts.

1917, 6 December. Off Halifax, Nova Scotia
The steamship, *Mont Blanc*, bound from New York to Halifax with a cargo of high explosive, collided with the Norwegian steamship, *Imo*, in fine weather and with plenty of room to spare. Twenty barrels of benzol were smashed by the impact and ignited the picric acid, causing sheets of flame to envelop the vessel. Time was wasted trying to put out the flames, instead of sinking her, and the crew reached the shore just as the ship exploded. The *Imo* was blown bodily ashore and the *Mont Blanc* was reduced to a mass of wreckage, but it was the city of Halifax which received the brunt of the explosion. Nearly all the wooden houses in the district were blown flat.

1918, 18 October. Off New York
The *Port Philip*, collided with the *Proteus*, and sank very quickly. She was carrying barbed wire for the trenches in France, and Ford cars and lorries for military transport. Salvage was started immediately, the barbed wire being raised first, causing a crop of minor injuries to the divers. On 11 November, the Armistice was declared and the *Port Philip*'s cargo no longer had any military value. The waterway, however, had to be cleared. The contractor brought up the crates of unassembled vehicles first, cleaned the parts and put them together, and sold the cars and lorries to dealers. When the whole cargo had been removed, the ship was cut up for scrap.

1918, 26 October. Vanderbilt Reef, Lynn Canal
The Canadian steamship, *Princess Sophia*, was bound from Skagway for Vancouver with 346 people on board, mostly from Dawson City and Alaska. The ship ran into a snowstorm and struck the reef, where she remained wedged for three days. Her anchors were unable to hold on the rocky bed, and eventually the vessel was swept off the reef and foundered with all on board.

1922, 8 August. Off Point Amour, Labrador
The British Navy cruiser, *Raleigh*, was wrecked here as she was cruising in the Straits of Belle Isle in dense fog. Seven hundred and twenty officers and crew reached shore safely, but as it was an uninhabited area, were not picked up until some days later by the Canadian Pacific liner, *Montrose*.

1922, 29 December. Race Point, Provincetown, Cape Cod
The wooden fishing schooner, *Annie L. Spindler*, of Nova Scotia, grounded here in a blizzard. The crew of six were taken off by breeches buoy. This was in the days of prohibition in the United States, and the ship was loaded with eight

hundred cases of whisky. A hundred cases were thrown overboard before the *Annie L. Spindler* went ashore. The remaining seven hundred were taken off by the coastguards and stored in a warehouse in Provincetown. Shortly afterwards, local people raided the warehouse and stole five hundred cases. The ship itself was stripped by wreckers and eventually boys set fire to the hull.

1923, 21 May. Off Pine Point, Newfoundland

The liner, *Marvale*, ran on to Freel's Rock in dense fog on a voyage from Quebec to Glasgow. Thanks to the excellent discipline on board 437 people were transferred to the shore in twenty-five minutes without loss of life.

1923, 9 September. San Miguel Island, California

The steamship, *Cuba*, was wrecked here in fog, with no loss of life. Eighteen ships of the US Navy were on manoeuvres close by. Their radio communication became confused with transmissions from the *Cuba* and seven of them piled up on Point Arguello one after the other. Only twenty-two of a total of 652 on board were lost. The findings of the Court of Enquiry were never published.

1924, 12 March. Sixty miles from Cape Hatteras, North Carolina

The American steamship, *Santiago*, was on a voyage from Cienfuegos to New York with a cargo of sugar when she ran into bad weather and began to fill with water after one of the hatches was damaged. Twenty-five crewmen were lost when the vessel sank, and ten were picked up later from a boat.

1924, 26 April. Cuttyhunk Island, Cape Cod

The barque, *Wanderer*, built in 1887, was the last square-rigged whaler to sail from the port of Bedford. She was driven ashore and wrecked during an exceptionally bad storm. The ship was stripped by wreckers.

1925, 19 April. Off coast of Massachusetts

The Japanese steamship, *Raifuku Maru*, 5867 tons, left Boston for Hamburg with a cargo of wheat. She met bad weather after leaving port and by next day was in distress. An SOS call from her was picked up by the White Star liner, *Homeric*, saying all the lifeboats had been smashed. The liner reached the vessel as she was listing heavily, and stood by to pick up survivors, but all forty-eight crew died in the mountainous seas.

1925, 17 October. Off Florida coast

The steamship, *Comanche*, was on the Florida–New York service and had just left Jacksonville with a cargo of resin when fire was discovered. Three hours later the ship had to be abandoned and lifeboats were launched. Survivors were picked up by the oil tanker, *Reaper*, and the pilot boat, *Mota*. The cause of the fire was spontaneous combustion of the resin in the hold.

1926, 19 November. Near Sorel, Province of Quebec

The Canadian steamship, *Montreal*, was destroyed by fire on a voyage from Montreal to Quebec with a general cargo and cattle. The fire started in the hay carried for the cattle.

1927, 4 March. Nauset Bar, Cape Cod

The lumber schooner, *Montclair*, left Halifax with a cargo of 25,000 bundles of laths, and was wrecked here in freezing weather. The captain and four of the crew were drowned when waves swept them overboard. Because of the conditions, the men at Orleans lifeboat station were unable to launch their boat. Telephone communication was also impossible, since the gale had brought the wires down.

1928, 23 November. Atlantic

The German ship, *Herrenwyk*, sprank a leak during a voyage from Hernosand to

New York with a cargo of wood pulp. Ships answering her distress call stood by in bad weather, and eventually thirteen survivors were taken off by the Danish steamship, *Estonia*.

1929, 29 August. Off Pigeon Point, California

The American steamship, *San Juan*, ran into dense fog during a voyage from San Francisco to Los Angeles and collided with the Standard Oil Company's tanker, *S.C.T. Dodd*. She foundered very quickly, with the loss of sixty-five lives.

1935, c. 15 February. Off Newfoundland

The Norwegian steamship, *Spec*, 2053 tons, was bound from Glasgow to Boston with coal, when a message received at the Sable Island wireless station said that the ship was in thick ice and a severe storm off the Newfoundland coast. Nothing more was heard from her.

1936, 6 June. Off Cape Race, Newfoundland

The Norwegian ship, *Magnhild*, went aground at Mistaken Point and sank in heavy seas. She was under charter to the Newfoundland-Canada SS Company and was on her way from St. Pierre, Miquelon to St. John's, Newfoundland, with a cargo of coal and cattle, as well as general supplies.

1938, 27 January. Cape Cod Canal

The tug, *Plymouth*, was pulling the barge, *Everett*, from New York to Salem. The barge was loaded with coal and early in the morning rammed the tug and sank her. Fifteen of the sixteen men on the tug were saved from the icy water and the tug herself was eventually lifted and salvaged.

1939, 3 February. North Beach, Chatham, Cape Cod

The 339-ton British freighter, *Lutzen*, was on her way from St. John, New Brunswick, to New York with a cargo that included 230 tons of frozen blueberries. She went aground in fog and after unsuccessful attempts to pull her off, local people were hired to unload the cargo. As a result of poor supervision, all the cargo on the starboard side was unloaded first, so that the next tide tipped the ship over on its port side and salvage operations had to be abandoned.

1940, 17 September. Atlantic

The Ellerman liner, *City of Benares*, was bound from England to Canada carrying 406 passengers and crew, among whom were ninety child evacuees. When the liner was six hundred miles out, she was torpedoed by a German submarine and sank within minutes. The weather was bad and several lifeboats capsized in the heavy seas. Many died of exposure during the night. Two hundred and forty-eight people lost their lives. After ten days a British warship picked up forty-six survivors, including six children.

1941, c. 24 March. Atlantic

The British cargo ship, *Koranton*, sailed from Philadelphia for Loch Ewe and Hull, via Halifax, Nova Scotia. She left Halifax on 10 March and was reported in the Atlantic on the 24 March, but nothing more was heard of her. She was carrying a crew of thirty-four and two gunners, and a cargo of pig iron.

1942, 14 January. Near Cape Race, Newfoundland

The steamship, *Dayrose*, was torpedoed and sunk by a German submarine on a voyage from St John's, Newfoundland to Portland, Maine. Three crewmen and six gunners died.

1942, 18 January. Off Cape Hatteras, North Carolina

The American tanker, *Allan Jackson*, 6635 tons, was bound from Cartagena, Colombia to New York with 72,870 barrels of crude oil, when she was struck by two torpedoes. The ship caught fire and broke in two, going down with the loss of twenty-two men.

1942, 19 January. Off Cape Hatteras, North Carolina
The American ship, *City of Atlanta*, was torpedoed and sunk by a German submarine off the Cape at night. The submarine surfaced and illuminated the scene with searchlights, but made no attempt to rescue survivors.

1942, 9 February. New York Harbour
The *Normandie*, 79,280 tons and 1029 feet long, was the second largest ship in the world. After Pearl Harbour, she had been 'borrowed' from the French and converted to an American troopship. While she was in harbour, a spark from an oxy-acetylene torch set fire to bales of kapok life-vests. During fire-fighting operations, so much water was poured into her that she sank. Raised at enormous expense, she was refitted but, with the war ending was never used again. She was sold for scrap for a mere fraction of what had been spent on raising her.

1942, 22 February. Off Nova Scotia
The Norwegian steamship, *Torungen*, was torpedoed and sunk on a voyage from Halifax to Charleston. Only one body was recovered, that of the chief engineer, which was found in a raft off the Nova Scotia coast.

1942, 23 February. Off St. Lawrence, Newfoundland
The US destroyer *Truxton*, 1193 tons, ran aground near here in a gale. The crew made several attempts to get a line ashore, but the lines were soaked in oil and could not be handled. A breeches buoy was rigged at sea level but when survivors landed on the rocks they were swept away by the heavy seas before they could climb the cliffs. Nearly a hundred officers and ratings died.

1942, 26 February. Atlantic coast
The American tanker, *R. P. Resor*, left Houston, Texas for Fall River, Massachusetts with 78,729 barrels of fuel oil. She caught fire after being torpedoed, and continued to drift for two days until she capsized and sank near the Barnegat Light. Only two men survived.

1942, 10 March. Off coast of New Jersey
Bound from Port Arthur, Texas, with fuel oil, the American tanker, *Gulftrade*, was torpedoed by a German submarine about five miles off the coast, broke in two and sank with the loss of nineteen lives.

1942, 23 March. South-east of Cape Race, Newfoundland
The tanker, *British Prudence,* was torpedoed and sunk by a German submarine off the Cape, while on a voyage from Halifax to the Clyde with twelve thousand tons of fuel oil.

1942, 28 June. Cape Cod Canal
The *Stephen R. Jones* was bound from Norfolk, Virginia, to Boston with a cargo of 7149 tons of coal. She hit the bank of the Canal, east of Bourne Bridge, and sank. The tide later pushed the ship round until she was across the canal, blocking it to other shipping, which had to go round Cape Cod and risk being torpedoed by German submarines. It took seventeen and a half tons of dynamite to blow up the ship and clear the waterway.

1942, 13 October. Four hundred miles south of Cape Farewell
The whale oil refinery vessel, *Southern Empress*, 12,398 tons, was torpedoed and sunk by a German submarine while on her way from New York to the Clyde with fuel oil. Twenty-four of her crew, 4 gunners and twenty passengers died.

1942, 14 October. Cabot Strait, Newfoundland
The Newfoundland railway steamship, *Caribou*, was torpedoed and sunk by a German submarine on a voyage from Sydney, Nova Scotia, to Port aux Basques. Thirty-one crew and 105 passengers died.

1942, 29 October. Atlantic
The Canadian steamship, *Bic Island*, 4000 tons, was torpedoed and sunk by a German submarine on a voyage from Halifax to Liverpool. Among those lost were forty-eight survivors from the American tanker, *Gurney E. Newlin*, which had been sunk two days before.

1942, 21 November. Three hundred miles east of Halifax, Nova Scotia.
The *Empire Sailor* was in convoy when she was torpedoed by a submarine. The explosion released deadly fumes from the phosgene and mustard gas which formed part of her cargo, and twenty-three officers and men died from its effects.

1943, 4 March. Atlantic
The British steamship, *City of Pretoria,* sailed from New York bound for Holyhead and Liverpool, and was hit by torpedoes from the German submarine U-172. She blew up immediately, with the loss of all hands.

1943, 17 March. One thousand miles east of Newfoundland
On a voyage from New York to the Clyde with over ten thousand tons of heavy fuel oil, the whale oil refinery ship, *Southern Princess*, was torpedoed and sunk. Four people lost their lives.

1943, 1 June. Near Passage Island, Lake Superior
The Canadian steamship, *Prindoc*, sank after a collision with the *Battleford* while trading in the Great Lakes. She was bound for Goderich, Ontario, with a cargo of wheat.

1943, 10 June. One hundred miles south-east of Savannah, Georgia
The tanker, *Esso Gettysburg*, 10,173 tons, was bound from Atreco, Texas to Philadelphia with a cargo of nearly 120,000 barrels of crude oil when she was torpedoed and caught fire. The water around was soon ablaze and only fifteen of the seventy-two men on board managed to reach a half-burned lifeboat. They were picked up after nineteen hours by the SS *George Washington*.

1945, 5 May. Narragansett Bay, Massachusetts
The American steamship, *Black Point*, was bound for Boston when she was torpedoed and sunk by the German submarine *U-853*. She sank with the loss of twelve lives. The *U-853* was destroyed by US frigates later the same day.

1946, 5 August. Jacksonville, Florida
The American tanker, *Homestead*, was struck by lightning while lying in harbour with a cargo of gasoline. Fire broke out, and burned for eight days.

1947, 16 April. Texas City
The steamship, *Grandcamp* was loading ammonium nitrate at Texas City when she caught fire and blew up, setting fire to the steamship, *Highflyer*, lying alongside. She also blew up and in turn destroyed the steamship, *Wilson B. Keene*, tearing away the hull of the ship above the waterline. A third of the port was destroyed and five hundred people were killed.

1947, 14 August. Juan de Fuca Strait, Vancouver Island
The 5525-ton freighter, *Diamond Knot*, was bound for Seattle with a cargo which included a large quantity of canned salmon. In thick fog, she was struck by the much larger *Fenn Victory*. Two tugs tried to tow her towards Crescent Bay, but she rolled over and sank. The captains of both ships were found to have been at

fault, and the day after the verdict was announced, the captain of the *Fenn Victory* hanged himself in his cabin. The *Diamond Knot's* cargo was sucked up through a pipeline and three-quarters of the cans were found to be resaleable.

1948, 4 March. Mississippi

The American steamship, *Natchez*, was towing six barges carrying sixty thousand barrels of oil in the Mississippi River when she struck the Greenville bridge and sank. Seventeen men lost their lives.

1950, 15 October. North coast of South Georgia

The Argentine whale oil refinery vessel, *Ernesto Tornquist*, ran aground between Cape Constance and Antarctic Point during a snowstorm. The ship later broke in two. There were no casualties among the 208 whaling factory workers aboard.

1954, 7 October. One hundred and forty miles off Cape Henry, Virginia

The American ship, *Mormackite*, foundered after her cargo of ore shifted during a voyage from Rio Grande to Baltimore and New York. Thirty-six people lost their lives.

1954, *c.* 7 December. Off South Carolina coast

The cargo carrier, *Southern Districts,* left Port Sulphur for Bucksport, Maine, carrying a cargo of sulphur, but after a message from her off the coast of South Carolina nothing more was heard from her.

1956, 25 July. Near Nantucket Island. Massachusetts

The Italian liner, *Andrea Doria*, was bound for New York from Europe and collided in fog with the Swedish ship, *Stockholm*. The *Stockholm* had strengthened bows for dealing with ice and drove deep into the *Andrea Doria*. She stayed afloat for eleven hours and then sank in 225 feet of water. An American coastguard cutter wanted to tow the ship into shallow water, which would have greatly simplified the task of salvage. The ship was foreign-registered, however, and special permission had to be granted for this. By the time the permission had been received, the ship had sunk.

1960, 27 June. Atlantic coast

The American tanker, *George MacDonald*, was bound from Houston to New York with 130,000 barrels of fuel oil when there was an explosion in her engine room. The vessel was taken in tow next day, but sank on 29 June.

1961, 7 November. Houston Ship Canal

The Chinese motorship, *Union Reliance*, was carrying a general cargo, which included vegetable oil, from Los Angeles to New Orleans when she collided with the Norwegian tanker, *Berean*, in the Ship Canal. Explosive chemicals on board the tanker burst into flames, and as the two vessels were locked bow to bow the flames spread to the oil barrels on the *Union Reliance*. The motorship had to be abandoned, and was towed out of the main channel three days later, where she continued to burn until she was completely gutted.

1969, September. Silver Beach, Falmouth, Cape Cod

The oil-barge, *Florida*, broke loose from her tug and was grounded on rocks, with her bottom holed. Twenty-five thousand gallons of diesel fuel polluted beaches and killed marine life over a wide area. Shell-fishing was banned for five years and the oil company had to pay the town of Falmouth a hundred thousand dollars in damages.

1970, 4 February. Chedabucto Bay, Nova Scotia

The Liberian tanker *Arrow*, went ashore here at full speed and in good visibility.

Eleven thousand tons of oil were spilled, the first large-scale oil pollution on the north-east American coast.

1976, 15 December. Nantucket Island, Massachusetts
The steam tanker, *Argo Merchant*, bound from Venezuela to Salem, Massachusetts, grounded on Middle Rip shoal, twenty-seven miles south-east of Nantucket Island. On 31 December she was sunk by cannon fire to stop her becoming a hazard to navigation.

1977, 10 January. Cape Ann, Massachusetts
The American motor tanker, *Chester A. Poling*, split in two in stormy seas and bad visibility. She was bound from New York to New Hampshire. Six men were rescued, one died later and an eighth was presumed drowned. The vessel sank three days later.

South America and the Caribbean

1911, 23 May. Off Punta Mala, Panama
The passenger steamship, *Taboga*, was on her normal run along the coast of South and Central America when she struck a rock off Punta Mala and sank soon afterwards, with the loss of sixty lives.

1914, 26–27 October. Off Maranhào, Brazil
The liner, *Vandyck*, was on her way from Buenos Aires to New York with more than three hundred passengers when she was sighted by the German light cruiser, *Karlsruhe*, and captured. The liner was sunk next day by the German vessel, after the passengers and most of the cargo had been removed. This included over a thousand tons of frozen meat.

1916, 5 March. Off Ponta Boi, Sào Sebastiào, Brazil
The liner, *Principe de Asturias*, ran into thick fog on a voyage from Las Palmas to Buenos Aires and struck the rocks with such violence that several of her boilers exploded and she broke in half. She foundered very quickly and 107 crew and 338 passengers died.

1922, 28 August. Off Coquimbo, Chile
The Chilean steamship, *Itata*, on a voyage from Valparaiso to Coquimbo was wrecked in bad weather. Of the two hundred passengers and crew on board, only thirteen reached shore. Three heavily loaded boats capsized in the heavy seas.

1926, 22 October. Off Bermuda
The sloop, *Valerian*, was caught in a hurricane here while on her way from Nassau to Bermuda. She had been taking the Acting Governor of the Bahamas on a round of visits to the outlying islands of the group. When the hurricane struck her water flooded into the vessel, the engines stopped and the boilers exploded, after which she sank. Four officers and eighty-two ratings drowned.

1927, 25 October. Near Abrolhos Island, off Brazil.
The Italian liner, *Principessa Mafalda*, was bound from the Cape Verde Islands to Rio de Janeiro with 971 passengers and 288 crew, when her port propeller broke. The boilers burst when water entered the boiler room and she started to list to port. The passengers panicked unnecessarily, crowded the boats and even jumped into the sea, turning a mishap into a disaster. The Blue Star steamship, *Empire Star*, was standing by after an SOS message from the liner and picked up as many survivors as she could. Despite this, 314 people were drowned. The ship

remained afloat for over four hours and then capsized and sank.

1930, 23 January. Beagle Channel, Tierra del Fuego

The German motorship, *Monte Cervantes*, struck an uncharted rock near Les Eclaireurs lighthouse and sank next day. She was bound from Buenos Aires to Ushuaia, Argentina, with 1517 passengers and 330 crew. There were no casualties except the captain, who stayed on board and drowned when the ship went down.

1932, 24 August. Off Itacoatiara, Brazil

The Brazilian ship, *Jaguaribe*, was seized by rebels while on a voyage from Rio de Janeiro to Manaos with a cargo of salt and gunpowder. The vessel was later intercepted by the Lloyd Brazileiro steamship, *Inga*, rammed and sunk.

1937, 24 September. Off Atico, Chile

The Chilean ship, *Pudeto*, was bound from Guayaquil to Valparaiso with a cargo of nitrate, cattle and timber when she caught fire after an explosion. She was towed to Atico but continued to burn until she sank on 9 October.

1938, c. 12 March. Near Navarin Island, Cape Horn

The four-masted steel barque, *Admiral Karpfanger*, was built in 1908 as the Belgian training ship, *L'Avenir*, and in the 1930s passed into Finnish hands. In 1937, she was acquired by the Hamburg-Amerika Line and set out for Australia. The outward voyage was uneventful, but when she was homeward bound from Port Germein, South Australia with a cargo of bags of wheat, and a crew of twenty-seven and thirty-three cadets, nothing was heard from her after thirty-two days at sea. The vessel had been recently overhauled and had up-to-date equipment, though the radio generator was known to be faulty. This might account for the fact that no distress signal was heard from her. Much ice was reported in the Cape Horn area, and wreckage from the ship was found at Windbound Bay, Navarin Island. It is probable that she hit an iceberg and sank immediately.

1939, 23 October. Yucatan Channel

The German tanker, *Emmy Friedrich*, 4372 tons, bound from Tampico, Mexico, scuttled herself on being stopped by the British cruiser, *Caradoc*.

1940, 22 May. Valparaiso, Chile

The Chilean steamship, *Chile*, was in a floating dock which capsized in a gale taking the ship with it. She went down in thirty fathoms of water.

1940, 22 May. Valparaiso, Chile

The Chilean ship, *Palena*, was lying at anchor when her cables were cut in a gale by the warship, *Almirante Latorre*, which was torn from her moorings. The *Palena* was driven ashore and broke up quickly.

1941, 21 May. Nine hundred and fifty miles from Cape St Roque, Brazil

The American steamship, *Robin Moor*, 4999 tons, was torpedoed and sunk by a German submarine while on her way from New York to Lourenço Marques.

1942, 18 May. Three hundred and twenty miles east-north-east of Barbados

The American steamship, *Quaker City*, 4961 tons, was bound from Table Bay to Norfolk Virginia with manganese ore when she was torpedoed and sunk by a German submarine. Ten crewmen died.

1942, 11 June. Caribbean

The American tanker, *Hagan*, was torpedoed and sunk by a German submarine on a voyage from Antilla to Havana with 900,000 gallons of molasses. Six crewmen were killed and three wounded.

1942, 12 June. Gulf of Mexico

The American tanker, *Cities Service Toledo*, 8192 tons, was torpedoed and sunk by a submarine between the Mississippi River and Calcasieu Pass. She was carrying 83,000 barrels of crude oil. Fourteen men lost their lives.

1942, 15 June. Caribbean

The American cargo liner, *Kahuku*, was in convoy when she picked up sixty-three survivors from the steamships, *Cold Harbor* and *Scottsburg*, which had been torpedoed. Later that evening the *Kahuku* was hit by a torpedo and the submarine, which had surfaced, opened fire on the steamship, killing the captain and fifteen men, including some of those rescued earlier in the day. The ship sank and survivors were picked up by escorting warships.

1942, 17 August. Off the coast of Cuba

The Egyptian steamship, *Samir*, was torpedoed and sunk by a German submarine on her way from Cristobal to Guantanamo Bay.

1942, 28 August. One hundred and twenty miles east of Jamacia

The Dutch tanker, *Rotterdam*, 8968 tons, was bound from Curaçao to Britain with 12,000 tons of refined spirit when she was torpedoed and sunk by the German submarine, *U-511*.

1942, 10 November. South Atlantic

The cargo ship, *Benlomond*, was bound from Cape Town to Paramaribo, Dutch Guiana (Surinam) when she was torpedoed six days from her destination. She sank quickly and only a Chinese steward survived floating on a raft for 133 days, living partly on provisions and partly on fish and seagulls which he caught. He was nearly dying when he was picked up by a Brazilian fisherman and taken to hospital at Belem.

1942, 15 December. Off the coast of Brazil

The Egyptian steamship, *Star of Suez*, 4999 tons, was torpedoed and sunk by a German submarine here.

1943, 23 May. Off Noumea, New Caledonia, South Pacific

The Panamanian tanker, *Stanvac Manila*, was on her way from Curaçao to Noumea with refined oil and a deck cargo of motor torpedo boats when she was sunk by a Japanese submarine. Eleven lives were lost.

1944, 4 March. One hundred and fifty miles north-west of Hollandia, Surinam

The steamship, *Kayo Maru*, was torpedoed and sunk by the US submarine, *Peto*.

1944, 7 August. Off Santa Catarina Island, Brazil

The Brazilian steamship, *Tiété*, bound from Imbituba to Rio de Janeiro with a cargo of coal, collided with the motorship, *Chuiloide*, and sank soon afterwards.

1944, 12 October. One hundred and fifty miles off Uraguay

The Norwegian motor vessel, *Braganza*, sank after catching fire following an explosion in her engine room. One boat with nine men reached shore south of the Rio Grande. The remainder of the crew in two other boats was lost.

1945, 4 July. North-east coast of Brazil

The Brazilian light cruiser, *Bahia*, built in 1909, was torpedoed and sunk with the loss of 333 crewmen.

1948 1 September. One hundred and fifty miles north of Puerto Columbia

The Honduran ship, *Euzkera*, a converted yacht, was bound from Cuba to Cartagena, Colombia with a cargo which included circus animals when she lost her rudder and capsized. Eight crew and thirty-six passengers lost their lives.

1950, 18 June. Near Tortuga lighthouse, Chile

The Chilean ship, *Lirquén*, had been sold for breaking up, but she had been recommissioned to take five hundred tons of manganese ore from Coquimbo to San Vicente. She struck a reef at Pajaros Rocks and foundered in deep water.

1954, 16 March. São Luiz, Brazil

The Brazilian motorship, *Maria Celeste*, was carrying one thousand drums of paraffin and three thousand drums of petrol when she blew up and caught fire in the harbour, sinking three days later. Thirteen men were killed, and three more were never found.

1957, 28 August. Martin Garcia Channel, River Plate

The Argentine ferry, *Ciudad de Buenos Aires*, collided with the steamship, *Mormacsurf*, and sank in eighteen minutes, with the loss of ninety-four passengers and crew.

1957, 21 September. Atlantic

The four-masted steel barque, *Pamir*, was six hundred miles west of the Azores on a voyage from Buenos Aires to Hamburg with fifty-one cadets, a crew of thirty-five and a cargo of barley, when she ran into a hurricane which blew away her sails. She was driven over on to her side and submerged. Only six survivors were picked up by ships which had answered her call for help. The *Pamir* had been built for the Chilean nitrate trade and made many voyages around Cape Horn before passing on to the Australian grain trade. The *Pamir* and another ship of similar design, the *Passat*, were bought by a group of West German shipowners to form the Pamir-Passat Foundation, an organization created to train officers for the German mercantile marine, refitted and given auxiliary engines.

1960, 22 May. Corral Bay, Chile

The Chilean steamship, *Carlos Haverbeck*, was driven ashore and wrecked here by a tidal wave following an earthquake.

1961, 22 October. St. George, Grenada, British West Indies

The *Bianca C.* was embarking passengers for England when there was an explosion in the engine room and fire broke out. Three men died and 11 were badly burned. The ship was towed from her berth, but sank before she could be taken outside the harbour.

1974, 9 August. Magellan Straits, Chile

The 206,000-ton tanker, *Metula*, went aground here, spilling oil which fouled seventy-five miles of the coast with oil up to three inches deep.

1976, 31 December. Off Bermuda

The motor container vessel, *Rio Haina*, struck the reefs off Bermuda and was holed in her port section. She docked at St. George's with the aid of tugs, where her containerised cargo was off loaded. The vessel sank by the stern.

Africa

1910, 23 October. Paternoster, South Africa.

The Portuguese liner, *Lisboa*, 7459 tons, was on a voyage from Lisbon to Mozambique when she struck the Soldier's Reef, about a hundred miles from Cape Town. The three hundred people on board reached shore safely, except for seven who were drowned when one of the boats overturned as it was being

79 *The wireless room of an Atlantic liner contemporary with the* Titanic. *Radio has never prevented ships from being wrecked but has made it much more likely that people on board a wrecked ship will be quickly rescued.*

No.	Words.	Origin. Station:	Time handed in.	Via.	Remarks.

To   *Titanic*   —H—M / 19—

CQD SOS SOS CQD CQD — MGY

We are sinking fast passengers are
being put into boats

MGY

J. L. Cennor.
J. G. Ward.

80 *The last message received from the White Star Liner,* Titanic, *after she had struck a submerged iceberg in mid-Atlantic on her maiden voyage in April 1912. Shortly afterwards she sank with the loss of 1490 of her total 2201 passengers and crew.*

81 *A contemporary interpretation of the end of the huge liner.*

82 *The luxury liner* Normandie *caught fire and capsized while being fitted out in New York harbour as an auxiliary for the United States Navy in 1942.*

83 *The Italian liner* Andrea Doria *sinking after colliding in fog with the Swedish ship* Stockholm *in July 1956, near Nantucket Island, Cape Cod.*

84 *Five hundred survivors from the* Andrea Doria *were carried back to New York on the* Stockholm, *which returned under her own steam with her bows completely crushed.*

85 *The tankers* Texaco Massachusetts *and* Alva Cape *on fire in the port of New York after a collision, June 1966. Three tugs were also set on fire.*

86 *In December 1976 the tanker* Argo Merchant, *bound from Venezuela to Salem, grounded on Middle Rip shoal, 27 miles south-east of Nantucket Island.*

87 *The four-masted steel barque* Pamir *ran into a hurricane 600 miles west of the Azores in September 1957. Only six survivors were picked up by ships which answered her call for help.*

88 *The 83,000-ton* Seawise University, *formerly the* Queen Elizabeth, *sinking in Hong Kong harbour after catching fire. The cause of the fire remains a mystery.*

89 *The Norwegian steel barque* Gunvor, *wrecked on the Black Rocks, Cornwall, in 1912. The crew managed to get on shore down a rope ladder thrown over the side of the ship.*

90 *The* Lusitania, *sunk by a German torpedo twelve miles off the coast of Ireland on 7 May 1915, on her way from New York to Liverpool.*

91 *A commemorative bronze medal was struck in Germany, the first issue of which was wrongly dated 5 May. (Left) the crowd clamouring for tickets, and (right) the ship sinking by the stern.*

92 *The* Vindictive, *seen after her return from battle on 4 May 1918 in Zeebrugge. Six days later she was deliberately sunk in Ostend harbour.*

93 *The last tense moments of the aircraft carrier* Ark Royal, *sinking off Gibraltar in 1941 after having been torpedoed by a German submarine.*

94 *The 20,235-ton luxury liner* Empress of Canada *on fire at Gladstone Dock, Liverpool, in January 1953.*

95 *The 118,000-ton Liberian tanker* Torrey Canyon *lying half-submerged on the Seven Stones reef on 27 March 1967. In daylight and in perfect visibility she struck the reef at speed.*

96 *The 230,000-ton* Amoco Cadiz *aground and breaking up on the Brittany Coast in March 1978. A large part of the cargo of oil drifted ashore, fouling beaches aver a wide area and causing serious losses to local fisherman.*

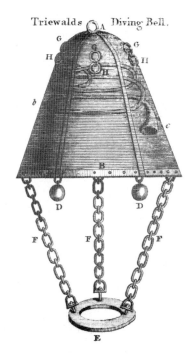

Triewalds Diving Bell.

97 *The first practical diving bell was invented by Dr Edmund Halley in 1717. Martin Triewald, a Swedish military officer, patented his lighter, less expensive diving bell in 1728.*

98 *Divers at work in 1700 using Freminet's apparatus. The men wore face masks with tubes connected to a reservoir of air – a remarkable foretaste of equipment to come.*

99 *Work in progress during the excavation of the* Wasa *in 1961. The ship sank in 1628; she was located with the help of Anders Franzen's underwater core sampler, raised in 1959, and floated into dry dock the following year. Her timbers were in a far better state of preservation than the iron-work, and many objects on board were well-preserved.*

100 *A frogman archaeologist at work on the submerged Kyrenia ship in 1968. Note the amphorae stacked on the left-hand side; there were about 400 of these on board and they were protected from the elements by coverings of woven matting.*

101 *The preserved remains of the Kyrenia ship. These timbers, over 2,200 years old, were recovered in an operation which took eight years to complete.*

lowered. In the first wireless message sent on the South African coast, news of the wreck was picked up by a ship in dock at Cape Town.

1911, 18 April. Cape of Good Hope

The Portuguese liner, *Lusitania*, 5537 tons, left Mozambique for Lisbon and struck the Bellows Rocks when rounding the Cape. She had nearly eight hundred passengers on board at the time, including a large contingent of indentured natives travelling to the cocoa plantations at São Thome. There were only four casualties. The *Lusitania* sank in deep water after being washed off the rocks.

1911, 9 August. Aden

The liner, *Fifeshire* was on a voyage from Melbourne to London with 105 passengers and crew, when she grounded near Cape Guardafui. She was battered by heavy seas and on 11 August the order was given to abandon ship. One lifeboat, containing twenty-four people, was lost.

1916, 27 June. West Africa

The French armoured cruiser, *Kléber*, struck a mine and sank off Cape St. Mathieu. Nearly all the men on board were saved by escorting torpedo boats.

1917, 20 October. Mozambique, East Africa

The British ship, *Ellerslie*, employed as an Admiralty collier, was bound from Cardiff and Durban with a cargo of coal and Government stores for Zanzibar when she was wrecked on Michel Reef.

1917, c. 31 December. Alexandria, Egypt

During the First World War the Royal Mail Steam Packet Company's liner, *Aragon*, 9588 tons, was employed as an auxiliary transport and in December 1917 was bringing reinforcements to the army in Palestine. On arrival at Alexandria she was ordered to anchor outside the harbour and was subsequently torpedoed and sunk by a submarine, with the loss of 610 persons.

1919, 28 June. Ras al Khebba, Oman

The British steamship, *Charles Tellier* 1366 tons, was bound from Port Said to the Arabian Gulf with a cargo of frozen meat when she was wrecked here.

1923, 24 April. Angola, West Africa

The liner, *Mossamedes*, ran aground on the Angolan coast after leaving Cape Town for Lisbon four days before. On hearing a wireless signal the liner, *Port Victor*, went to the scene and found the striken vessel high and dry, but no sign of passengers or crew. The boats had decided to make for Porto Alexandre, but one was lost with twenty-four people on board, and the others were picked up after being at sea for nearly a week.

1928, 17 August. Baleur Bank, Nigeria

The tanker, *Gustave Schindler*, with a cargo of 2972 tons of palm oil in bulk, ran aground on the bank. She was pulled free by a tug, but then sank in forty-two feet of water. She was declared a total loss but the underwriters, having paid up, decided to salvage the oil. A team sent out from England lowered steam coils into the hold to melt the semi-solid oil, pumped it out into boats and transported it to Port Harcout. The divers worked thirty feet deep in the oil.

1928, c. 22 December. South West Africa

The Danish motorship, *København*, left Buenos Aires on 14 December bound for Melbourne. After a wireless message on 21 December nothing more was heard from her. Seven years later the remains of a lifeboat and skeletons were found half buried in sand on the south-west African coast and it is thought these may have come from the vessel. The *Kobenhavn* carried forty-five cadets and fifteen crew.

1937, 29 January. Mozambique, Africa
The British-registered ship, *Baron Polwarth* was bound from Vishakhapatnam to Workington with a cargo of iron ore when she went aground on the Juan de Nova Reef and broke her back.

1939, 15 November. Off Madagascar
The tanker, *Africa Shell*, 706 tons, was sunk by the German pocket battleship, *Admiral Graf Spee.*

1941, 30 March. West Africa
The liner, *Umona*, bound from Durban to London, was torpedoed and sunk by a German submarine, about ninety miles south-west of Freetown. Three survivors were picked up, and a hundred people lost their lives, including the captain.

1941, 20 June. Casablanca, Morocco
The Portuguese-registered steamship *Ganda*, 4333-tons, was torpedoed off Casablanca, on a voyage from Lisbon to Mozambique three hundred miles from land and was taken to Huelva. One lifeboat with twenty-six on board reached Lisbon two days later, and forty-two survivors in a motor lifeboat were picked up by a Spanish trawler.

1941, 17 October. North Africa
The British tanker, *Pass of Balmaha*, 758 tons, blew up and sank when she was torpedoed on her way from Alexandria to Tobruk with petrol, with the loss of all on board.

1942, 16 April. Beirut, Lebanon
The British tanker, *Caspia*, 6018 tons, bound from Haifa to Tripoli with a cargo of seven thousand tons of benzine, was torpedoed and sunk, with a loss of twenty-six lives.

1942, 6 June. East Africa
The steamship, *Susak*, 3889 tons, was on her way from Aden to Laurenço Marques when she was torpedoed, shelled and sunk by a German submarine. Six of her crew were killed by gunfire and one died later.

1942, 14 June. Indian Ocean
The Dutch tanker, *Olivia*, bound from Abadan to Fremantle with nine thousand tons of benzine and kerosene was sunk by Japanese warships about one thousand miles south-east of Mauritius. On 13 July, a boat containing four survivors reached Madagascar, eight men having died on the way. The survivors reported that the Japanese had machine-gunned the boats.

1942, 27 June. East African coast
On a voyage from Aden to Lourenço Marques, the Norwegian steamship, *Goviken*, 4854 tons, was torpedoed and sunk by a German submarine, with the loss of thirteen lives. Some of the survivors were taken on board the British steamship, *Mundra*, and died when that ship was sunk nine days later.

1942, 1 July. Madagascar
The Swedish motorship, *Eknaren*, was bound for Table Bay from Suez when she was torpedoed and sunk by a submarine off the west coast of Madagascar. Five men, including the captain, were picked up by a passing whaler, but survivors rescued by the British steamship, *Mundra*, were lost when she herself was sunk.

1942, 12 September. Two hundred miles north of Ascension Island
The *Laconia* was homeward bound to Britain, not in a convoy, because of her

speed. She had come from Alexandria via the Cape, with four thousand people on board, including 1800 Italian prisoners of war. She was torpedoed and sank within fifty minutes. Many of the survivors were picked up by German U-boats.

1942, 27 October. West of Canary Islands
The liner, Stentor, left Freetown for England, the leading ship in a convoy of forty vessels. Two hundred miles west of the Canary Islands she was torpedoed and sunk by a German submarine. Twenty-one crew and twenty-three passengers were killed.

1942, 30 November. Lourenço Marques, East Africa
The Union Castle liner, *Llandaff Castle*, was sunk one hundred miles from here by a submarine. At the time she was serving as a troopship, mostly employed on the East African coast and the Red Sea.

1942, 21 December. Off Oran, North Africa
The P&O liner, *Strathallan*, converted to a troopship, was torpedoed sixty miles from the African coast, with six thousand soldiers on board. She caught fire and everyone on board was taken off. A fire-fighting crew from HMS *Laforey* fought the flames until it was considered too dangerous to remain on the liner. The ship went down as a result of water entering portholes which had been carelessly left open.

1943, 6 January. Algiers
The *Benalbanach*, bound from the Clyde to North Africa was attacked in convoy by a German aircraft carrying torpedoes. She sank almost immediately, with the loss of fifty-seven crew and 340 men of the Motor Transport section. Her captain died from exhaustion just as he was about to be rescued by a destroyer. The vessel was carrying a cargo of motor vehicles, tanks, petrol, ammunition and general military stores, as well as troops.

1943, 3 March. East London, South Africa
The steamship, *Nirpura*, was in a convoy from Durban, with 737 horses, mules and donkeys on board, when she was torpedoed by a submarine off East London, broke in two and sank.

1943, 19 March. Atlantic
The British steamship, *Lulworth Hill*, was in a convoy bound for the Mersey from Mauritius, when she fell behind and was torpedoed and sunk by a German submarine, about eight hundred miles east of Ascension Island. Forty-three men died, one was taken prisoner and two were picked up from a raft by a British warship on 7 May.

1943, 19 March. Tripoli, Libya
The British steamship, *Ocean Voyager*, was at anchor at Tripoli when she was bombed by German aircraft. The ship caught on fire and her cargo of munitions and aviation spirit blew up.

1943, 27 March. North African coast
The British steamship, *City of Guildford*, bound from Alexandria to Tripoli with a cargo of aviation spirit and munitions, was torpedoed and sunk by a German submarine off the north African coast. Thirteen survived out of a total complement of 140 passengers and crew.

1943, 28 March. Rio de Oro, West Africa
The motorship, *Silverbeech*, was in a convoy bound for Lagos with munitions and explosives when she was sunk by a German submarine. The vessel blew up and sixty-two people were killed.

1943, 1 May. Benghazi, Libya

The 8466-ton tanker, *British Trust* was in convoy off Benghazi when she was bombed and sunk by enemy aircraft. Ten men lost their lives.

1943, 4 October. Algeria

The steamship, *Fort Fitzgerald*, bound from New York to Alexandria, was bombed by German aircraft and set on fire. Five crewmen were killed. The burning vessel was sunk by gunfire.

1947, 1 April. Cape Town, South Africa

The Greek ship, *George M. Livanos*, went aground at Mouille Point near Cape Town, catching fire as a result. She was carrying wool and nickel ingots to Antwerp and Havre from Newcastle, New South Wales.

1952, 22 December. Beirut, Lebanon

The French liner, *Champollion*, bound from Marseilles to Beirut with 108 passengers and 250 crew ran into a sandbank off Beirut in bad weather. Most of the passengers were pilgrims and priests travelling to the Holy Land for Christmas. The vessel began to break up and it was not until the following day that small craft could take off survivors. Fifty people attempted to swim for the shore in their panic, but seventeen drowned in the attempt.

1956, 27 April. Zululand coast, Natal, South Africa

The Portuguese ship, *Luabo*, sank off the coast in heavy seas when her cargo shifted. She was bound from Durban to Lourenço Marques with a crew of fifty-seven. Fourteen men were drowned.

1961, 8 April. Dubai, Persian Gulf

The British India liner, *Dara* was at Dubai unloading cargo and disembarking passengers when a storm hit the port. The ship rode out the storm outside harbour, but while returning to port there was an explosion and she caught fire. Many people jumped overboard in the panic and 238 were burned or drowned. Survivors were picked up by vessels in the area and landed at Bahrain.

1961, 7 July. East Africa

The Portuguese motorship, *Save*, ran on to a sandbank in the mouth of the River Linde during a heavy storm, when she was seeking shelter while on a voyage from Beira to Quelimane. Her cargo included petrol, diesel fuel and explosives, and among her 495 passengers were two hundred African troops. She freed herself next day, but on 9 July fire broke out and she was driven inshore again by gales. Several explosions then wrecked the ship. Sixteen crew and 243 passengers were killed.

1961, 29 September. Malagasy, Madagascar

The Norwegian motorship, *Starcarrier,* caught fire in Diego Suarez harbour and her cargo of dynamite exploded, killing twenty-seven crew and the crew of a tug trying to tow her clear of the berth.

1971, 28 February. Off Cape Agulhas, South Africa

The Liberian tanker, *Wafra*, 28,339 tons, broke down, with complete loss of power, and ran on to a reef. Half her cargo of 63,000 tons of crude oil was spilled into the sea, in an area which is one of the principal breeding grounds for many of the bird and penguin species of the Antarctic. The vessel had to be destroyed.

1977, 2 January. Durban, South Africa

The suction dredger, *Claus*, sank in Richards Bay while berthed alongside the repair quay, before being taken back to the Netherlands on the completion of a contract.

1977, 2 January. Alexandria, Egypt
The *El Giza*, with a cargo of cotton and peanuts, caught fire five miles off Alexandria. The blaze spread quickly and the crew abandoned the ship, which sank two days later.

Europe to the Far East

1915, 23 February. Komuriya Ridge, Ceylon (Sri Lanka)
The British ship, *City of Mysore*, was wrecked here on a voyage from Calcutta to London and Dunkirk with a cargo of jute and tea.

1915, 7 April. Falloden Shoal, near Singapore
The British cargo ship, *Glenroy*, was wrecked here on a voyage from Portland, Oregon, via Vladivostok, to London. She was carrying a general cargo, which included soya beans.

1917, 1 July. Off Baruva, India
The British ship, *Chilka*, was bound from Madras to Rangoon when she caught fire and had to be beached. She was carrying fifteen European and 1600 native passengers at the time, some of whom drowned when they jumped overboard.

1919, 17 January. Syriam Flats, Rangoon, Burma
The British cargo ship, *Glenogle*, was wrecked here while on a voyage from Rangoon to Calcutta with a cargo of rice.

1919, 24 August. Huknang Channel, Yangtze River
The British steamship, *Tamsui*, was wrecked here on her way from Hankow to Swatow with a cargo of beancake.

1921, 3 March. Lamock Island, off Swatow, China
The British steamship, *Hong Moh*, was wrecked on the White Rocks here while on a voyage from Singapore to Arroy with about 1100 Chinese passengers. The British warship, *Foxglove*, took off twenty-eight men before the weather worsened and 230 more were taken off by means of a line from the *Carlisle*.

1923, 6 May. Bay of Bengal
During a cyclone in the Bay the British India cargo steamship, *Okara*, sent out an SOS message but foundered while help was still nine miles away. The crew of eleven Europeans and seventy Indians drowned.

1923, 23 August. Yellow Sea
The British cargo ship, *Mylie*, sank during a typhoon while bound from Chingwantao to Shanghai with a cargo of coal, with the loss of all hands.

1924, 6 June. Ten miles south-east of Hainan Head, China
The steamship, *Yahiko Maru*, was wrecked here during a storm, on a voyage from Haiphong to Hong Kong with a cargo of limestone. Thirty-two people died and three survivors were picked up by a Japanese naval vessel.

1927, 14 July. Fifty miles off the Sandheads, Calcutta, India
The steamship, *Shahzada*, was fifty miles from Calcutta on her way to Akyab with a cargo of coal when she began to sink, going down before the boats could be launched. As she went down some boats broke free from their fastenings and fifty-one survivors in them were picked up by the *Clintonia* and taken to Calcutta. Twenty-one men died, mainly because of the suction caused when the ship went down.

1927, 19 October. East China Sea

The Chinese steamship, *Irene*, was captured by pirates during a voyage from Shanghai to Amoy with 258 passengers and crew. The pirates set a course for Bias Bay but were intercepted by a British submarine, and when they refused to stop a shell was fired into the engine room, setting it on fire. The *Irene* sank two days later. Fourteen passengers lost their lives.

1928, 10 March. Off Cape Inuboye, near Tokyo Bay

The *Kohryu Maru* was wrecked in a typhoon here with the loss of all hands. She was on a voyage from Tacoma to Yokohama with a cargo of timber.

1929, 16 January. Off Wanglan Island, China

The steamship, *Hsin Wah*, was on a voyage from Shanghai to Hong Kong when she struck the rocks here. Panic broke out when the lighting system failed and one of the boats was swamped as soon as it was launched. The lighthouse keepers on Wanglan Island called Hong Kong for assistance, but it was two hours before a tug arrived, by which time the vessel had foundered. Four hundred and one people lost their lives.

1930, 7 July. Off Shantung Promontory, China

The Norwegian steamship, *Dampto*, was sunk in a collision with the *Hoten Maru* in thick fog while on a voyage from Chinwangtao to Shanghai with a cargo of coal.

1931, 5 January. Off Colombo, Ceylon (Sri Lanka)

The Norwegian motor ship, *Tricolor*, was bound from Oslo and Hamburg to Yokohama with a large consignment of chemical products when she exploded. The vessel sank in five minutes, with the loss of six lives.

1931, 21 April. Saddle Island, Heishan Group, China

The Chinese ship, *Hwah Yang*, was attacked by pirates when she grounded on the island. The passengers and crew were rescued by the Chinese steamship, *Kung Ping*, which drove off the pirates.

1931, 9 August. Fuyan Island, near Fuchou, China

The steamship, *Kwong Sang*, was wrecked here during a typhoon while bound from Shanghai to Shan-t'ou with a crew of six British officers and forty-four Chinese. All but three men died and they fell into the hands of pirates. A search was made for the vessel and the destroyer, *Sepoy*, and the Chinese gunboat, *Tung Chi*, landed in the pirate area between Santuao Bay and Funing Bay, rescued the three men and recovered some of the ship's gear.

1932, 13 April. Twenty-two miles north-east of Lungkou Lighthouse

The Chinese steamship, *Tsieh Fa*, bound from Shanghai to Lungkhow, ran on to an uncharted rock and caught fire. She was carrying a cargo of ten thousand small drums of petrol and the ship was totally destroyed.

1932, 2 May. Cape Shantung, near Dairen

The steamship, *Tyne Maru*, on a voyage from Dairen to Yokohama with a cargo of pig iron and cereals, collided with the steamship, *Kirin Maru*, in dense fog and sank with the loss of five lives.

1933, 1 May. Chusu Island

The Chinese steamship, *Yungshin*, was bound from Fuchou to Shanghai when she struck a reef and started to list heavily. The three hundred passengers were put ashore in bad weather and were attacked by pirates, who seized thirteen of them for ransom and then boarded the ship to loot it. An armed Customs cruiser arrived on the scene and drove them off. The ship later broke up.

1933, 10 July. Off South East Promontory, Shantung, China

The Chinese steamship, *Toonan*, was sunk by a collision with the Japanese steamship, *Choshun Maru*, in fog. She was bound from Newchwang to Shanghai with a consignment of silver valued at one and a half million dollars. One hundred and sixty-eight passengers and crew died.

1934, 2 November. Near Mokpo, Korea

The Chinese steamship, *Tung Foo*, foundered during a typhoon on a voyage from Hokkaido to China with the loss of all hands.

1938, 23 June. Near Yochow, Yangtze River

The Chinese steamship, *Kiang Hsin*, was bombed and sunk here by Japanese aircraft. Over a thousand refugees on board were killed. The ship was later raised but was destroyed by bombing at Shanghai on 5 September 1949.

1939, 13 November. Off Singapore

The steamship, *Sirdhana*, struck a mine three miles off shore and sank in twenty minutes. She was carrying a large number of passengers, of whom 137 were Chinese deportees. Twenty Asian deck passengers were killed.

1941, 10 December. Off Padan, Philippine Islands

The steamship, *Takao Maru*, was in service as a transport, carrying troops to the Philippines. The convoy was bombed by aircraft of the US Army Air Force and the *Takao Maru* caught fire and was forced ashore.

1941, 24 December. Manila, Philippines

The French steamship, *Si Kiang*, was confiscated by the Americans at Manila on the outbreak of war with Japan. On 24 December she was bombed and set on fire by Japanese aircraft and burnt for two days, her cargo of petrol adding to the conflagration. Ten crewmen died and eight were seriously injured.

1942, 9 January. Eighty miles south of Tjilatjap

The Dutch steamship, *Van Rees*, was sunk by a Japanese submarine on her way from Tjilatjap to Emmahaven. Six crew members died.

1942, 22 January. Near the Gulf of Martaban, Burma

The steamship, *Chak Sang*, was intercepted by a Japanese submarine, which opened fire and sank the steamship from the surface. Five men died.

1942, 3 February. Java Sea

The British steamship, *Loch Ranza*, was on a voyage from Singapore to Batavia (Djakarta) when she was bombed and set on fire by Japanese aircraft. She was beached and blew up soon afterwards.

1942, 5 February. Off Singapore

The liner, *Empress of Asia*, 16,909 tons, was transporting 2200 troops to the Far East when she was attacked by Japanese dive-bombers. The ship sustained five direct hits and caught fire, later drifting ashore and burning out. The Australian sloop, *Yarra*, took off many hundreds of those on board. Seven were killed and 153 taken prisoner by the Japanese.

1942, 17 February Off Banka Island, Sumatra

The Dutch destroyer, *Van Ness*, was bombed and sunk by Japanese aircraft. She was part of the ill-fated Allied East Indies Squadron which was almost entirely destroyed by the Japanese in February and March 1942.

1942, 6 April. Off Masulipatam, India

The British steamship, *Gandara*, 5281 tons, was bombed by a Japanese aircraft and disabled, while on her way from Calcutta to Suez. She was accompanied by the SS *Dardanus*. Shortly afterwards three Japanese cruisers sank both ships.

1942, 1 May. Pacific

The Russian cargo ship, *Angarstroi*, was torpedoed and sunk by a submarine about thirty-two miles from the Japanese coast. The previous week she had been stopped by a Japanese warship and ordered to go to a Japanese port for examination. The Japanese later denied that the submarine was one of theirs.

1942, 8 May. Two hundred miles south-south-west of Nagasaki, Japan

The liner, *Taiyo Maru*, escorted by naval vessels, was carrying 700 people from the Mitsui industrial organisation, who were to help reorganise the countries of South East Asia seized by Japan, after her entry into the Second World War. The ship was sunk by the US submarine, *Grenadier*, with a heavy loss of life.

1942, 1 December. Timor, East Indies

The Australian fleet minesweeper, *Armidale*, was bombed and sunk by Japanese aircraft off Timor while carrying Dutch troops to the island. About a hundred casualties were reported, including men said to be machine-gunned by the Japanese while swimming in the water.

1942, c. 2 December. South Indian Ocean

The US motorship, *Sawokla*, bound from Calcutta to New York, was sunk by enemy action between 29 November and 4 December. Nothing was heard of her until a crew member was reported to be a prisoner-of-war in Japan.

1942, 29 December. Off Billiton Island, Java Sea

The steamship, *Hachian Maru*, was torpedoed and sunk near here by the US submarine, *Thresher*. She was formerly the *Kinshan*, captured by the Japanese at Hong Kong in December 1941.

1943, 5 June. Indian Ocean

The British India Steam Navigation Company's liner, *Dumra*, 2304 tons, was torpedoed by a Japanese submarine between Durban and Madagascar. The ship was abandoned but did not sink, but then a second torpedo was fired and the vessel began to go down. Twenty-seven people died, including the captain, who was blown into the sea by the second torpedo.

1943, 17 June. Indian Ocean

The Norwegian motorship, *Ferncastle*, was torpedoed and sunk by a German raider while on a voyage from Fremantle to Abadan with a cargo of wheat. She went down about seven hundred miles south of Cocos Island. Two men were killed on board, and another sixteen were never seen again after boarding one of the boats. The other reached Madagascar 30 days later, six of the nineteen men on board having died during the 2800-mile voyage.

1944. Near Manila Bay, Philippines

The Japanese hospital ship, *Moro Maru*, plainly marked with red crosses, illuminated at night, was sunk fifteen miles off Manila Bay in shallow water during the Battle of the Philippine Sea. The Japanese government issued a formal complaint to Geneva about what it alleged was a deliberate act on the part of the United States. American divers sent to investigate the wreck found no serious damage and no bodies. The Captain's full-dress uniform was laid out on his bunk. The Americans concluded that the Japanese had scuttled the ship.

1944, 26 February. One hundred and fifty miles south-east of the Chagos Archipelago

The British motorship, *Sutlej*, 5189 tons, was torpedoed and sunk on a voyage from Kosseir to Fremantle with seven thousand tons of phosphate. The Japanese submarine shelled the sinking ship and the boats in the water. Five survivors were picked up after forty-two days, and eighteen after forty-nine days.

1944, 13 March. Two hundred miles south-west of Karachi
The American tanker *H. D. Collier*, 8298 tons, was bound from Abadan to Bombay with a cargo of 11,600 tons of aviation spirit and kerosene when she was torpedoed by a Japanese submarine and caught fire, burning for three days.

1944, 29 March. Five hundred miles west of Mormugao, India
The steamship, *Richard Hovey*, was torpedoed and sunk by a Japanese submarine on a voyage from Calcutta to the United States. Twenty-five survivors were landed at Karachi, the captain was taken prisoner and forty-five men died.

1944, 14 April. Bombay docks, India
The British steamship, *Fort Stikine*, 7142 tons, was in the docks with a cargo of cotton and 1400 tons of munitions, when she caught fire and blew up. Eighteen merchantmen and three warships were either sunk or badly damaged, and warehouses nearby were wrecked, blazing cotton setting fire to a wide area.

1944, 7 May. Off Kyushu Island, Japan
The Norwegian steamship, *Madrono*, was captured by the Germans and taken to Japan, where she was renamed *Rossbach*. She sailed from Kobe to try and reach a German controlled port in Europe in 1943, but was ordered to return to Japan when she was off the coast of Brazil. She was eventually torpedoed and sunk by the US submarine, *Burrfish*.

1944, 22 September. Fifty miles from Olongapo, Philippines
The steamship, *Shun Yuan*, was formerly Chinese, and was seized by the Japanese. She was subsequently sunk by the US submarine, *Lapon*.

1944, 12 October. Formosa Strait
The liner, *Asaka Maru*, was taken over by the Japanese Admiralty during the Second World War and was used as an auxilliary cruiser. She was bombed and sunk by US carrier-borne aircraft, with an undisclosed loss of life.

1945, 12 April. Off Okinawa, Japan
The United States destroyer, *Mannert L. Abele*, was attacked by a glide bomb and sank rapidly while on a radar picket station off Okinawa. Seventy-nine officers and men died.

1945, 9 June. Off Honshu Island, Sea of Japan
The Japanese steamship, *Hokutu Maru*, was torpedoed and sunk here. She was the first victim of a 'wolf pack' raid by US submarines into the Sea of Japan.

1947, c. 18 April. Andaman Sea
The steamship, *Sir Harvey Adamson* 1030 tons, was lost on a voyage from Rangoon to Tavoy and Mergui. A radio message was received from her saying she could not reach port because of gale-force winds, but no wreckage or bodies were ever washed up. She carried a crew of sixty-four and 205 passengers.

1948, 9 May. T'ung-ch'ou, China
The Chinese steamship, *Chang Hsing*, ran aground and sank here. She was carrying soldiers and horses at the time, as well as passengers.

1948, 2 November. River Lino, near Yingkow, China
The Chinese ship, *Hsuan Huai*, sank near the mouth of the river when her cargo of petrol exploded, with the loss of ten lives.

1949, 27 January. Bonham Strait, north of Chusan Island
The Chinese steamship, *Tai Ping*, was in collision with the *Kien Yuan* while on her way from Shanghai to Keelung with 1500 passengers and a large consignment of

Nationalist Government securities and currency. Both ships sank within fifteen minutes and only thirty-five people were saved.

1949, 23 August. Kaohsiung, Taiwan

The Chinese steamship, *China Victor*, was in harbour unloading her cargo of ammunition when fire broke out on board and the ship blew up and sank. Extensive damage was caused in the port, and some five hundred people were killed or injured.

1951, 15 February. Two hundred miles from Tokyo

The Swedish motor tanker, *Christer Salen*, struck a submerged rock in bad weather and broke in two. Forty-seven survivors on the after part kept afloat and reached Yokohama three days later.

1954, 13 March. Off Khanderi Island, Malabar coast

The Indian cargo ship, *Janaki*, was bound from Bombay to Calicut and capsized. She drifted bottom up for several days before finally sinking off Khanderi Island.

1954, 26 September. Tsugaru Strait, Japan

The train ferry, *Toya Maru*, on her way from Aomori to Hokkaido with passengers and freight cars, dragged her anchors during a typhoon and capsized. She was driven inshore and wrecked outside Hakodate. Seven hundred and ninety-four people lost their lives, and there were 196 survivors.

1956, 2 June. River Meghna, India

The Indian river steamship, *Badora*, was carrying over two hundred passengers and a general cargo from Chittagong to Sandwip when she was sunk by heavy seas off Sandwip Island, with the loss of 194 lives.

1956, 27 November. Three hundred and forty miles south-south-east of Okinawa

The steamship, *Towa Maru*, was carrying a cargo of logs from Mindanao to Osaka when she sprang a leak in bad weather and called for assistance. Ships answering the call could not find the ship in the heavy rainstorms and no bodies were ever found.

1959, 6 October. East China Sea

The Panamanian ship, *Malaya*, sank after her cargo of scrap had shifted and knocked a hole in her side. She was bound from Hong Kong to Kobe, Japan.

1966, 19 September. Hallanuja Island, Indian Ocean

The 134,000-ton tanker, *Mare Nostrum*, ran into rocks at full speed, ripping open all but thirty of her tanks. The crew abandoned her, in the belief that she was breaking up. Dutch salvage experts worked out an ingenious method of saving her, by filling her tanks with compressed air. Prepared in this way and without any further repairs, she was towed the 3400 miles back to La Spezia, Italy.

1972, 9 January. Hong Kong harbour

The 83,000-ton liner, *Queen Elizabeth*, sank in Hong Kong harbour, after catching fire. An enquiry failed to find the cause of the fire, but came to the conclusion it was 'the act or acts of a person or persons unknown'. The *Queen Elizabeth* was commissioned just before the outbreak of the Second World War and started life sailing to New York as one of the world's largest troopships. Hitler offered U-boat captains a reward of about 83,000 pounds and the Iron Cross to the man who sank her. After the war she spent thirty years as the pride of Britain's passenger fleet, retiring to become a floating hotel at Port Everglades, Florida. She was bought by a Hong Kong shipping magnate for conversion into a floating university and cruise liner.

1972, 21 August. Indian Ocean, north-east of Cape Town
The 95,608-ton tanker, *Oswego Guardian*, and the 100,000-ton *Texanita* collided off Cape Town. The Liberian-registered *Texanita*, which was empty, exploded, rocking buildings sixty miles away, broke in two and disappeared in less than five minutes. Both ships were travelling at high speed in thick fog.

1973, 12 March. South China Sea, near Singapore
The Italian oil and ore carrier, *Igara*, hit an uncharted reef and sank. It was at that time the largest marine insurance loss ever recorded.

1975, 30 December. South of Mindanao, Philippines
The 224,000-ton Norwegian ship, *Berge Istra*, sailed from Tubarao, Brazil, to Japan in November 1975, with a cargo of iron ore. After a routine radio call to her owners on 29 December nothing more was heard from her. Two survivors were afterwards picked up, after spending nineteen days adrift on a raft. They reported that the ship had exploded and gone to the bottom in three minutes. They themselves had survived only because they were in a group scraping paint on the bows. She was insured at Lloyd's for 18.2 million pounds.

1977, 23 January. Indian Ocean
The Panamanian motor vessel, *Gulf Star*, bound from Hong Kong to Singapore, sank 350 miles off Singapore. The crew abandoned ship and during this operation the ship's log and documents were lost. The survivors were picked up by the motor vessel, *Strathcarron*, and taken to Singapore.

1977, 2 March. Hong Kong
The triple-decker motor ferry, *Man Tack*, was in collision with the hydrofoil, *Flying Albatross*, while returning to Hong Kong from Cheung Chau, in foggy conditions. The ferry had a hole torn in her side and listed badly. A hundred and sixty-eight survivors were picked up, twenty-one injured and twenty unaccounted for, though there was some confusion about the number of casualties.

1977, 27 November. Shibushi Bay, Japan
The motor vessel, *Tensho Maru*, 2969 tons, was en route from Sandakan to Osaka with a cargo of logs when her deck cargo collapsed, causing a severe list. The ship anchored, but sank in 260 feet of water. The crew were rescued.

Europe

1910, *c.* 24 January. Atlantic
The Dutch steamship, *Prins Willem II*, was lost in the Atlantic during a voyage from Amsterdam to Paramaribo with a general cargo and fifty-three passengers and crew on board. Lifebuoys, oars and a case of varnish from the *Prins Willem II* were washed ashore on the west coast of France nearly two months later.

1910, 5 September. Near Pendeen Lighthouse, Cornwall
The 2660-ton *William Cory* was on her way from Uleaborg to Newport with a cargo of pitprops. In good weather and for no apparent reason she hit the Vynecs off Cape Cornwall and, in an attempt to save her, she was beached further down the coast. The crew got off in the boats, but the ship became a total loss.

1910, 7 November. Off Spanish coast
The British India liner, *Abhona*, 4066 tons, was on her maiden voyage to Rangoon from Plymouth, having completed her steam trials on the Clyde, when she was sighted in difficulties in lat. 44°N, long. 90°W by a Danish steamship,

listing heavily to port. The weather was too bad for the other ship to assist her and the *Abhona* disappeared from sight. From the description of her black funnel with a white ring the Company was certain of her identity, and three weeks later flotsam was washed up off Gijon, Spain. On this voyage she did not carry any passengers, but the crew of ninety were presumed lost.

1911, 25 September. Toulon, France

The French battleship, *Liberté*, was at anchor in the harbour here when she blew up without any warning. When the smoke and flames cleared away the ship was seen to have broken in two. Two hundred and four officers and men were killed and 184 injured.

1911, 13 November. Housel Bay, near the Lizard.

In 1896 the *Aberfoyle* built in Scotland and an unfortunate ship, had been found drifting off the Tasmanian coast, after the captain had been lost overboard and the first mate had committed suicide. On her last voyage, from Sweden to Australia with timber and pig iron, she went ashore on the Cornish coast in a gale. The crew were taken off by breeches buoy and the cargo was absorbed locally. When a salvage party eventually boarded the ship, they found two goats asleep in one of the bunks.

1912, c. 18 January. North Sea

The steamship, *Genoa*, was bound from Hull and Blyth to Riga with a cargo of coal and a crew of twenty-four, when she was caught in heavy gales and sank with all hands.

1912, 8 November. In the English Channel

The P&O liner, *Oceana*, bound for Bombay, sank in fifteen fathoms after a collision. She was carrying 771,000 pounds in bullion in wooden chests. The salvage divers were unwilling to blast their way into the strong room, in case the explosion should scatter the gold inside. They eventually found the strong room keys in a desk in the captain's cabin, but they fitted only three of the five locks. The other two had to be smashed open with an axe. Hoisting the gold up in baskets, the divers rescued all but three thousand pounds of the gold.

1913, 11 February. Off Tcherkess, Bulgaria

The Turkish ironclad, *Assar-I-Tewfik*, built 1867, was used by the Turks in landing operations and coastal fighting during the Balkan War. In stormy weather she stood in too close to cover the landing of some Turkish irregulars and ran on to a submerged rock.

1913, 5 May. The Lizard, Cornwall

The steel barque, *Queen Margaret*, 2144 tons, built in Scotland in 1893, was returning from Sydney with a cargo of wheat. The weather was calm, with no fog, but the captain decided to run the ship close to the lighthouse in order to shout to the keeper. The ship ran on the rocks and was wrecked.

1914, 31 January. Falmouth, Cornwall

The four-masted square-rigger, *Hera*, of Hamburg, was bound for Falmouth from Pisagua, Chile with a cargo of nitrate and twenty-four crew, most of them Scandinavians. The chronometer was faulty and the ship missed the St Anthony light at Falmouth and struck a submerged reef surrounding Gull Rock, off Portscatho. She sank in ten minutes and nine men were left clinging to the mast. The ship's flares had been seen by the coastguards at Portloe, and the Falmouth lifeboat was launched. After great difficulties in finding the remains of the wreck, it was located by the sound of the mate's whistle being blown vigorously.

1914, _c._ 25 August. Gulf of Finland
The German light cruiser, _Magdeburg_, ran aground off the island of Odensholm during an engagement with a small Russian squadron, and was then quickly despatched. The secret signal code of the German navy fell into Russian hands and was subsequently passed to the British.

1914, 5 September. Near the mouth of the Tyne, Northumberland
The steamship, _Runo_, was bound from Hull to Archangel with a large number of passengers, many of them Russian, when she struck a mine and sank twenty-two miles from the mouth of the River Tyne. An enquiry found that the ship had deviated from the course laid down by the Admiralty.

1914, 26 October. Off Cap Gris Nez
The French liner, _Amiral Ganteaume_, was bound from Ostend to Havre with two thousand Belgian refugees when she was torpedoed off the French coast. Most of the passengers were transferred to the steamship, _Queen_, and the vessel was taken in tow and brought into Boulogne. Thirty refugees died.

1914, 30 October. Whitby, Yorkshire
The 7400-ton _Rohilla_, of the British India Line, had been taken over for use as a hospital ship during the First World War, and sailed from Queensferry in the Firth of Forth bound for Dunkirk, with 229 people on board. In a south-east gale she was swept on to a dangerous reef half a mile from Whitby. She broke in half very quickly, the after part being demolished and washed away. No lifeboat crew could row out of harbour and through the surf in the conditions, and the people of Whitby combined in the herculean task of manhandling the smaller of their two boats to the foot of the cliffs opposite the wreck. Here the _John Fielden_ was launched and took off five nurses and twelve men in one journey and eighteen men on a second, before she was declared no longer seaworthy. The Upgang lifeboat was brought overland to the top of the cliffs and lowered down, but the sea was too rough to launch her.

1915, 22 January. Off Antrim, Ireland
The steamship, _Hydro_, was bound from Liverpool to Trondheim with a cargo of cotton, rubber and other goods. Heavy seas washed away the hatches and the boat began to sink, going down off the Giant's Causeway.

1915, 4 April. Longpeak, Devon
The Dutch steamer, _Flora_, 725 tons and built in 1894, was bound from Amsterdam to Swansea in ballast. To protect her against submarine attack, she had her name and port of registry painted in large letters on her side. She met her end from rocks, not torpedoes, however. In fog, she went aground two miles south of Hartland Point. The crew waited for low tide and walked ashore.

1915, 8 April. Cape de la Hague, Channel Islands
The steamship, _Guernsey_ was bound for Southampton with a cargo of flowers and vegetables when she ran on to rocks in darkness and sank rapidly. Because of wartime conditions the warning light on the Cape was not operating. The violence of the impact flung the captain into the water and he was never seen again. Twelve survivors were rescued by the steamship, _Cherbourg_.

1915, 7 May. St George's Channel, twelve miles off south-east coast of Ireland
The Cunard liner, _Lusitania_, was on her way from New York to Liverpool when she was hit by a German torpedo. She sank within twenty minutes in 310 feet of water. 1198 passengers and crew died, out of a total of 1959. World reaction to the sinking was very damaging to the German cause and did much to alienate

neutral countries, as well as to arouse great feeling in the United States. The American millionaire, Alfred Vanderbilt, was among the casualties. There were rumours that the *Lusitania* was carrying gold worth six million dollars, but there was no firm evidence of this.

1915, 1 June. North Foreland area, Kent coast

The British steamship, *Saidieh*, was bound from Alexandria to Hull with a cargo of eight thousand tons of onions and cotton seed when she was torpedoed and sunk by a German submarine near the Elbow Buoy.

1916, 27 February. Off Dover, Kent

The P&O liner, *Maloja*, was bound from London to Bombay with 456 people on board when she struck a mine two miles from Dover and foundered. A hundred and fifty-five people died. The Canadian liner, *Empress of Fort William*, was also mined when she tried to give assistance, but suffered no casualties.

1916, 20 March. Thirty miles from Dutch coast

The Dutch liner, *Tubantia*, 14,400 tons, left Amsterdam, for Buenos Aires with 360 passengers and crew and seven hundred tons of general cargo, which included cheese. Soon after reaching the open sea, she was hit by a German torpedo and sank within three hours. The International Committee of Enquiry at The Hague ordered Germany to pay 800,000 pounds in compensation, but the money was not finally paid until 1922. Salvage companies began work in 1922 and continued until 1931, without finding anything of value. Their aim was two million pounds in smuggled gold, reputed to be packed inside the cheeses.

1916, 2 August. Outside Taranto Harbour, Italy

The 24,000-ton Italian battleship, *Leonardo da Vinci*, was blown up by a German time bomb, hidden in the powder magazine. She sank rapidly and was soon covered by thirty feet of mud. After operations lasting more than two and a half years, she was raised and righted at the end of 1919.

1916, 27 October. Salcombe, Devon

The Salcombe lifeboat, *William and Emma*, was called out to the wreck of the schooner, *Western Lass*, which was ashore in Lannacombe Bay. The crew of the *Western Lass* were saved by a rocket line to the ship, but the message failed to reach the lifeboat, which continued to make its way to the wreck in very heavy seas. On its return to Salcombe, it was capsized by a huge wave and swept out to sea. Only two of the fifteen members of the crew survived.

1916, 21 November. Aegean Sea

The White Star liner, *Britannic*, was taken over for use as a hospital ship and was sailing to Salonika to take on wounded when she struck a mine in the Zea Channel and sank. The mines had been laid only an hour previously by the U-73.

1917, 24 January. Lough Swilly, Northern Ireland

The 15,000-ton White Star liner, *Laurentic*, had been converted into an armed cruiser. Carrying gold ingots from Liverpool to Halifax, Nova Scotia, to pay for food and war supplies, she went round the north of Ireland to avoid German submarines. She struck a mine laid near the mouth of Lough Swilly and sank immediately, with the loss of 354 out of the 745 on board. By 1924, 99.2 per cent of the ingots had been recovered, in more than five thousand salvage dives, without any loss of life or serious injury.

1917, 10 April. Near Le Havre, France

The steamship, *Salta*, was a former French ship taken over by the British

Admiralty during the First World War as a hospital ship. She struck a mine north of the Whistle Buoy and sank with the loss of eighty-six lives.

1917, 28 April. Lyme Bay, Dorset

The P&O liner, *Medina*, 12,350 tons, was completed in 1912 and was put into service between London, the Far East and Australia. She called at Plymouth and then left to complete her voyage to London. Soon afterwards she was hit by a torpedo and sank in less than an hour.

1917, 19 July. Near Portland Bill, Dorset

The P&O liner, *Salsette*, was on her normal run from London to Bombay when she was torpedoed fifteen miles from Portland Bill and sank within five minutes. Her speed had been thought sufficient protection against enemy attack. Thanks to the excellent discipline on board no passengers were lost, and the only casualties were one European and fourteen Indian members of the crew, killed when the torpedo exploded.

1917, 24 November. Saroka Bay, Russia

The 6000-ton *Ulidia* went ashore here in a gale, three hundred miles from Archangel and within the Arctic Circle. The crew and a Russian salvage company failed to refloat her and in July 1919 a British salvage expert arrived. Having hired a Russian tug and crew, he patched the hull with cement, pumped her out and towed her to a small Russian port, where a box patch was put on, held in place by a chain. The Russians intended to confiscate the ship, but this act was forestalled by getting her to sea and bringing her 2200 miles back to England.

1917, 28 November. Off Lynas Point, near Liverpool

The Elder Dempster liner, *Apapa*, was torpedoed by a German submarine while returning home from West Africa. A number of boats were launched in the calm conditions, but a second torpedo struck one of the boats and shattered it.

1918, 24 March. English Channel

Two tankers, the *War Knight* and the *Jennings*, were in a large convoy sailing without lights. The *Jennings*, which had a cargo of naphtha, accidentally cut across the bows of the other ship, which collided violently with her. The naphtha exploded, killing nearly all the *War Knight*'s crew and setting her on fire. A destroyer got a hawser on board her and attempted to tow her to safety but she struck a mine. The destroyer managed to get her into shallow water, with a sandy bottom, and then sank her with gunfire, in the hope that salvage might be possible later. The *Jennings*, too, was taken in tow. At anchor in Sandown Bay, she burnt for ten days until she was sunk by a torpedo. She was sealed by divers, refloated and repaired, and joined another convoy to America. When she was a hundred miles from New York, she was torpedoed again and sank for good.

1918, 10 May. Ostend Harbour, Belgium

The cruiser, *Vindictive*, went into Ostend harbour to try to prevent German submarines from using it. German shore batteries fired at her and she was taken close to the eastern pier, filled with cement and sunk with explosive charges, blocking the channel. The Germans stripped all usable metal from the exposed parts of the wreck, and she was eventually raised by British salvage experts in 1920, beached and presented to the Belgian government as a monument of the occasion.

1919, 8 January. Plymouth, Devon

The schooner, *Fair City*, was carrying stone blocks and china clay as ballast. A wave knocked her on to the breakwater and she became a total loss. The records show that her crew included two naval gunners, although the First World War had ended several weeks earlier.

1920, 9 January. Off St Alban's Head, Dorset

The steamship, *Treveal*, was driven off course in bad weather and struck the Kimmeridge Ledge, lying exposed to the heavy waves. At the time she was bound from Calcutta to Dundee with a cargo of jute and manganese ore. Next morning the captain decided to abandon ship and launched two boats, which were both immediately swamped. Thirty-six men, including the captain, lost their lives.

1920, 11 January. Bay of Biscay

The French liner, *Afrique*, was bound for West Africa when she developed engine trouble in the Bay, and was swept towards the Roche-Bonne Reefs about fifty miles from La Rochelle. Other vessels came to the liner's aid, but could do nothing in the choppy seas, and after striking the reef the *Afrique* sank. Five hundred and fifty-three passengers and crew died.

1921, 1 January. Near Kingswear, Devon

The oil-tanker, *Broadmayne*, bound empty for Newport News, went ashore in thick fog and very rough weather. The Brixham lifeboat could not be launched, but its coxwain and signalman located the wreck, climbed down the cliffs in darkness and talked to the crew, sixteen of whom climbed up the cliffs to safety. The remaining twenty-eight were later taken off by lifeboat. The wreck broke up.

1922, 3 March. Talland Bay, Cornwall

The French steam trawler, *Marguerite*, approaching Plymouth with her catch, ran aground in a gale. The Looe lifeboat, which was normally rowed, was towed to the scene by a motor-lugger and took off the crew, including the captain's ten-year-old son, who had been tied to his father's back for several hours, to prevent him from being washed overboard.

1922, 20 May. Off Armen Lighthouse, Finistère, France

The 7941-ton P&O liner, *Egypt*, was on her way from London to Bombay, when she was rammed by the 1383-ton French freighter, *Seine*. The *Seine* had originally been built as an ice-breaker and her reinforced bows cut so deeply into the *Egypt* that she sank within twenty minutes, settling on the seabed in sixty-six fathoms of water. The *Egypt* had been carrying gold insured for more than one million pounds. Most of it was recovered.

1924, 31 August. The Lizard, Cornwall

The White Star freighter, *Bardic*, struck the rocks near the Lizard Light in fog. The crew got off safely but the salvage ship arrived to find the *Bardic* badly holed and flooded. The wool and beef on board were unloaded, but the wreck had to be abandoned as the gale got worse. Later, however, she was pulled off by tugs and taken into dry dock in Falmouth. A hundred and forty of her hull plates were completely destroyed and much of the interior framing damaged, but she was satisfactorily repaired and put back into service.

1927, 28 October. Point Lynas, Anglesey

The ketch *Excel*, was reported in distress in very heavy seas seven miles north-east of Point Lynas. The lifeboat, *Charles and Eliza Laura*, in a spectacular rescue, sailed right over the waterlogged vessel and snatched the crew of three from the rigging. The lifeboat was damaged and could not get back to Moelfre until the following day. Conditions were so severe that two men died during the night, one of the survivors and one of the lifeboat's crew.

1928, 17 September. Bennan Head, Isle of Arran
The tanker, *Olva*, ran aground here, with a cargo of 5500 tons of benzine. The salvage crew first had to disperse large quantities of benzine that were floating round the wreck and then with compressed air, forced out what remained in the tanks and pumped it into another tanker. The *Olva* was got off the rocks twelve days after going ashore. She was then taken into dry dock at Elderslie.

1929, 6 October. Stanfjorden, Florö, Norway
The passenger and mail ship, *Haakon VII*, struck the rocks here in gale-force conditions travelling at twelve knots. Of the seventy-five people on board, sixty-six survived by climbing on to a narrow ledge of rock, from which they were later picked up by the Norwegian steamship, *San Lucar*.

1929, 7 December. North Devon coast
The 2280-ton collier, *Radyr*, ran into severe storms off the Devon coast and sent out an SOS message which was relayed to the Clovelly and Appledore lifeboat stations. The sea was so rough, however, that neither boat could get to the *Radyr* before she went down, and all twenty-one of the crew were drowned.

1930, 19 December. Off coast of Finland
The Finnish steamship, *Oberon*, left Hangö, bound for Hull with eighty-one passengers and crew. She collided with the Finnish steamship, *Arcturus*, near the Laesö Trindel lightship and sank rapidly. Forty survivors were picked up.

1931, 28 March. Hannafore Point, Cornwall
At the time she was wrecked, the iron-hulled schooner, *Naiad*, was one of the oldest ships still in service, having been built at Llanelly in 1867. She was carrying 110 tons of granite for works at Looe harbour. Anchored off Looe to wait for a pilot, she was caught by a gale, dragged her anchors and finished up on the rocks.

1931, 14 June. Loire estuary, France
The passenger steamer, *St. Philibert*, with 467 passengers and crew on board, left Nantes for a day excursion to the island of Noirmoutier. On the return trip the boat was capsized by a squall and sank with the loss of 368 on board.

1934, 13 February. North Sea
The Russian icebreaker, *Cheliuskin*, 3607 tons, left Murmansk in August 1933, bound for Wrangel Island with a Soviet scientific expedition on board. From September onwards she was caught in the ice and was finally crushed and sank 44 miles from the Bay of Wellen. The crew took to the ice and were eventually picked up by aircraft.

1934, 22 March. Port Jerome, River Seine
The French tanker, *Girafe*, was loading petroleum when an explosion killed twelve men and seriously injured another eight. The tanker sank but was later raised and broken up.

1934, 21 June. Boku Island, Norway
The cruise liner, *Dresden*, struck a rock at Klepp, during a Norwegian cruise and was beached at Blikshavn on Karmøy Island. Shortly after the last passenger had been taken off she turned over and sank.

1935, 18 January. Near St. Ives, Cornwall
The 79-ton ketch, *Cicelia* was built in Jersey in 1867. For many years she sailed the Atlantic in the Newfoundland salt trade, and then came back to Britain as a coaster. On her last voyage, from Lydney to St. Ives with coal, she broke her moorings at the pier at St. Ives, drifted on to the headland nearby and broke up.

1936, 25 April. Near Salcombe, Devon

The four-masted steel barque, *Herzogin Cecilie*, 3242 tons, was built at Bremerhaven in 1902 as a training ship for the Norddeutscher Lloyd line. She was sold to the Finnish shipowner, Gustaf Erickson, in 1921 and then won the annual grain race from Australia eight times in succession. She went aground in Soar Mill Cove, near Salcombe, in thick fog. A few weeks later she was refloated and beached in Starehole Cove, so that her rotting cargo could be unloaded. She broke up in a gale early in 1939.

1936, 1 November. Near St. Ives, Cornwall

The American cargo ship, *Bessemer City*, 5687 tons, was en route to London from the United States via Liverpool. She went ashore during the night at Pen Enys Point, near St. Ives. The crew were taken off by lifeboat and local people took good care of the cargo of tinned peaches and tinned salmon.

1936, 25 November. Baggy Point, Devon

At the time when she met her end, the *Ceres* may well have been the oldest ship still in service. Built in 1811 as a sailing ketch, she operated as a munitions carrier during the Napoleonic Wars. At some time early in the present century she was motorised, although she continued to use sail as well. On her last voyage, she was carrying a cargo of slag from Swansea to Bude. She sprang a leak off the Devon coast, sank about half a mile from Baggy Point and broke up.

1937, 23 January. Dartmouth, Devon

The *English Trader*, 3953 tons, was built in 1934 as the *Arctees*. The steering gear failed as she was entering Dartmouth for bunkers with a cargo of wheat from the Argentine. She ran on to the rocks on the Checkstone Ledge, near Dartmouth Castle. The bow section was cut away and left on the rocks and the rest of the ship was refloated a month later, to allow new bows to be built on. She was finally wrecked in October 1941, when she went ashore at Hammond Knoll, Norfolk.

1937, 1 July. Near St Just, Cornwall

The *Radnor*, 4538 tons, was bound for Hull from West Africa, and her cargo included groundnuts. She ran ashore in thick fog and darkness on the north Cornish coast. The crew were taken off safely, but the ship broke her back and went to pieces. Large quantities of peanuts were washed up on shore and were greatly appreciated by the local inhabitants.

1939, 18 April. Le Havre, France

The French liner, *Paris*, was in harbour here when fire broke out simultaneously in the bakery and on A deck. The following morning she capsized and lay on her side, but art treasures on board for the New York World Fair were salvaged. The wreck was damaged by air attacks in 1944 and she was broken up after the war.

1939, 30 June. Liverpool Bay, North Wales

The newly-launched submarine, *Thetis*, left the builder's yard at Birkenhead to carry out diving trials in the bay. With a crew of forty-four and fifty technicians on board she failed to surface from her first dive. Four men escaped through a hatch by means of Davis apparatus, but then the submarine sank suddenly and the ninety-nine men still on board were drowned. All subsequent attempts to raise her failed. When war broke out later in the year, submarines were urgently needed and the *Thetis* was successfully raised and refitted. Renamed *Thunderbolt*, she served with distinction in the Mediterranean until sunk by enemy action off Sicily in 1943.

1939, 27 July. Near Fowey, Cornwall
The French tanker, *Sunik*, bound from Constanza and Stockholm for Liverpool with a cargo of benzine, was in collision with the Swedish steamship, Grängesberg, twenty-five miles from Fowey. The tanker caught fire and sank later. Twenty-four survivors from her crew were picked up.

1939, 3 September. Rockall Bank, North Atlantic
The British passenger liner, *Athenia*, 13,581 tons, was mistaken for an auxiliary cruiser south of Rockall and was torpedoed by the German submarine, *U30*. About 1300 passengers were rescued.

1939, 18 November. Off Harwich, Essex
The liner, *Simon Bolivar*, was on a voyage from Holland to Paramaribo when she struck two mines and sank by the stern, with the loss of eighty-four lives. She was carrying four hundred passengers and crew at the time.

1939, 13 December. Stadt, Norway
The steamship, *Deptford*, was torpedoed by a German submarine near the Honningsvaag Lighthouse while on a voyage from Kirkenes to England with a cargo of iron ore. She sank immediately, with the loss of thirty lives.

1940, 21 January. Near Toulon, France
The Italian liner, *Orazio*, was reported on fire off the French coast while on her way from Genoa to South America. French destroyers were despatched to the scene and took off forty-eight survivors, while two other liners in the area saved another 391. A hundred and six people died in the disaster.

1940, 14 February. North-east coast of Scotland
The tanker, *Gretafield*, was torpedoed twelve miles east of Wick and caught fire. She was navigated as far as the coast where she was beached and blazed for some days. Eleven men were killed and thirty were taken off by nearby trawlers.

1940, 14 February. Two hundred miles off Land's End, Cornwall
The liner, *Sultan Star*, 12,306 tons, was sunk by a German submarine on a voyage to England with a cargo which included a thousand tons of butter and eight thousand tons of frozen meat. The crew were picked up by a British warship, which chased the submarine and dropped depth charges. After a while the submarine came to the surface, turned turtle and sank.

1940, 8 April. Off Norway
The British destroyer, *Glowworm*, became detached from the main force covering a minelaying operation off the Norwegian coast in a storm and met German landing forces heading for Trondheim. After ramming the cruiser, *Admiral Hipper*, the destroyer was sunk by the German vessel.

1940, 9 April. Oslofjord, Norway
Carrying troops for a landing at Oslo, the German heavy cruiser, *Blücher* tried to force her way up the Dröbak Narrows. After being hit by shells and torpedoes of the Norwegian defences she capsized, with heavy loss of life.

1940, 29 May. Off Dunkirk, France
The paddle-steamer, *Gracie Fields*, was taken over by the Admiralty during the Second World War for duties as a minesweeper. She was engaged in the evacuation from Dunkirk when she was sunk by German aircraft.

1940, 2 July. Seventy-five miles off Bloody Foreland, Ireland
The Blue Star liner, *Arandora Star*, was carrying 1178 German and Italian internees to Canada, together with 254 troops and 176 crew, when she was torpedoed and sunk by a German submarine. Panic broke out and many were

forced overboard and drowned. Six hundred and thirteen internees lost their lives.

1940, 24 July. Off Portland, Dorset
The French liner, *Meknes*, 6127 tons, left Southampton with 1281 French sailors on board. France had capitulated the previous month, and the seamen were being repatriated. Although her marking were unmistakable, she was intercepted by a German torpedo boat, which opened fire. The *Meknes* stopped her engines, identified herself and waited for the torpedo boat to acknowledge her, but instead was torpedoed and sank in ten minutes. Eight hundred and ninety-eight survivors were taken to England.

1940, 26 July. Off the west coast of Ireland
The Elder Dempster liner, *Accra*, was on her way to West Africa in convoy when she was torpedoed by a German submarine and sank in thirty minutes. A Norwegian vessel stood by at great risk to herself and picked up 137 survivors, and 313 got away in boats.

1940, *c.* 11 December. Three hundred miles west of Orkney Islands
The Swedish motorship, *Stureholm*, became detached from a convoy travelling from Boston and Halifax to Grangemouth with a cargo of steel, and was presumed to have been sunk by an enemy submarine, with the loss of all hands.

1941, 21 January. Three hundred miles west of Inishtrahull, Northern Ireland
The British steamship, *Temple Mead*, bound from Rosario to Britain with a cargo of grain, was bombed and sunk by German aircraft with a loss of fourteen lives.

1941, 10 February. North Atlantic
The steamship, *Brandenburg*, was torpedoed and sunk by a German submarine while in convoy some hundreds of miles west of Portugal. The entire crew of twenty-four lost their lives, together with thirty survivors from the steamship, *Courland*, sunk the previous day.

1941, 13 March. River Mersey, England
The steamship, *Ullapool*, was struck by a parachute mine while she lay off Princes Stage in the Mersey. She broke in two and sank with the loss of sixteen lives.

1941, 26 May. Crete
The Greek steamship, *Rokos*, was driven ashore and wrecked in Suda Bay after being bombed by German aircraft during the invasion of Greece.

1941, 19 August. Gulf of Finland
The Russian motorship, *Sibir*, fitted out as a hospital ship, was set on fire by German aircraft and sank with the loss of 400 of the 1300 on board.

1941, 21 September. Thames estuary
The tanker, *Vancouver*, struck a mine, broke in two and caught fire near the Sunk Lightship, while on a voyage from Halifax to Shell Haven with 7500 tons of gasoline. Thirty-nine crew members died and the tanker burned for several days.

1941, 14 November. Off Gibraltar
The aircraft carrier, *Ark Royal*, 22,000 tons, was returning to Gibraltar after a cruise in the Mediterranean when she was torpedoed by a German submarine. She was taken in tow but she was badly holed below the waterline and sank twenty-five miles east of Gibraltar. The crew were transferred to a destroyer.

1942, 24 February. The Bosphorus, Turkey
The Bulgarian steamer, *Struma*, sailing under the Panamanian flag with 764 Jewish refugees on board, was sunk by the Soviet submarine, Shch-213, north of

the Bosphorus. Only one refugee survived. The ship had set out from Constanza with 769 refugees and had not been allowed to land them on Turkish soil 'because the British mandatory government in Palestine did not grant immigration visas'. On 24 February the Turkish authorities forced the ship to put to sea.

1942, 24 March. Murmansk, USSR

The steamship, *Lancaster Castle*, was part of a convoy to Northern Russia, and was attacked by German bombers as she lay at anchor at Murmansk. She was set on fire and badly damaged, but remained afloat until 15 April, when she was again attacked and sunk. Twelve men were killed and seventeen were wounded.

1942, 29 March. North Sea

The Panamanian steamship, *Bateau*, was torpedoed and sunk by German destroyers on her way from Iceland to Murmansk, USSR. Forty men died, and six survivors were picked up by the destroyers.

1942, 9 June. Mediterranean

The Swedish steamship, *Stureborg*, was chartered by the Swedish Red Cross to carry food supplies to Greece, and was on her way from Piraeus to Haifa when she was bombed and sunk by aircraft. One survivor on a raft reached Gaza nineteen days later.

1942, 24 September. Near Iceland

The Belgian steamship, *Roumanie*, was torpedoed and sunk by a German submarine off the coast of Iceland while on her way from Halifax to Loch Ewe. Thirty-seven crew and six gunners died.

1943, 1 April. Off Gothenburg, Norway

The Norwegian motorship, *Storsten*, was bombed by German aircraft and a patrol ship while trying to escape to England. The crew opened the seacocks and abandoned ship, seventeen of them being killed during the battle.

1943, 10 July. Sicily

The British steamship, *Talamba*, was in service as a hospital ship when she was bombed and sunk by a German aircraft three miles from the anchorage at Avola. All 400 wounded on board were taken off safely.

1943, 25 July. Syracuse Harbour, Sicily

The motor vessel, *Fishpool*, was lying in harbour, loaded with a thousand tons of aviation spirit and four thousand tons of munitions, when she was bombed and set on fire by enemy aircraft. The vessel blew up and sank.

1944, 14 August. Brest

The German Government tanker, *Sudetenland*, was sunk by Allied aircraft at Brest. She was formerly the Canadian vessel, *Canadolite*, and had been captured by German raiders in the North Atlantic on 25 March 1941.

1944, 7 September. Off Trieste, Italy

The liner, *Rex*, 51,062 tons, was used as a blockship outside Trieste harbour. She was attacked by British aircraft there, caught fire and was completely wrecked when she ran ashore. The *Rex* was built with the object of gaining the 'Blue Riband' of the Atlantic and in 1933 she made the fastest west bound passage of four days thirteen hours fifty-eight minutes.

1944, 14 October. Near Honningsvaag, North Norway

The whale oil refinery ship, *Südmeer*, was torpedoed and sunk here by Russian aircraft.

1944, 10 November. Off Vestmann Islands, Iceland

The British tanker, *Shirvan*, was bound from Bowling to Reykjavik with a cargo of 7500 tons of motor spirit when she was torpedoed and sunk by a German submarine 150 miles from the Vestmann Islands with the loss of eighteen lives.

1945, 11 February. Bigbury Bay, Devon

The 5030-ton *Persier* was built at Newcastle in 1918. In 1940 she took part in the evacuation from Dunkirk. She then went to New York to collect a cargo of steel. On her return voyage, she was attacked and hit by German aircraft while she was at anchor off Oban. She was patched up, but on her next voyage, to Baltimore with scrap iron and steel, she sprang several leaks as a result of bomb damage to her hull. Sailing back in convoy, she fell behind as a result of having to slow down to seal leaks. Her cargo shifted, her steering-gear broke down, three of her lifeboats were smashed and her electrical system failed. She was beached in Iceland and in 1942 was towed back to England for repairs. Back in service, she completed five more voyages and was selected for sinking as a blockship off the Normandy beaches, but the orders were reversed and she became a merchant ship again. In 1945, she was torpedoed off Cornwall, with a cargo of soap and foodstuffs for Belgium, eventually going down in Bigbury Bay.

1945, 18 April. Off Bay of Biscay

The 8028-ton tanker, *Empire Gold*, was carrying a large cargo of white spirit when she was torpedoed by a German submarine. She broke in two, caught fire and sank with the loss of five gunners and thirty-eight of her crew of forty-two.

1947, 23 April. Mount's Bay, Cornwall

The 27,000-ton battleship, *Warspite*, went aground on a reef off Prussia Cove while being towed to Clydeside from Portsmouth to be broken up. She had been launched in 1915, taken part in the Battle of Jutland, and in the Second World War had been Admiral Cunningham's flagship at the Battle of Matapan. The *Warspite* ended her days beached on St. Michael's Mount, being slowly broken up for scrap.

1947, 23 April. Porthcawl, Wales

The British steamship, *Samtampa*, was wrecked at Sker Point on a voyage from Middlesborough to Newport in ballast, with the loss of all hands. The Mumbles lifeboat capsized trying to reach the ship, and her crew were drowned.

1949, 31 October. Baltic Sea

The East German cargo ship, *Hansa*, 2800 tons, was on a voyage from Rostock to Tallinn with a cargo of sugar when she found herself in the middle of Soviet navy manoeuvres. She was boarded by two Russian officers and while they were on board the ship was hit by two torpedoes and sank. Four of the crew of fifteen were rescued, but the dead included the two Russians.

1952, c. 22 December. West of the Hebrides, Atlantic

The German motor cargo ship, *Melanie Schulte*, was bound from Narvik to Mobile with a cargo of iron ore, when she met bad weather off the coast of Scotland and all contact with her was lost. On 17 February 1953, one of the ship's lifebuoys was washed ashore on Benbecula Island.

1953, 16 April. Menai Straits, North Wales

The training ship, *Conway*, was wrecked on the Swillies, near the Menai Bridge, as she was being towed to Liverpool for dry docking. The *Conway* was one of the last of the old 'wooden walls'. Built originally as HMS *Nile*, she had been stationed off Rock Ferry as a training ship for Merchant Navy cadets. In 1940, during the German blitz on Liverpool, she had been towed to the Straits for safety. After grounding, she broke her back and while she was being moved by a firm of salvage contractors she caught fire and burnt to the waterline.

1955, 19 February. Genoa, Italy
The Swedish motorship, *Nordanland,* was in the harbour here when she smashed against the quay and began to leak. Two days later her cargo of calcium carbide exploded, and a further explosion on 11 March wrecked the ship completely.

1955, 16 June. Portland Harbour, Dorset
A torpedo inside the hull of HMS submarine, *Sidon,* exploded. The ship was sunk and thirteen men killed.

1957, 18 June. Off Ushant
The Liberian tanker, *Stony Point,* 10,506 tons, was bound from Sidon to Antwerp with a cargo of oil when she collided with the Greek motorship, *Ioannis,* loaded with potash, in thick fog. Both vessels caught fire. Fourteen men were killed and many more seriously injured.

1957, 20 August. Off Gibraltar
The Liberian tanker, *World Splendour,* 25,583 tons, bound from Fawley to Mena al Ahmadi, caught fire after two explosions. The fire was eventually put out and next day the tanker was taken in tow, but sank before reaching port. Seven crewmen died.

1959, 23 August. Off Flamborough Head, Yorkshire
The British trawler, *Staxton Wyke,* was in collision with the *Dalhanna* on her return journey to Hull from the Icelandic fishing grounds. She sank with the loss of five of her crew of sixteen.

1959, 6 September. Gironde estuary, France
The Spanish steamship, *Tarragona,* sank after an explosion in her engine room, with the loss of thirteen lives. She was bound from Gijon to Bordeaux with a cargo of pyrites.

1960, 24 August. Off the south coast of Spain
The Lebanese ship, *Halcyon Med,* was cut in two after a collision with the *Esso Switzerland* and both parts of the vessel sank within twenty-four hours.

1960, 14 December. Bosphorus, Turkey
The Greek tanker, *World Harmony,* 20,992 tons, collided with the Yugoslav tanker, *Petar Zoranic,* loaded with benzine and petrol, both vessels catching fire. They drifted on to the Turkish steamship, *Tarsus,* and all three ships were eventually totally destroyed, with a loss of fifty-two lives.

1961, 18 October. Twenty miles off Flamborough Head
The Hull trawler, *Arctic Viking,* was returning from the White Sea when she met a gale north-east of Flamborough Head and capsized. The vessel floated bottom up for some hours, then sank by the stern. Fourteen men escaped on rafts and were later picked up by the Polish trawler, *Derkacz,* which brought them into Hull.

1962, 7 January. Off Dover, Kent
The Yugoslav steamship, *Sabac,* was in collision with the British motorship, *Dorington Court,* in dense fog six miles off the Kent coast. She was badly holed and sank almost immediately. The *Sabac* was bound from Ploce to Rotterdam with a cargo of bauxite.

1967, 18 March. Seven Stones Reef, Cornwall
The 118,000-ton Liberian tanker, *Torrey Canyon* was bound for Milford Haven from the Persian Gulf with 120,000 tons of crude oil. In daylight and with perfect visibility she hit the rocks at speed. Attempts to pull her off failed, she broke in

three sections, with appalling pollution over a wide stretch of coast. She was bombed and set on fire from the air. The coast-clearing operation cost nearly two million pounds. The main cause of the wreck appears to have been the captain's anxiety to meet his timetable. To avoid missing the tide at Milford Haven, he attempted to take a short cut.

1968, 31 October. Adriatic

The 1134 ton Dutch ship, *Oostmeer*, was carrying steel billets from Belgium to Monfalcone, on the Adriatic. She was new and recently surveyed. After passing Gibraltar and being last seen off Cape Bougaroni, all trace of her was lost. She apparently foundered in a gale in the lower Adriatic.

1969, 24 March. Off the coast of the Peloponnese

The Turkish tanker, *Aygaz*, was proceeding to Italy to pick up a cargo of crude oil and was caught in a storm off the coastal islands along the Peloponnese. Another ship reported her as apparently being in trouble and on 26 March she was discovered overturned, with no sign of her crew. She was towed into Pylos harbour, where cries were heard coming from the inside of the hull. Naval frogmen cut a way in and pulled out four bodies and one man still alive. They had been trapped in the engine room when the ship overturned.

1970, 5 May. Muxieirio Point, Bay of Vigo, Spain

The 50,000-ton Norwegian tanker, *Polycommander*, with a full load of crude oil, ran aground and burst into flames here on the Spanish Atlantic coast. The burning oil created a 'fire-storm', which caused a black, oily rain to fall over a wide area, causing extensive damage to crops and killing livestock. The crew of forty were taken off safely, but a Spanish fishing boat, approaching the wreck, caught fire, killing all on board.

1970, 24 October. Off the Isle of Wight

The 42,000-ton tanker, *Pacific Glory*, and the 46,000-ton *Allegro*, both fully loaded, collided. *Pacific Glory* exploded and was burnt out, with the loss of thirteen lives. A number of the officers on both ships were afterwards shown to have had no certificates.

1971, 11 January. English Channel, off Folkestone

The 12,000-ton Peruvian freighter, *Paracas*, took the wrong lane down the Channel and collided with the tanker, *Texaco Caribbean*, which exploded, shattering windows five miles away in Folkstone. Nine of the tanker's crew were killed. The site of the wreck was immediately marked with lights, but the next day the German freighter, *Brandenburg*, hit the wreck and sank. A lightship and extra light buoys were added to the site, but on 28 February the Greek freighter, *Niki*, hit the wreck and sank, with the loss of her entire crew.

1971, 3 March. Berry Head, Torbay, Devon

The Liberian-registered tanker, *Trinity Navigator*, carrying 32,000 tons of oil, ran aground, but was fortunately refloated five hours later. The Channel pilot who supervised the operation reported that the ship's radar was out of order, that she had no VHF radio and that the Chinese crew spoke no English.

1971, 4 April. Goodwin Sands, Kent coast

The Liberian tanker, *Panther*, carrying 25,000 tons of oil, grounded here. She was freed two weeks later by tugs. The pilot who boarded her reported her radar out of order.

1972, 5 November. Land's End. Cornwall

The Cypriot motor vessel, *Nefeli*, lost her rudder after striking Kettles Bottom in

146

dense fog after fire had put her radar out of action. She drifted ashore in Dollar Cove, right on top of the wreck of the *La Varenne*. The crew of eleven were rescued, but the ship went to pieces by the end of the month.

1976, 27 December. Bosphorus, Turkey

The motor bulk carrier, *Lok Prabha*, sank after colliding with the motor vessel, *Matesesta*. She broke in two and each part sank seperately in 275 feet of water.

Appendix 1
Wrecks and the Law

The principal authority on the law relating to shipping in all its aspects is C. J. Colombos, *International Law of the Sea*, 6th ed, London, Longman, 1976.

The law distinguishes between a wreck, which is the loss of the ship herself, and wreck, which is 'property cast ashore within the ebb and flow of the tide after shipwreck'. In common law, such property is not wreck so long as it remains floating on the sea; it becomes wreck once it has been cast up on the shore or deposited on the bottom of the sea within the territorial waters of a particular country. It is not easy to establish long-term, let alone perpetual rights to the cargo or structure of a wrecked ship, but if it can be shown that the insurers or their agents are taking active steps to recover goods from a wreck, they can usually rely on the courts to protect their interests against outsiders.

The law regarding ownership and salvage is similar throughout the world. Where a ship is wrecked, stranded, or in distress at any place on or near the coast a local official is placed in charge of operations. He has powers to require the assistance of any person necessary, or the use of any vessel near at hand, or of any vehicle. He may legally pass over adjoining lands for the purpose of rendering assistance and may use armed force to suppress any disorder or plunder of the vessel. The local official, the Receiver, must pass over the property to the owner, provided he establishes his claim satisfactorily within a year. A receiver may sell any perishable goods and hand over the proceeds to the owner. Except in cases where a grant has been made to any other person, all unclaimed wreck belongs to the State. It may be sold and the proceeds paid to the national treasury. Plundering a wreck is punishable as a felony.

Freebooting divers may be restrained in two ways, first by the insistence of governments that no salvage work or diving is to be carried out in their territorial waters without their express permission and without strict safeguards as to what is to happen to any discoveries, and second, by the decision of particular governments to support an international code of practice relating to underwater archaeology. It is fair to say that most underwater archaeology at the present time is reputable and legal, although there are certainly pirates and criminals in it.

A case of great importance was decided in connection with the steamship, *Schiller*, wrecked near the Bishop Rock in 1875, when she was carrying, among other items of cargo, specie to the value of three hundred thousand dollars. Two years later, Lord Justice Brett was required to decide whether this part of the cargo could be construed as 'wreck', or whether it belonged, in fact, to those who had attempted to save the crew, passengers and cargo before the ship went down, and who might therefore have established a claim to what they asserted was 'wreck'. Lord Justice Brett referred to the Merchant Shipping Act 1854, which declared that 'wreck shall include jetsam, flotsam, lagan and derelict found in or on the shores of the sea or any tidal water', and which went on to say:

Flotsam, is when a ship is sunk or otherwise perished, and the goods float on the sea. Jetsam, is when the ship is in danger of being sunk, and to lighten the ship the goods are cast into the sea, and, afterwards, notwithstanding, the ship perish. Lagan (*vel potius* ligan) is when the goods are so cast into the sea, and afterwards the ship perishes, and such goods cast are so heavy that they sink to the bottom, and the mariners, to the intent to have them again, tie to them a buoy or cork, or such other thing that will not sink, so that they may find them again.

Lord Brett ruled:

This specie never was within any of those definitions, and even if it were, would be taken out of them by the fact of its being in the possession of the owner before it was or would be taken possession of by any one else. . . . This specie was once 'derelict' but ceased to be so the moment the true owners of it resumed the exercise of their rights of ownership and began to endeavour to recover it, whilst no one else was endeavouring to save it.

This appears to have settled the point for all those cases in which the ownership of a ship or its cargo is clear and beyond doubt. It may well be, however, that, especially in the case of a ship which was wrecked a long time ago, the owners no longer exist and their title has not passed to any discoverable person. In that case, what remains of either the ship or its cargo can usually be presumed to belong to the government in whose territorial waters it is to be found, and that government may or may not be willing to give an individual or an expedition permission to carry out diving or salvage. Even if such permission should be given, it is extremely unlikely, in the present climate of opinion, that, as 'cultural property', any material of archaeological importance would be allowed to leave the country. The best that the marine archaeologist can usually hope for nowadays is the opportunity to make a reputation. The days when he might dream of making a fortune as well have almost gone, assuming, of course, that he remains within the bounds of the law.

Appendix 2
Some Notable Achievements by Underwater Archaeologists

The first excavation and restoration of an ancient ship which can be considered in any way methodical was carried out in 1863 by a Danish archaeologist, Conrad Engelhardt. Engelhardt was not required to dive; he recovered the fourth-century Nydam ship from a peatbog in Slesvig. His success was followed soon afterwards by the discovery and conservation of the ninth-century Viking ships from Gokstad and Oseberg in Norway and, in the present century, by similar no-diving archaeological work on such sites as Sutton Hoo and Lake Nemi. For this type of work, archaeologists were able to use techniques already developed on other kinds of dry-land sites.

Until the 1940s, such work as had been carried out on underwater wrecks had been limited to little more than surveying and haphazard salvaging of objects. No thorough *in situ* examination had been found possible and no detailed, accurate recording had taken place. The situation was completely changed in 1943 by Jacques Cousteau's development of the aqualung, a portable breathing device which gave the diver complete freedom of movement under water. This relatively simple apparatus allowed diving to be de-professionalised and within a few years created a body of several hundred people, all more or less expert, who were able to find their way around under the water, to stay there for considerable periods, and to work there. Two areas were particularly popular, the Mediterranean and the Caribbean. Until recently, the Mediterranean has been the main centre of archaeologist-divers, the Caribbean for treasure-hunting archaeologists. The entry of the serious archaeologist into the Caribbean is a welcome development of the past ten years.

The scientific techniques made possible by the aqualung took some years to work out and apply. In 1948, Cousteau and his team discovered a Roman ship off Mahdia, in Tunis, by this means, but soon moved over to the other side of the Mediterranean, where they located and worked on the second-century BC ship at Grand Congloué, using a water-gun to clear mud and sand from the wreck. Here and at La Chrétienne a little later, the archaeologists were learning new methods and getting used to the excitement of having new tools, such as the suction pipe used to remove debris. Their recording system remained very crude, however. They were using the aqualung to help them to find wrecks and to bring up materials from the site, but their treatment of the site itself was clumsy and cavalier to an extent which no land-archaeologist of the period could possibly have tolerated.

The first underwater wreck to be properly investigated from an archaeological point of view was that of the Bronze-Age ship at Bodrum, in Turkey, from 1959 onwards, with George Bass of the University of Pennsylvania in overall charge, Frédéric Dumas as chief diver, Joan du Plat Taylor, of the Institute of Archaeology in London, as chief conservator, and Peter Throckmorton as technical adviser. Bass insisted on a very high standard of recording, using a steel-grid plotting frame laid on the sea-bed, or where the ground was too rough for this, triangulation. The position of everything found was marked by the divers on sheets of plastic and from these sheets it was possible to make a complete and accurate photographic montage of the site, the first time this had been done and the first deliberate attempt to raise the standard of underwater recording to something comparable to what was normally achieved by land-archaeologists.

Two other Mediterranean wrecks allowed the techniques of underwater archaeology to be considerably refined and improved. The first, the Yassi Ada wreck, found off the south coast of Turkey, sixteen miles from Bodrum, was surveyed and excavated by a team from the University of Pennsylvania, again led by George Bass, during four seasons of work in 1961–64. There were fifteen specialists on the site, which had a large barge moored over it as a base of operations. The ship had settled down at a depth of 120 feet and it was heavily encrusted with weed, which had to be removed before recording could begin. Nine hundred amphorae were visible and each was numbered for photographing where it lay. Wire grids were laid over the wreck. Artists hovering over the wreck made drawings on sheets of plastic of whatever lay below them and, once this had been done, the amphorae themselves were lifted off. The remainder of the wreck was then plotted, recorded and removed, layer by layer, until the hull itself was reached. This was photographed, stage by stage, by placing a camera on nine towers made from angle-iron along the length of the ship. While this was being done, every piece of timber was spiked to the sea-bed with more than two thousand sharpened bicycle spokes.

The second excavation which has become a classic was at Kyrenia in Cyprus. It was carried out during 1967–69 by Michael and Susan Katzev, who were also from the University of Pennsylvania and who had learned the job while working on the Yassi Ada project. They laid down a cord grid over and around the pile of amphorae which marked the site of the wreck and by working over this with a proton magnetometer and a metal detector established the outline of the ship. Everything discovered was meticulously recorded and it was then decided to lift the hull and to transfer it to Kyrenia Castle for conservation. In order to do this, the wreck had to be cut up into sections small enough to go through the doorway of the castle. This was done by means of a compressed-air underwater saw. Before this happened, however, photogrammetry was used to record the shape of the hull on the sea-bed. A study of the timbers showed how the planks had been mortised together, with the outside of the hull sheathed with lead fixed on with copper nails. The wood was dated by radio-carbon tests as 389 BC ± 44, but the cargo of almonds gave quite a different date, 288 BC ± 62, showing that the ship was probably about eighty years old when she was wrecked.

As a result of this pioneering work carried out in the Mediterranean during the twenty years between 1947 and 1967, the science of underwater archaeology was established on a sound basis by the beginning of the 1970s. It will certainly be transformed during the next few years by new techniques such as midget submarines and underwater television, which will greatly simplify the task of locating wrecks, and by methods which will make it possible for men to work for much longer periods on the site and at much greater depths.

Maps

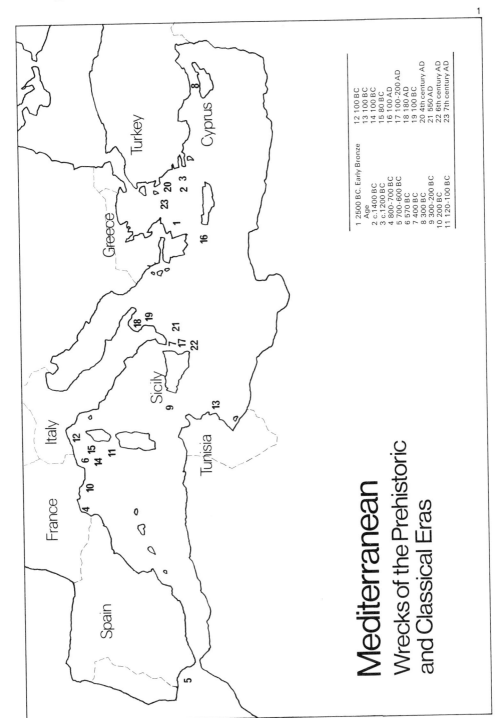

Mediterranean
Wrecks of the Prehistoric
and Classical Eras

France
Italy
Spain
Tunisia
Sicily
Greece
Turkey
Cyprus

1 2500 B.C. Early Bronze
  Age
2 c.1400 BC
3 c.1200 BC
4 800-700 BC
5 700-600 BC
6 570 BC
7 400 BC
8 300 BC
9 300-200 BC
10 200 BC
11 120-100 BC

12 100 BC
13 100 BC
14 100 BC
15 80 BC
16 100 AD
17 100-200 AD
18 180 AD
19 100 BC
20 4th century AD
21 550 AD
22 6th century AD
23 7th century AD

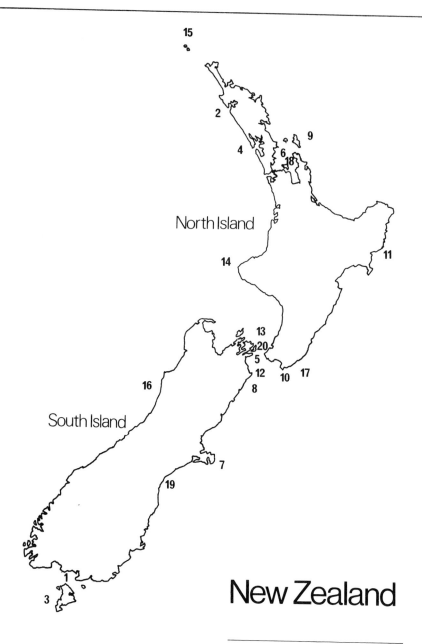

North Island

South Island

New Zealand

1 *Lynx*, 1837
2 *Osprey*, 1846
3 *Emilie*, 1890
4 *Northern Star*, 1893
5 *Torva*, 1909
6 *Tauranga, Enterprise*, 1870
7 *Clyde*, 1884
8 *Taiaroa*, 1886
9 *Wairapa*, 1894
10 *Zuleika*, 1897

11 *Tasmania*, 1897
12 *Ohau*, 1899
13 *Timaru*, 1902
14 *Ventnor*, 1902
15 *Elingamite*, 1902
16 *Penguin*, 1909
17 *Kairaki*, 1914
18 *Ripple*, 1924
19 *Niagara*, 1940
20 *Holmglen*, 1959

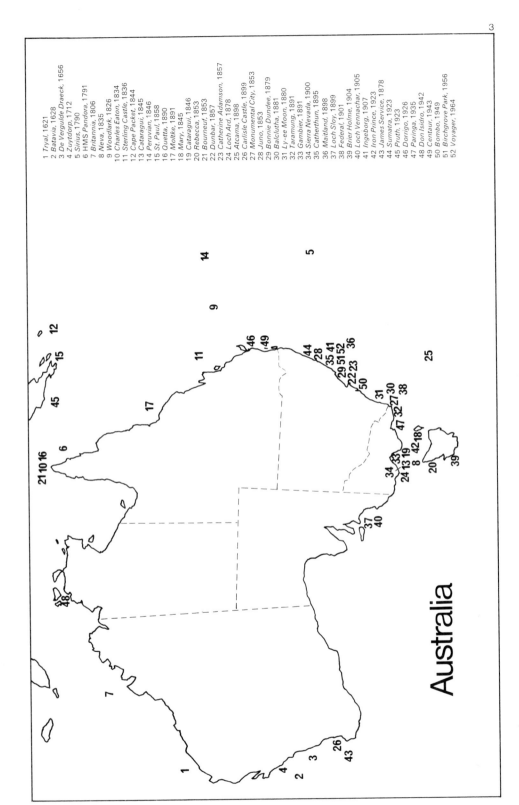

1 *Tryal*, 1621
2 *Batavia*, 1628
3 *De Vergulde Draeck*, 1656
4 *Zuytdorp*, 1712
5 *Sirius*, 1790
6 *HMS Pandora*, 1791
7 *Britannia*, 1806
8 *Neva*, 1835
9 *Woodlark*, 1826
10 *Charles Eaton*, 1834
11 *Sterling Castle*, 1836
12 *Cape Packet*, 1844
13 *Cataraqui*, 1845
14 *Peruvian*, 1846
15 *St. Paul*, 1858
16 *Quetta*, 1890
17 *Moltke*, 1891
18 *Mary*, 1845
19 *Cataragui*, 1846
20 *Rebecca*, 1853
21 *Bourneuf*, 1853
22 *Dunbar*, 1857
23 *Catherine Adamson*, 1857
24 *Loch Ard*, 1878
25 *Atcama*, 1898
26 *Carlisle Castle*, 1899
27 *Monumental City*, 1853
28 *Juno*, 1853
29 *Bonnie Dundee*, 1879
30 *Balclutha*, 1881
31 *Ly-ee Moon*, 1880
32 *Taramung*, 1891
33 *Gambier*, 1891
34 *Sierra Nevada*, 1900
35 *Catherthun*, 1895
36 *Maitland*, 1898
37 *Loch Sloy*, 1899
38 *Federal*, 1901
39 *Brier Holme*, 1904
40 *Loch Vennachar*, 1905
41 *Ingeborg*, 1907
42 *Iron Prince*, 1923
43 *James Service*, 1878
44 *Sumatra*, 1923
45 *Pruth*, 1923
46 *Dorrigo*, 1926
47 *Paringa*, 1935
48 *Don Isidro*, 1942
49 *Centaur*, 1943
50 *Bombo*, 1949
51 *Birchgrove Park*, 1956
52 *Voyager*, 1964

Australia

4

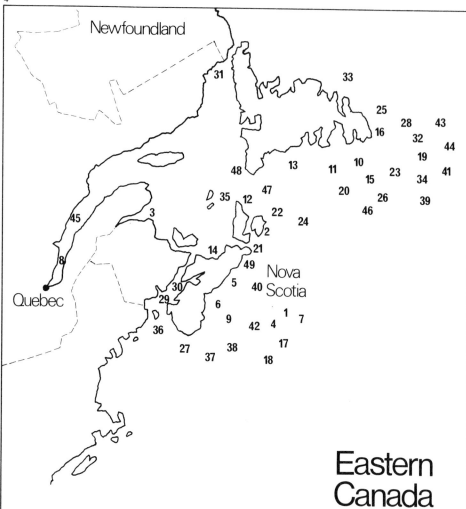

Newfoundland

Quebec

Nova Scotia

Eastern Canada

1 *Buchanan*, 1757
2 *Tilbury, Ferret*, 1757
3 *Marchault, Bienfaisant,
Marquis Marloze*, 1700
4 *Aurora*, 1777
5 *La Tribune*, 1797
6 HMS *Chubb*, 1812
7 HMS *Barbadoes*
1812
8 *Catherine*, 1845
9 *Humbolt*, 1853
10 *Arctic, Vesta*, 1854
11 *John Rutledge*, 1856

12 *Pallas*, 1856
13 *Niobe*, 1874
14 *Melmerby*, 1890
15 *Cashier*, 1892
16 *Indian*, 1859
17 *Hungarian*, 1860
18 *State of Virginia*, 1879
19 *Bath City*, 1881
20 *Asdrubal*, 1882
21 *Colombo*, 1885
22 *Benona*, 1886
23 *Acton*, 1886
24 *Bessie Morris*, 1889

25 *John Knox*, 1887
26 *Aslacoe*, 1890
27 *Bamboro*, 1894
28 *Calitro*, 1894
29 *Belgravia*, 1896
30 *Assaye*, 1897
31 *Baltimore City*, 1897
32 *Bernica*, 1898
33 *Lucerne*, 1901
34 *Assyrian*, 1901
35 *Sovinto*, 1906
36 *Orinoco*, 1907
37 *St. Cuthbert*, 1908

38 *Ben Earn*, 1911
39 *Southern Cross*, 1914
40 *Mont Blanc*, 1917
41 *Marvale*, 1923
42 *Concordia*, 1934
43 *Magnhild*, 1936
44 *Dayrose*, 1942
45 *Truxton*, 1942
46 *British Prudence*, 1942
47 *Arlyn*, 1942
48 *Caribou*, 1942
49 *Arrow*, 1970

Maine

Lake Erie
23

Massachusetts

New York

Pennsylvania

Long Island

New Jersey

Delaware

Maryland

Virginia

Cape Cod

5
25
43
24 46
28 39 31 36
16 30
17 6
15 12 3 11
33 8 32
2 42 21 18
35 19 9 37
29 10 13 40
45 38
34
14 1 44
27 22
41
26
4
20
7

North-East United States

1 *Herbert*, 1710	12 *Messenger*, 1894	24 *Alfred*, 1812	36 *Kate Harding*, 1892
2 *Prinzessin Augusta*, 1738	13 *Culdoon*, 1898	25 *Hanover*, 1849	37 *Biela*, 1900
3 *Somerset*, 1778	14 *Fort Philip*, 1918	26 *Powhattan*, 1854	38 *Canonbury*, 1888
4 *San Joseph*, 1794	15 *Belfast*, 1918	27 *New Era*, 1854	39 *Père Marquette 5*, 1917
5 *Warren, Diligent, Hazard,*	16 *Annie L. Spindler*, 1922	28 *Maritana*, 1861	40 *Oregon*, 1941
Tyrannicide, 1779	17 *Everett*, 1938	29 *A. G. Roper*, 1888	41 *Arundo*, 1942
6 *Frances*, 1872	18 *Lutzen*, 1939	30 *Jason*, 1893	42 *Black Point*, 1945
7 *Albert Dailey*, 1883	19 *Andrea Doria*, 1956	31 *Charles A. Campbell*, 1895	43 *Daytona*, 1955
8 *Viking*, 1884	20 *African Queen*, 1958	32 *Haroldine*, 1895	44 *Gwendoline Steers*, 1962
9 *Oregon*, 1885	21 *Florida*, 1969	33 *Walter Miller*, 1897	45 *Argo Merchant*, 1976
10 *Austin Locke*, 1885	22 *Palatinate*, 1710	34 *General Slocum*, 1904	46 *Chester A. Polling*, 1977·
11 *Hannah E. Schubert*, 1886	23 *Le Jean Florin*, 1721	35 *City of Columbus*, 1884	

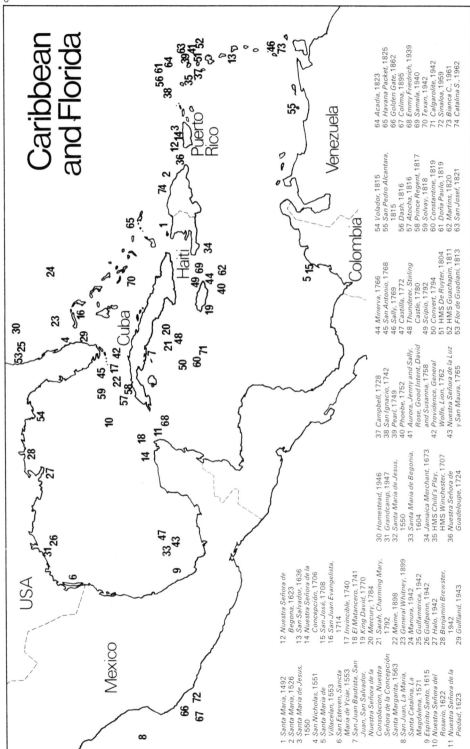

Caribbean and Florida

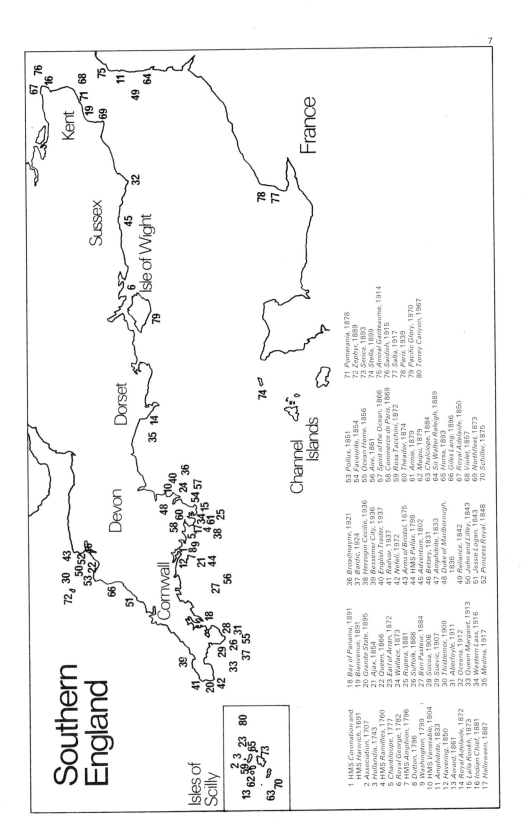

Southern England

Isles of Scilly

Kent

Sussex

Isle of Wight

Dorset

Devon

Cornwall

Channel Islands

France

1 HMS Coronation and HMS Harwich, 1691
2 Association, 1707
3 Hollandia, 1743
4 HMS Ramillies, 1760
5 Chantloupe, 1777
6 Royal George, 1782
7 HMS Amphion, 1796
8 Dutton, 1796
9 Washington, 1799
10 HMS Venerable, 1804
11 Amphitrite, 1833
12 Havering, 1850
13 Award, 1861
14 Royal Adelaide, 1872
15 Lalla Rookh, 1873
16 Indian Chief, 1881
17 Halloween, 1887

18 Bay of Panama, 1891
19 Bienvenue, 1891
20 Granite State, 1895
21 Ajax, 1854
22 Queen, 1866
23 Earl of Arran, 1872
24 Wallace, 1873
25 Rupera, 1881
26 Suffolk, 1886
27 Bon Pasteur, 1884
28 Socoa, 1906
29 Suevic, 1907
30 Thistlemor, 1909
31 Aberfoyle, 1911
32 Oceana, 1912
33 Queen Margaret, 1913
34 Western Lass, 1916
35 Medina, 1917

36 Broadmayne, 1921
37 Bardic, 1924
38 Herzogin Cecilie, 1936
39 Bessemer City, 1936
40 English Trader, 1937
41 Radvor, 1937
42 Nefeli, 1972
43 Arms of Bristol, 1675
44 HMS Pallas, 1798
45 Adventure, 1802
46 Betsey, 1831
47 Amphitrite, 1833
48 Duke of Marlborough, 1836
49 Reliance, 1842
50 John and Lilley, 1843
51 Jessie Logan, 1843
52 Princess Royal, 1848

53 Pollux, 1851
54 Favourite, 1854
55 Ocean Home, 1856
56 Aire, 1861
57 Spirit of the Ocean, 1866
58 Commerce de Paris, 1869
59 Rosa Tacchini, 1872
60 Theador, 1874
61 Annie, 1879
62 Maipu, 1879
63 Chalciope, 1884
64 Sir Walter Raleigh, 1889
65 Horsa, 1893
66 Giles Lang, 1896
67 Royal Adelaide, 1850
68 Violet, 1857
69 Northfleet, 1873
70 Schiller, 1875

71 Pomerania, 1878
72 Zephyr, 1889
73 Serica, 1893
74 Stella, 1899
75 Amiral Ganteaume, 1914
76 Saidieh, 1915
77 Salta, 1917
78 Paris, 1939
79 Pacific Glory, 1970
80 Torrey Canyon, 1967

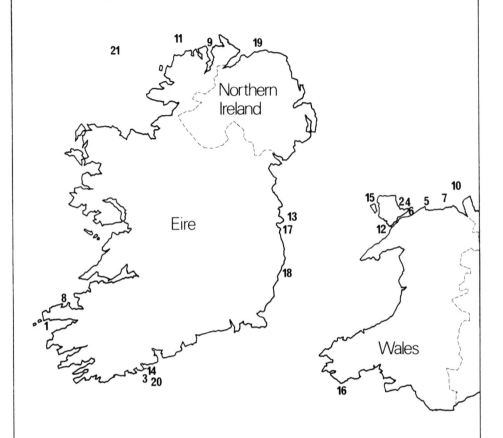

Irish and
Welsh Coasts

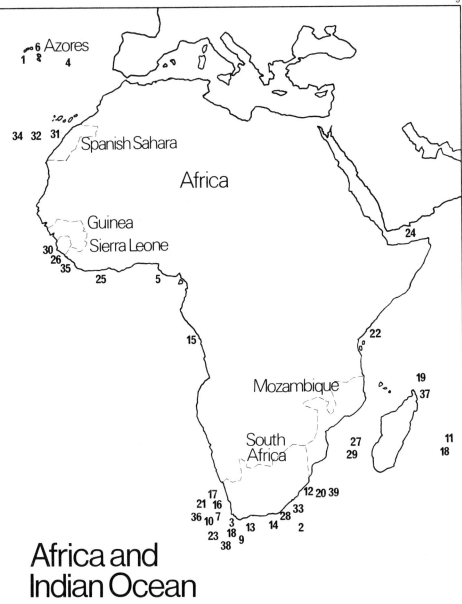

6 Azores

34 32 31 Spanish Sahara

Africa

Guinea
30 Sierra Leone
26
35   25   5

15

22

Mozambique

19
37

South
Africa

27
29

11
18

17
21 16
36 10 7
23   3
18 13   14   2
38 9

12 20 39
33
28

Africa and Indian Ocean

1 *Las Cinque Chagas*, 1594	11 *Randolph*, 1851	20 *Newark Castle*, 1908	30 *Umona*, 1941
2 *Grosvenor*, 1782	12 *Fairfield*, 1852	21 *Maori*, 1909	31 *British Yeoman*, 1942
3 *Guardian*, 1790	13 *Queen of the Thames*,	22 *Ahmadi*, 1909	32 *Empire Attendant*, 1942
4 *Marie Celeste*, 1872	1871	23 *Lusitania*, 1911	33 *Nirpura*, 1943
5 *Gustave Schindler*, 1928	14 *Strathblane*, 1890	24 *Fifeshire*, 1911	34 *Silverbeech*, 1943
6 *Pamir*, 1957	15 *Matadi*, 1896	25 *Winneba*, 1913	35 *Fernhill*, 1943
7 *Birkenhead*, 1852	16 *Mexican*, 1900	26 *Fulani*, 1914	36 *George M. Livanos*, 1947
8 *Teuton*, 1881	17 *Sybille*, 1901	27 *Ellerslie*, 1917	37 *Starcarrier*, 1961
9 *Grace*, 1822	18 *Taher*, 1901	28 *Cape Recife*, 1929	38 *Walfra*, 1971
10 *Waterloo*, 1842	19 *Hardwick Hall*, 1903	29 *Baron Polwarth*, 1937	39 *Claus*, 1977

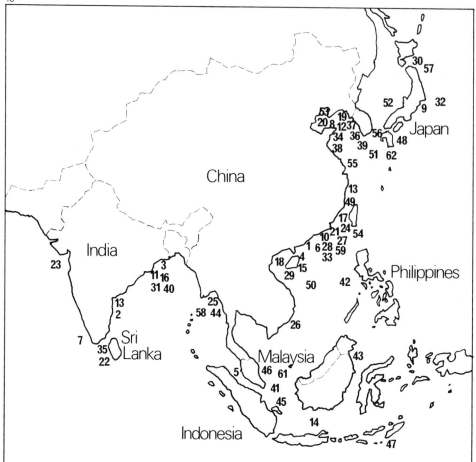

China

Japan

India

Philippines

Sri Lanka

Malaysia

Indonesia

Far East

1 *Donna Maria II*, 1850	17 *Bokhara*, 1892	33 *Hsin Wah*, 1929	49 *Asaka Maru*, 1944
2. *Successor*, 1852	18 *Mombassa*, 1902	34 *Dampto*, 1930	50 *Ryoei Maru*, 1945
3. *Eagle Speed*, 1865	19 *Stereguschi*, 1904	35 *Tricolor*, 1931	51 *Mannert L. Abele*, 1945
4. *Charterhouse*, 1845	20 *Stroini*, 1904	36 *Takasago Maru*, 1932	52 *Hokutu Maru*, 1945
5. *Pasha*, 1851	21 *St. Kilda*, 1905	37 *Tyne Maru*, 1932	53 *Hsuan Huai*, 1948
6. *Charlemagne*, 1857	22 *Sir John Jackson*, 1908	38 *Toonan*, 1933	54 *China Victor*, 1949
7. *Colombo*, 1862	23 *Shrewsbury*, 1909	39 *Tung Foo*, 1934	55 *San Antonia*, 1950
8. HMS *Racehorse*, 1864	24 *Sung Kiang*, 1919	40 *Sumatra*, 1939	56 *Ayikawa Maru*, 1954
9. *Oneida*, 1870	25 *Glenogle*, 1919	41 *Sirdhana*, 1939	57 *Seikan Maru II*, 1954
10. HMS *Stanley*, 1870	26 *Lien Shing*, 1919	42 *Si Kiang*, 1941	58 *Aung Tiza*, 1961
11. *Ava*, 1879	27 *Hong Moh*, 1921	43 *Prins van Oranje*, 1942	59 *Queen Elizabeth*, 1961
12 *Foochow*, 1883	28 *Wing Shing*, 1923	44 *Chak Sang*, 1942	60 *Ingar*, 1973
13 *Miramar*, 1884	29 *Yahiko Maru*, 1924	45 *Van Ness*, 1942	61 *Man Tack*, 1977
14 *Bengal*, 1885	30 *Kenkon Maru*, 1928	46 *Empress of Asia*, 1942	62 *Tenshu Maru*, 1977
15 *Lorne*, 1887	31 *Shahzada*, 1927	47 *Armidale*, 1942	
16 *Anglia*, 1892	32 *Kohryu Maru*, 1928	48 *Madrono*, 1944	

Further Reading

The books listed below are intended for the general reader. Those marked with an asterisk have particularly good bibliographies, which make it easy to follow up particular points and special interests.

1. Ship's design, navigation, cargoes, trade routes, wrecks in general

Allen, Kenneth S., *The World's Greatest Sea Disasters*, London, Odhams, 1969.

* Bass, George F. (ed.), *A History of Seafaring* Omega/Thames & Hudson, 1972.

Bradford, Ernle, *The Mediterranean: Portrait of a Sea*, London, Hodder & Stoughton, 1971.

Calvert, James, *Surface at the Pole*, New York, McGraw-Hill, 1960.

Casson, L., *The Ancient Mariners*, London, Gollancz, 1959.

Collinder, P., *A History of Maritime Navigation*, London, Batsford, 1954.

Cowburn, P., *The Warship in History*, London, Macmillan, 1966.

Greenhill, Basil and Giffard, Ann, *The Merchant Sailing ship: a photographic history*, Newton Abbot, David & Charles, 1972.

Greenhill, Basil and Giffard, Ann, *Travelling by Sea in the Nineteenth Century*, London, Adam & Charles Black, 1972.

Landström, Björn, *The Ship*, London, Allen & Unwin, 1961.

de Latil, P. and Rivoire, J., *Sunken Treasure*, London, Rupert Hart-Davis, 1962.

The Life and Times of Columbus, London, Paul Hamlyn, 1967.

Meiggs, Russell, *Roman Ostia*, Oxford, Clarendon Press, 1960.

Mostert, Noël, *Supership*, London, Macmillan, 1975.

Neatby, Leslie H., *The Search for Franklin*, London, Arthur Barker, 1970.

Ortzen, Len, *Stories of Famous Disasters at Sea*, London, Arthur Barker, 1969.

Padfield, Peter, *An Agony of Collisions*, London, Hodder & Stoughton, 1966.

Parry, J. H., *The Discovery of the Sea*, New York, The Dial Press, 1974.

Skelton, R. A., *Explorers' Maps: Chapters in the Cartographic Record of Geographical Discovery*, London, Spring Books, 1958.

Stackpole, Edouard A., *Those in Peril on the Sea*, New York, Dial Press, 1962.

Tavernier, Bruno, *Great Maritime Routes: an illustrated History*, London, Macdonald, 1972.

Torr, Cecil, *Ancient Ships*, Cambridge University Press, 1894.

Wood, Walter, *Survivors' Tales of Famous Shipwrecks*, Wakefield, E.P. Publishing, 1974.

2. Wrecks in particular areas

Bateson, Charles, *Australian Shipwrecks*, Vol. 1: 1622–1850, Artarmon, A. H. & A. W. Reed, 1972.

Behenna, John, *Westcountry Shipwrecks: a Pictorial Record, 1866–1973*, Newton Abbot, David & Charles, 1974.

Edwards, Hugh, *The Wreck on the Half-Moon Reef*, London, Robert Hale, 1971.

Fowles, John, *Shipwreck*, London, Jonathan Cape, 1974.

Holthouse, Hector, *Ships in the Coral*, London, Macmillan, 1976.

* Horner, Dave, *The Treasure Galleons: clues to millions in sunken gold and silver*, London, Robert Hale, 1971.

Larn, Richard, *Devon Shipwrecks*, Newton Abbot, David & Charles, 1974.

Martin, Colin, *Full Fathom Five: wrecks of the Spanish Armada*, London, Chatto & Windus, 1975

* Marx, Robert F. *Shipwrecks of the Western Hemisphere*, New York, David McKay Inc., 1975.

Quinn, William P., *Shipwrecks Around Cape Cod*, Privately printed, 1973.

3. Underwater archaeology and the archaeology of ships

Barker, T. F., *Roman Galley Beneath the Sea*, Leicester, Brockhampton Press, 1964.

Bascom, Willard, *Deep Water, Ancient Ships*, Newton Abbot, David & Charles, 1976.

* Bass, George F., *Archaeology under Water*, London, Pelican, 1970.

Cleator, P. E. *Underwater Archaeology*, Robert Hale, 1973

Cousteau, Jacques-Yves and Diolé, Philippe, *Diving for Sunken Treasure*, London, Cassell, 1971.

Diolé, Philippe, *4,000 Years Under the Sea*, London, Sidgwick and Jackson, 1953.

Dumas, F. *Deep-Water Archaeology*, London, Routledge & Kegan Paul, 1962.

Dumas, F., *30 Centuries Under the Sea*, New York, Crown Publishers, 1976.

Frost, H., *Under the Mediterranean*, London, Routledge & Kegan Paul, 1963.

Johnstone, Paul, *The Archaeology of Ships*, London, The Bodley Head, 1974.

McKee, Alexander, *History Under the Sea*, London, Hutchinson, 1968.

4. Rescue and wreck prevention

Elder, Michael, *For Those in Peril: the story of the lifeboat service*, London, John Murray, 1963.

Fry, Eric C., *Lifeboat Design and Development*, Newton Abbot, David & Charles, 1975.

Gibbs, Jim, *West Coast Lighthouses: a pictorial history of the guiding lights of the sea*, Seattle, Superior Publishing Co., 1974.

Gores, Joseph N. *Marine Salvage*, Newton Abbot, David & Charles, 1972.

* Hague, Douglas B. and Christie, Rosemary, *Lighthouses: their Architecture, History and Archaeology*, Llandysul, Gomer Press, 1975.

Holland, Francis Ross, Jr., *America's Lighthouses: their Illustrated History since 1716*, Brattleboro, The Stephen Greene Press, 1972.

Ortzen, Len, *Famous Lifeboat Rescues*, London, Arthur Barker, 1971.

Parry, Henry, *Wreck and Rescue on the Coast of Wales 2: the story of the North Wales lifeboats*, Truro, D. Bradford Barton, 1973.

Stevenson, D. Alan, *The World's Lighthouses before 1820*, Oxford University Press, 1959.

Index

Ships wrecked

166

General

170